Context:

Executing Strategy in a Developing Economy

Songhai Business Publishing
Bellevue, Washington

Context:
Executing Strategy in a Developing Economy

www.songhai.com

ISBN: 978-0-9767241-1-7
Library of Congress Card Number:
A PUBLICATION OF THE SONGHAI GROUP, BELLEVUE, WA, USA

Songhai Business Publishing
Bellevue, Washington

Context:

Executing Strategy in a Developing Economy

Edited by

Kwaku Appiah-Adu
Head of the Delivery Unit, Vice President's Secretariat, Office of the President
and
Mahamudu Bawumia
Vice President, Republic of Ghana
and
Hene Aku Kwapong
Managing Partner, The Songhai Group

Contents

COMPLIMENTS

Context: Executing Strategy in a Developing Economy

A must read for those interested in national and business transformational development and are keen to share the experiences of authors who have been at the nuts and bolts level.

~*Kwame Pianim, Economist and Founder, New World Investments; Chairman, Airtel Communications (Ghana) Ltd; and Former Chairman, United Bank for Africa (Ghana) Ltd.*

It is most refreshing that these three fine brains and great talents from Ghana have collaborated with experts in selected fields to write this compendium "Context: Executing Strategy in a Developing Economy". I commend this book to leaders in the private and public sectors and pray the authors will all be fully involved in the future governance of Ghana.

~*Sam Okudzeto, Founder and Senior Partner, Sam Okudzeto & Associates, Legal Practitioners.*

This book is an essential material for understanding, initiating and translating a value chain activity into business functional activity. In totality, it will definitely serve as a springboard for focused leadership and transformational success for any business. This is the kind of scintillating work required for academic astuteness and business performance based on planned and executed strategy.

~*Joyce Rosalind Aryee, Executive Director, Salt and Light Ministries; Former CEO, Ghana Chamber of Mines; Former Minister of State, Ghana.*

A compelling guide for forward-thinking and high performing entrepreneurs and leaders, who appreciate diligent efforts towards ultimate growth, progress and success.

~*Elizabeth Joyce Villars, Founder & Chairman, Camelot Group*

Appiah-Adu, Bawumia, Kwapong and the contributors have put together a masterful discussion of the relationship between the way organisations operate and business performance, keeping in mind the significance of environment. Skillfully and insightfully, they consider the impact of strategies in the context of various dimension of management. This is a must read for serious academics and practitioners concerned about the future of organisational performance in Africa and the world over.

~*Kofi Lomotey, Bardo Distinguished Professor of Educational Leadership at Western Carolina University.*

I congratulate the editors and contributors for this truly classic scholarly work all of whom are accomplished in their respective fields. The book's concept is appropriately placed in the cultural setting of developing economies, thus, making it highly relevant to scholars, practitioners and investors in such economies. I recommend this book to all who desire to see the developing world competing effectively in the global economy.

~*Christian Tetteh Sottie, Former Controller and Accountant-General, Ghana; and President of the Institute of Chartered Accountants, Ghana.*

About the Editors

Kwaku Appiah-Adu (PhD) is Head of the Delivery Unit, Vice President's Secretariat, Office of the President, Republic of Ghana, Professor of Strategy, immediate past Dean of the Business School, Central University and Partner Emeritus of the Songhai Group. Previously, he was Head of Policy Coordination, Monitoring and Evaluation at the Office of the President, Chairman of the Oil and Gas Technical Committee, Director of Ghana's Central Governance Project and member of the President's Investors' Advisory Council, as well as the Advisory Board for the UN Initiative on Continental Shelf Delineation. Prior to that, he worked as a consultant with PricewaterhouseCoopers and lectured at the Universities of Cardiff and Portsmouth. An author of several books, he has recently edited a book entitled Governance of the Petroleum Sector in an Emerging Developing Economy, and another book co-edited with Mahamudu Bawumia titled Key Determinants of National Development, both published by Gower, UK. With over 100 publications, he has facilitated workshops and presented papers at several international forums. Kwaku has been elected to the ANBAR Hall of Excellence for outstanding contribution to the Literature and Body of Knowledge. He has also served on various boards in the public and private sectors. Currently, he is the Board Chairman of GLICO Pensions Trustee Company Ltd, Director of Switchback Developers Ltd, Advisory Board member of the Lupcon Centre for Business Research (Germany), and the Independent Director of Shell Pensions Fund. He has received many awards, including the President's Award for exceptional contribution to national development.

Mahamudu Bawumia (PhD) is the Vice President of the Republic of Ghana. A former Visiting Professor of Economic Governance at Central University, Ghana, he has extensive experience as a senior policy maker, policy advisor, and has worked with governments as well as international organisations. Dr. Bawumia was Resident Representative for the African Development Bank in Zimbabwe from 2011-2012. He served as Deputy Governor of the Central Bank of Ghana between 2006 and 2009. Between 2009 and 2010, Dr. Bawumia was a visiting professor at the University of British Columbia (Canada), and a Senior Associate Member of St. Antonys College, University of Oxford. Dr. Bawumia served as an Assistant Professor of Economics at Hankamer School of Business, Baylor University, Texas, USA (1996-2000) where he received the Young Researcher Award in 1998. Dr. Bawumia has published several articles in refereed journals and has also published a book on Monetary Policy and Financial Sector Reform in Africa. He holds a BSc. Economics (First Class Honours) degree from the University of Buckingham, UK, an MSc. in Development Economics from Oxford University and a PhD in Economics from Simon Fraser University (Canada). Dr. Bawumia holds the Chartered Institute of Bankers (UK) diploma (ACIB) and is a Fellow of the Chartered Institute of Bankers (FCIB), Ghana.

Hene Aku Kwapong (PhD) holds a BS, MS in Chemical Engineering and an MBA in Finance Engineering (all from MIT, Cambridge, MA) and a PhD in Systems Dynamics (Columbia University, New York). He is currently a Managing Partner of Songhai, a corporate development company and Chief Restructuring Officer of Park Street Advisors, a London real-estate private equity company. Dr. Kwapong is a director of both Nordicom-Denmark and Ecobank, Ghana Ltd. He is a former Senior Vice President of the New York City Economic Development Corporation and has more than 25 years of strategy and operational experience from several Fortune 50 companies including Microsoft, GE, Exxon Mobil, Deutsche Bank and Royal Bank of Scotland. He has a wealth of experience from the financial services industry including multi- asset securitisation platform management, value-based management leadership, and architecting control frameworks for fixed income businesses. Dr. Kwapong served as COO with Royal Bank of Scotland's Global Credit Business, where he led the restructuring of its global credit and ABS business. Until recently, he served as the head of strategy and new markets overseeing global credit electronic trading business, overseeing operational execution of strategy; including regulatory imperatives, risk management, implementing supervisory framework, and overall profitability of the Europe, Middle East & Africa Credit & Mortgage Markets.

About the Contributors

Alex Addae-Korankye holds a BA (Hons) in Economics, an MBA and a Doctor of Business Administration degree. He is pursuing a PhD in Finance at Cardiff Metropolitan University in the UK. He has researched and written a number of books/papers in the area of Economics, Finance, Microfinance, and General Management. His areas of interest include but not limited to Finance, International Business, Strategic Management, Information Management, Microfinance, Economics, Monetary and Financial Systems, Money and Banking, Managerial Economics, Quantitative Methods/Management Science, and Research Methods. He has lectured in both the United Kingdom and Ghana on several academic & professional programmes including ABE, ACCA, CIMA, ICAG, BA/BBA/BSc, MBA and University of London programmes.

Ebenezer Ofori Agbettor is the Executive Director of Institute of Human Resource Management Practitioners (IHRMP)-Ghana (HR Professional Body). Previously, he worked as General Manager/HR Business Partner for Vodafone Ghana. He also worked as Head/Human Resource Management, Head/Customer Service and Senior Overseas Operations Manager at different times for Ghana Airways Ltd; Tutor & Learning Advisor on Henley Management College (UK)'s MBA distance learning programme; Senior Management Consultant for Lexcroft Consulting Ltd; and Management Consultant (OD) for PwC. Ebenezer holds an MBA (Distinction) from London South Bank University (UK), is a Fellow of Ghana Institute of Management and member of the IHRMP-Ghana. He is Chairman of the National ISO Committee on Human Resource Management in Ghana. Ebenezer serves on a number of evaluation panels and committees for organisations such as Minerals Commission, National Petroleum Authority, Ghana Statistical Service, and Public Services Commission. He has managed several consultancy projects and facilitated numerous Management Development programmes for various organisations in Ghana and abroad. Ebenezer has ten publications to his credit and is married with two children. Ebenezer serves as the Head of the Counselling Department of Believer's Temple, ICGC.

Hazel Berrard Amuah (DBA, PhD) has over fifteen years of human resource experience in several multinational organisations whose operations have covered twenty two countries in West and Central Africa. These experiences in the areas of HR and business include but are not limited to HR Strategy Development and Implementation, Talent Acquisition, Compensation, Learning/Training, Executive Coaching, Cross Cultural Leadership and Coaching, Talent Management and Retention Strategy, Organisational and Management Development, Performance Management, Career Design and Management, Employee Relations and Welfare and Policy formulation in multinational organisations across Central and West Africa. The values that drive her actions are trust, respect, integrity, credibility, discipline, hard work and a focus on achieving results. These values have been Hazel's key success drivers in every endeavour that she has undertaken and have enabled her succeed and gain the exposure highlighted above. As an HR professional, Hazel facilitates identifying potential and uses performance management techniques to enable employees unleash this potential to excel in their work.

Samuel Aning is currently Director of the African University College of Communications Pensions Academy and is also a part-time senior lecturer in Contemporary Issues at the Methodist University. Additionally, Sam lectures in Media and Governance and Social Entrepreneurship, and was educated at Mfantsipim School and University of Science of Technology in Ghana, London School of Economics, UK and Galilee College, Israel. Prior to assuming his current position, Sam was a Policy Advisor in the Policy Coordination, Monitoring and Evaluation Unit of the Office of the President, Ghana, where he provided policy advice and evaluated a number of government programmes for six years. He has also served as a consultant on a number of projects. When Ghana discovered oil in 2007, Sam was appointed a member of the Oil and Gas Technical Committee that developed the country's Oil and Gas Master Plan and Policy. He also served as a Board Member of the National Identification Authority, the President's Special Initiative on Distance Learning and the Review Committee on the upgrade of Senior Secondary Schools. Sam serves on the NAGRAT Fund Board and the GAPOHA Pensions Fund Board, the AUCC Pensions Academy Governing Council and the Board of the Centre for Advanced Strategic Analysis.

Albert Antwi-Boasiako is the Founder & Principal Consultant at e-Crime Bureau & a Cyber Security Expert with the Interpol Global Cybercrime Expert Group (IGCEG). Albert attended the University of Trento in Northern Italy where he graduated with a first class before pursuing his graduate studies at the University of Portsmouth, UK where he graduated with distinction, receiving overall post-graduate best student award from the School of Computing of the University. Prior to founding e-Crime Bureau in 2011, Albert was responsible for Europe, Middle East & Africa (EMEA) Market of DFLabs, a global information security firm based in Milan, Italy. Albert is currently a PhD Research Fellow with the University of Pretoria in South Africa. He consults for law enforcement/security agencies, public sector institutions and private sector organisations across Africa. Albert has also consulted for a number of international organisations including the UN Office on Drugs & Crime, UN Conference on Trade & Development, Council of Europe (CoE), Commonwealth Cybercrime Initiative (CCI), the Inter-Governmental Action Group against Money Laundering in West Africa and the Royal Institute of International Affairs (Chatham House). Apart from overseeing e-Crime Bureau activities in the region, Albert also serves as a Visiting Lecturer - Cybercrimes, Cyberterrorism & Cyber Security ,at the Kofi Annan International Peacekeeping Training Centre (KAIPTC), Accra, Ghana; Adjunct Lecturer – Cybercrime, Cyberterrorism & Digital Forensics, Kwame Nkrumah University of Science & Technology (KNUST), Kumasi, Ghana; Research Associate, African Centre for Cyberlaw & Cybercrime Prevention (ACCP), Kampala, Uganda and a Faculty Member, Ghana Police Command & Staff College (GPCSC), Winneba, Ghana.

Nana Kegya Appiah-Adu (Mrs) is a lawyer by profession and a lecturer at the Ghana School of Law. She holds a BA degree in languages and an LLB (Hons). In addition, she holds a Master's degree in commercial and maritime law from the University of Wales, Cardiff. After qualifying as a lawyer in Ghana, she worked at the Central Bank of Ghana for several years. Owing to her interest in education, she left the Central Bank and started a career as a lecturer at the Ghana School of Law where she is a lecturer in banking law. Mrs. Appiah-Adu has published in the area of banking law as well as oil and gas management. In addition to being a law lecturer, Mrs. Appiah-Adu is a pastor and a director of Ace Educational Services.

Williams Abayaawien Atuilik (PhD) is a Senior Lecturer at the Heritage Christian University College. He is also a PFM Consultant with the Ghana Oil & Gas for Inclusive Growth programme. He has lectured in a number of universities in Ghana and abroad. He has provided PFM consulting services in a number of countries including: Ghana, Liberia, Somalia, Sierra Leone, South Africa and Botswana with organisations such as: The African Development Bank, World Bank, USAID, and WHO. He holds a PhD (Accounting) from Capella University, USA; MSc. (Finance) from GIMPA; MA (Economic Policy Management) from the University of Ghana; LLB from the University of Ghana; and BSc. (Administration) from the University of Ghana. Dr. Atuilik is a member of the Institute of Chartered Accountants, Ghana; Ghana Bar Association, Chartered Institute of Taxation, Ghana; Chartered Institute of Bankers, Ghana; Chartered Institute of Public Finance & Accountancy, UK; Liberian Institute of Certified Public Accountants; and the Association of Certified Chartered Economists, USA. He serves on the Council of the Institute of Chartered Accountants-Ghana and on the Board of Hope College.

Douglas Boateng (MSc, EngD, FCILT, FIPlantE, FSOE, FIOD,FCMI, FIC, FIOM, FCIPS, Finst.D, CDIR). He is the CEO PanAvest International & Partners, Professor Extraordinairus, Supply and Value Chain Management, Graduate School of Business Leadership, UNISA.; Independent Distinguished Extraordinary Chair in Operations and Supply Chain Management, Professional Development: Institute of Operations Management (IOM) Africa. Douglas is an International Professional Chartered Director, a vertical specific executive coach, mentor and an adjunct academic. He is a Fellow of the: Institute of Directors (UK); Society of Operations Engineers (UK); Institution of Plant Engineers (UK); Chartered Institute of Logistics and Transport (UK), Chartered Institute of Procurement and Supply (UK); Institute of Operations Management (UK); Chartered Institute of Logistics and Transport, Southern Africa. Professor Douglas Boateng is Africa's first ever appointed Professor Extraordinarius for Supply and Value Chain Management. Douglas is Chairman of the Advisory Board of Chartered Institute of Procurement and Supply (Africa); President of the Institute of Operations Management (Africa); Editorial Board Member of Smart Procurement. Douglas was honoured with the Life Time Achievers Award in 2013 by the Chartered Institute of Purchasing and Supply for ongoing local and international contribution to supply chain management practice in industry and for director level skills development; and honoured by the Commonwealth Business Council for contribution to international supply chain management executive leadership development and emerging long term world economic development.

Vincent Kwapong holds a BS Electrical Engineering (MIT); MS (Carnegie Mellon); MSE & MBA Finance and Strategy (Michigan, Ann Arbor). He is a Managing Partner of the Songhai Group, a business development company. Prior to this, Vincent was Director of Operations Excellence at United Technologies Corporation and was responsible for the operational integration of 13 business acquisitions into the parent company. He is a certified Lean Six Sigma expert with a record of accomplishment at GE, Johnson & Johnson and Sony Electronics where he also led or supported implementation of Enterprise Resource Planning systems to improve workflow management and execution. In his roles as Lean Six Sigma leader at GE, he led business process simplification efforts to turn around GE's Security Division. Between 2003 and 2007, Vincent was Global Operations Leader at Johnson & Johnson. Previously, he was Process Engineering Manager at Corning Incorporated. He has over 25 years' experience in Operations Excellence, Business Process Simplification and New Product Commercialization. Vincent is the author of "OAK – Business Principles of Strategic and Operational Excellence". He holds a US patent on Dielectric Drying.

Theophilus Maloreh-Nyamekye (PhD, MBA, MSc, MCIPS, PgDip, PgCert, BAHons) is an international scholar and a scientific writer. His expertise is in the area of procurement and supply chain management, health services management and systematic reviews of healthcare evidence. He has served as a scientific writer and a reviewer of works of Joanna Briggs Institute of the University of Adelaide, South Australia and the Robert Gordon University in the UK. Theophilus has also served as a consultant in the development of a curriculum on BSc Procurement and Supply Chain Management programmes. He is currently coordinating the development of an MSc Procurement and Supply Chain Management programme at the University of Ghana Business School. He also teaches project management for ALTIS University of Milan, Italy/CIBT on a Global MBA in Entrepreneurship and Sustainability programme and supervises PhD Student projects. Theophilus is currently a lecturer at the University of Ghana, teaching Purchasing and Materials Management, Healthcare Financing, Supply Chain Management for Health Services (MBA programme) Partnership and Collaboration in Health Services Management and Strategic Management for Health Care (PhD programme). Prior to joining University of Ghana Faculty, Theophilus was a health services administrator in the Ministry of Health in Ghana, a consultant/Lecturer at GIMPA where he was involved in management training, research and consultancy, including projects for World Health Organisation, Ghana AIDS Commission, Ministry of Health/Ghana Health Service and Ministry of Education. Theophilus pursued his BA (Hons) in Nursing and Psychology and MBA (Health Services Management) at the University of Ghana. He later studied for a Postgraduate Diploma in Marketing at CIMG, and then MSc Purchasing and Supply Chain Management and PhD in Health Services Management at Robert Gordon University in UK.

Francis Mensah Sasraku BA Hons (Econ), MBA, LLM, FCCA, ACMA, ACIB, ACIM, DBA, is the Head of Risk and Regulation at the National Banking College in Ghana. Previously, he worked as an accountant and management consultant with KPMG and also as Head of Customer Management and Marketing Division of the Ghana Commercial Bank, Ghana's largest bank. He is an economist, a certified chartered accountant, management accountant, a chartered banker and chartered marketer. An expert in energy economics and finance, Francis holds an MBA (Oxford Brooks University) and an LLM with Distinction in Energy Policy from the Centre for Energy, Petroleum and Mineral Law and Policy (Dundee University), Doctor of Business Administration (Bradford University) and is currently completing a PhD programme with specialisation in petroleum finance and law (Dundee University). He has authored several papers in academic and professional journals. Two of his papers (i) Risks in Gas-Power Project Financing and (ii) Ghana's Petroleum Tax Regime and its Strategic Implications were published in a book titled "Governance of the Petroleum Sector in an Emerging Developing Economy".

Acknowledgments

The editors wish to express their sincerest gratitude to the contributors who spent numerous valuable hours of their time writing the chapters of this book, thus making it possible for this project's dream to become a reality – Prof. Douglas Boateng, Vincent Kwapong, Dr. Williams Abayaawien Atuilik, Francis Mensah Sasraku, Dr. Theophilus Maloreh-Nyamekye, Ebenezer Ofori Agbettor, Dr. Hazel Berrard Amuah, Mrs. Nana Kegya Appiah-Adu, Sam Aning, Albert Antwi-Boasiako and Alex Addae-Korankye.

To our wives: Nana Kegya, Samira, and Nana Aba; our children: Afua, Kwaku and Akua; Abdul Mumin, Nadia, Mahmoud and Aidan; Justin, Jonathan, and Jeremy; who gave us the time and breathing space to complete the project on schedule. Words cannot express our appreciation for your patience and encouragement which were more than adequate to propel us to higher levels of motivation when the going got tough.

On behalf of the whole team, we wish to thank the following eminent citizens who inspired the team by demonstrating their confidence in the project: Sam Jonah, KBE, who wrote the foreword; Sam Okudzeto, Kwame Pianim, Mrs. Elizabeth Joyce Villars, Rev. Dr. Joyce Rosalind Aryee, Prof. Kofi Lomotey, and Christian Sottie, who provided compliments.

Our sincere gratitude also goes to Festus Hagan and Frank Harry Junior, the research assistants on this project as well as Ace School of Languages, the proof readers, for their meticulous approach to work and attention to detail. Finally, to all others that time and space would not permit us to list, we say a big thank you for the various roles you played in making this project see the light of day.

Foreword

This is a book that is timely for the current set of challenges facing companies which find their beginnings in the African environment. The authors have taken great pains to bring to light business frameworks that have been largely part of high-performance companies for quite some time, but are largely absent as part of management philosophy and discussions in Africa.

There is no doubt that the challenges in managing companies in Africa present a unique problem because of the peculiarities of the varied culture across the continent. Some of these peculiarities are also present in other developing economies so instances can be found elsewhere where great companies have emerged. The ones that are unique to Africa, on the other hand, need to be understood in a much more fundamental way that allows formulation of effective solutions. For that to happen, businesses in developing economies have to be familiar and highly conversant in management frameworks that have been a result of years of problem-solving.

The authors have done exactly that, bringing together a set of management frameworks and insights gathered from experiences dealing with challenges within the context of a developing economy.

Context, the lack of it or the prevalence of it, is what determines successful outcomes from applying these frameworks. Having an understanding of the context and how to execute strategy however depends on having a fundamental understanding of the frameworks the authors bring together in this book.

Executing strategy without context is a recipe for failure of a company's strategy. This is the unitary lesson from this book, one worth taking seriously.

Sam E. Jonah, KBE
Former Executive President, AngloGold Ashanti

Chapter 1

Introduction

Kwaku Appiah-Adu, Mahamudu Bawumia & Hene Aku Kwapong

The introduction to this book commences by establishing the roots of the *concepts and topics* being addressed, that is, how time-honoured strategic and operational organisational practices contribute to competitive performance within the context of a developing economy. This book's theoretical foundations are derived from Michael Porter's value chain for strategic and operational efficiency and effectiveness as well as McKinsey's 7-S paradigm for strategy implementation within the context of an organisation.

For an organisation to be successful in the marketplace, it does not only need to be rigorous in developing corporate, business and operational strategies but also has to be effective in the implementation of these strategies. Since firms operate within a wider economic environment, an added dimension to the issues explored in this book relates to the impact of the macro-economic environment on competitive performance.

Porter's Value Chain Framework

How does a firm create value? How does a firm change business inputs into business outputs such that it has a greater value than the original cost of creating those outputs? This is not merely a mundane question: it is a subject of major significance to organisations, because it focuses on the economic logic of why a firm exists.

Different types of organisations have unique sets of activities that are employed to create value. Manufacturing firms create value by procuring raw materials and utilising them to develop products that meet specific needs. Retailers assemble an array of products and offer them to customers in a convenient manner, often supported by services such as fitting rooms or personal shopper's advice. Service firms such as insurers provide customers with policies that are underwritten by larger re-insurance policies. This way, these weightier policies are packaged in a customer-friendly manner, and distributed to their clients.

How do we measure the value that is generated and captured by an organisation? It is simply the profit margin that is derived from the difference between: Value Created and Captured minus Cost of Creating that Value. The greater the value created by the firm, the higher the likelihood of its profitability and higher value delivered to customers, which ultimately results in the development of a competitive advantage. To achieve a competitive edge, Porter suggested that paying attention to the chain of a firm's activities will add greater value to the products and services than the sum of the added cost of these activities.

The ability to appreciate how one's organisation creates value, and the development of insights relating to further value addition, are essential prerequisites to developing a competitive strategy. In his seminal book titled *Competitive Advantage,* Michael Porter discussed the competitive strategy concept in which he first presented the value chain model. A value chain is a set of activities that a firm undertakes to create value for its customers. Porter advanced a general-purpose value chain that organisations can employ to analyse their activities, and determine how they are interrelated. The manner in which value chain activities are conducted influences costs and profits, so this model can help a firm to better appreciate its value sources.

The value chain concept can be used as a great diagnostic framework for strategic planning and to develop the organisational paradigm that facilitates an effective leadership model. The value chain notion can also be utilised in distinct business units, as well as the complete supply chain and distribution networks. For a firm to develop an unbeatable offering, it is vital to add value in each activity that the product undergoes in the course of its life cycle. One excellent area in which to achieve this is to add value at each phase during the product development process. In order for this to happen, the right synchronisation of the value chain activities is required. A sound organisation of the functional departments involved in these activities and a proper communication strategy is needed to synchronise the activities of these functional units economically, efficiently and effectively.

To make the models underpinning this book easier to understand we start with the question: how does a firm map Porter's value chain activities into its business functional activities? Porter classified the generic value added activities into two classes which are presented in

Figure-1 below. These activities are: primary activities which are classified as products; and market related activities and support activities that are related to infrastructure, technology, procurement, and human resource management.

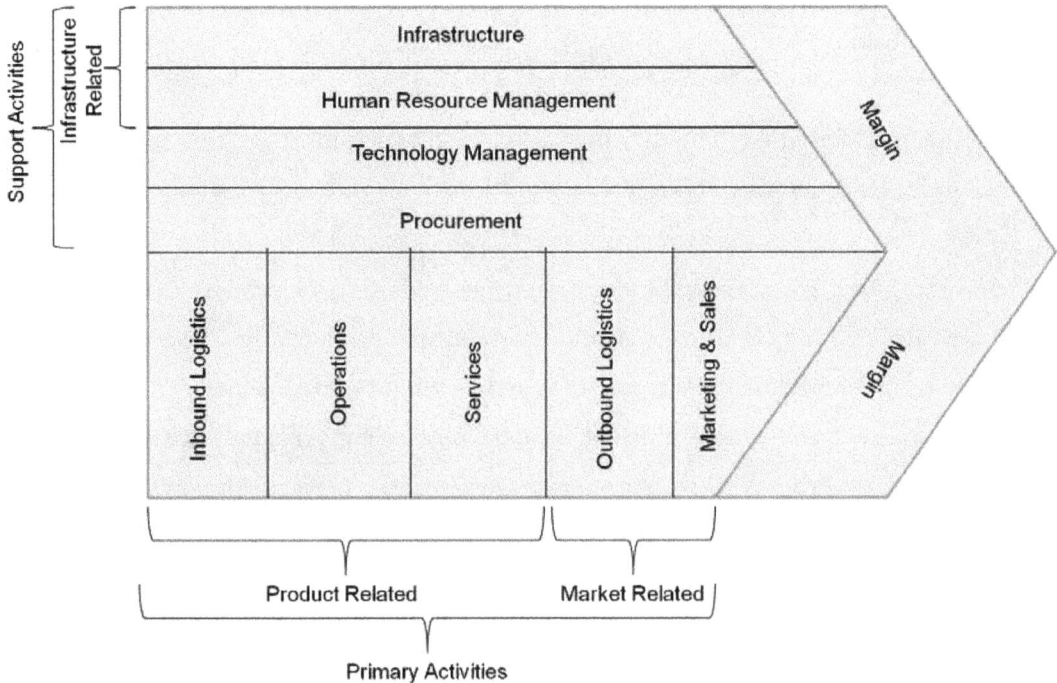

Figure-1.1: The Generic Value Chain (Source: Michael E. Porter, 1985)

Product related activities: The activities that the organisation performs to add value to the products and services itself. The activities are classified as:

1. *Inbound Logistics*: For the production and development activities, organisations need inputs such as goods which are received from the suppliers. Inbound logistics refer to all the activities related to goods received from the suppliers, decision about the transportation scheduling, storing the goods as inventory, managing the inventory, and making the inputs ready to use for the production of end products.

2. *Operations*: These include the production process, development activities, testing, packaging, maintenance, and all other activities that transform the inputs into finished product.

3. *Services*: An Organisation offers services after the products and/or services have been sold.

These service activities enhance the product's value in the form of after sales guarantees, warranties, spare parts management, repair services, installation, updating, trainings, etc.

Primary activities can be classified into product related and market related activities which are described below:

Market related activities: The activities that the organisation performs to transfer the finished products or services to the customers. The activities are classified as:

1. *Outbound Logistics:* The finished products are developed using the product related activities. Now activities are required to transfer the finished products to the customers via warehousing, order fulfilment, transportation, and distribution management.

2. *Marketing and Sales:* These activities include advertising, channel selection, product promotion, selling, product pricing, retail management, etc. The activities are performed to make sure that the products are transferred to targeted customer groups. Marketing mix can be an instrument to take the competitive advantage to the target customers.

Support activities: The activities that the organisation performs to assist the primary activities to gain the competitive advantage. The activities are classified as:

1. *Procurement:* This is the purchasing activity of inputs to transform these into finished products or services. Procurement adds value by the acquisition of appropriate goods or services at the best price, at the right time, and in the desired place with the desired quality and quantity.

2. *Technology Management:* This is very important in today's technological driven environment. Technology can be used in production to reduce cost, to develop new products, increase customer service facility, build up cost effective process, etc. It supports the value chain activities such as research and development, process automation, process design, etc.

3. *Human Resource (HR) Management:* The key roles of HR are to support the attainment of the overall strategic business plan and objectives. As a strategic business partner, HR designs the work positions by hiring, recognition, rewarding, providing appraisal systems, career planning, and employee development. They act as advocates of the employees to motivate them and create a happy working environment. For organisational changing situations, the

HR executes the strategic needs of the organisation with minimum employee dissatisfaction and resistance to change.

4. *Infrastructure*: This includes planning management, legal framework, financing, accounting, public affairs, quality management, general management, etc. These are required to perform the value added activities efficiently to drive the organisation forward to meet its strategic plan and objectives.

To form a successful product for an organisation, it is important to add value in each activity that the product goes through during its life cycle. The best possible value can be achieved in the product development process by adding value at each stage. For that it needs all, or a combination of, value chain activities and a proper synchronisation among all the related activities. A proper organisation is required to contain all the required functional departments to perform these activities; and a proper communication approach is required to synchronise the activities of these functional units efficiently. In the solution section below, Porter's value chain activities are mapped into the related business functions.

Following an expose on the value chain, we attempt to answer the question asked earlier about how a firm can successfully map Porter's value chain activities into business functionalities:

The product related activities can be divided among functional units: production performs operational activities, partly inbound logistics, and services activities. Software production includes activities such as product development, testing, packaging, maintenance, installation, updating, training, etc. A sale is part of service activities (e.g. guarantees, warranties). Inbound logistic activities can be shared between the logistics department and the production function as an inventory management activity. In SMEs, the logistics department can be merged with marketing and sales unit. Production process and production value means profitability analysis is decided by production management functionality. In brief, the function of the production management is to manage the production activities to meet strategic goals.

Market related activities can be classified as functions of marketing and sales. In many organisations, marketing and sales are two independent departments that work in

5

collaboration. But in SMEs both departments can be merged into one department to perform all   related activities. The decision process of marketing and sales depends on the revenue and cost element of all the marketing and sales activities. These decision making functionalities can be defined as marketing and sales management functionalities to manage marketing and sales activities and more importantly, the decision is taken where the marketing and sales add value to the products, or services, and the organisation.

Technology management activities can be presented as a research and development (R&D) function which increases the stock of knowledge for the organisation. **Infrastructure related activities** can be divided into key business functions of finance and accounting, quality management, and general management. **Procurement activities** may belong to the marketing and sales department in collaboration with production operation for scaling the need for quality and quantity, depending on the size of the organisation (e.g., for small and medium firms). **Human resource management activities** can be performed by the human resource (HR) department.

On its practical impact, after mapping Porter's value chain activities to the required business functionality we can summarise the value chain business functions into the following categories:

The *Primary Business Functions* perform product and market related activities. These are production, production management quality management, marketing and sales, and marketing and sales management. The *Supportive Business Functions* perform processes that are necessary for the effective and efficient execution of value added primary activities. These are research and development, accounting and finance, human resource management, and general management. As a summary, the Porter value chain model can be generally defined as nine major functions of business. These business functions are in brief:

1. Production: This is the process of producing a good or service from the inputs collected from the supplier using the resources that carry a cost determined by production factors.

2. Production Management: This is the decision process about the profitability of the production activity to produce a good or service. The profitability measurement can be done

by assessing the revenue and cost of production factors. The outcomes are the management of the all the production functions as well as the heartbeat (day-to-day operations) and integration of operations to achieve a desired strategic outcome.

3. Quality Management: The quality of a product is an integral part of production itself. But maintaining quality at all corporate levels increases confidence that the quality requirements of the product or service will be met. To some extent, to ensure the quality of a product is part of production management functionality but globally, quality management provides the process of quality assurance by fulfilling the requirement of quality management systems like ISO 9000 for achieving the desired quality of the products, services, and the entire corporate activities.

4. Marketing and Sales: Marketing is the social process by which individuals and groups obtain what they need through creating and exchanging products and value with others. In brief, marketing is the process that identifies, anticipates, and satisfies customer requirements and profitability. Sales perform all the exchange processes of goods or services to the customers in return for money or its equivalent.

5. General Management: It has overall responsibility for an organisation. It also has profit and loss responsibility of the company. Essentially, general management oversees all the firms' functions as well as day-to-day operations to sustain the company's integrity and growth.

6. Marketing and Sales Management: This is the decision process related to the profit and loss elements of marketing and sales activities. It also oversees the production functions including day-to-day operations to synchronise marketing and sales activities with production activities.

7. Accounting and Finance: Finance creates value from the company's capital budgeting, financing, and net working capital activities. Accounting is the process of analysing and summarising financial activities as well as interpreting and communicating the financial results to internal and external stakeholders.

8. Research and Development: This comprises the creative activity in a systematic way for the creation of new business, improving knowledge for the efficient usage of existing resources, and in general for diversifying the applications of the stock of knowledge.

9. Human Resource Management: This is the workforce management process of the organisation to build up a desirable working environment and the competence to achieve the strategic goals of the company.

The success of a company is measured by its profitability, which is closely connected to the efficiency of the performed activities. All the activities in an organisation have cost and generate a return. If the rate of returns is greater than the cost, then the activities add value to the organisation. To achieve the premium rate of returns, businesses need to perform economic activities efficiently. According to Porter the efficiency of the activities depends on the finalisation processes in the interrelated areas of organisation, strategy, and tactics. The platform for performing activities is the business organisation. The pre-condition to accomplish value added activities is efficient organisation. Efficient organisation must have all the value added functions of business for the proper interrelations of value added activities.

Individually, all the single business functions also produce results and perform value creation activities. To achieve Porter's value added efficiency, it is important to include all nine major functions as sub-functions in each major business function.

In terms of implementation there are five steps a firm needs to embark on:
1: Depending on the business model, it is vital to identify the organisation's value chain activities.
2: Defined value chain activities have to be assigned into proper value added business functions.
3: Definition of a proper organisational structure such that each business unit can generate effective maximum value by performing all needed value added activities.
4: A proper synchronisation mechanism for the efficient synchronisation of business functional activities to achieve common business goal.
5: *Effective* communication mechanism has to be defined among the business functional units.

The McKinsey 7-S Framework

This model was developed in the 1980s by Tom Peters, Robert Waterman and Julien Philips with help from Richard Pascale and Anthony Athos. The model, made famous by McKinsey Consulting, is good for a thorough discussion around an organisation's activities, infrastructure, and interactions. The 7-S framework is a strategic model that can be used for any of the following purposes: organisational alignment or performance improvement; understanding the core and most influential factors in an organisation's strategy; determining how best to realign an organisation to a new strategy or other organisational design; and examining the current workings and relations an organisation exhibits.

Since its introduction, the model has been extensively applied by scholars and practitioners and is one of the most utilised strategy implementation tools. It tends to focus on human resources (Soft S), rather than the conventional mass production tangibles of capital, infrastructure and equipment, as a major determinant of superior business success. The aim of this framework was to demonstrate how seven facets of the firm; Structure, Strategy, Skills, Staff, Style, Systems, and Shared values, can be synchronised to attain organisational effectiveness. The major purpose of the framework is that all the seven facets are interlinked and a change in one facet calls for change in the others for an organisation to function successfully.

Below is the McKinsey 7-S framework, which represents the connections between seven areas and classifies them into 'Soft Ss' and 'Hard Ss'. The shape of the model reflects interconnectedness of the seven components.

The model can be applied to many situations in the firm and is a valuable tool when organisational design is under consideration. The most common uses of the framework are:

- To facilitate organisational change.
- To help implement new strategy.
- To identify how each area may change in future.
- To facilitate the merger of organisations.

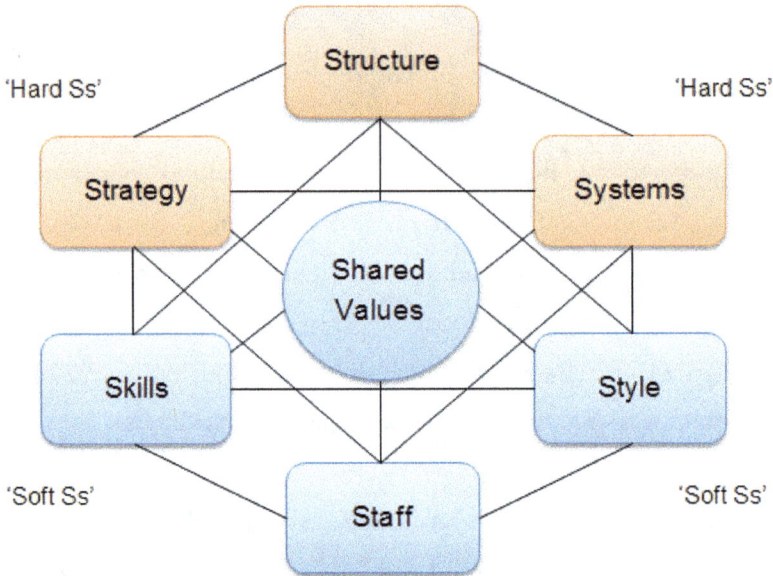

Figure 1.2: McKinsey 7-S Framework (Source: Peters and Waterman, 1982)

In the McKinsey model, the seven areas of an organisation are divided into the 'soft' and 'hard' areas. Strategy, structure and systems are hard elements that are much easier to identify and manage when compared to soft elements. On the other hand, soft areas, although harder to manage, constitute the foundation of the organisation and are more likely to create sustained competitive advantage.

Hard 'Ss'

Strategy is a plan developed by a firm to achieve sustained competitive advantage and successfully compete in the market. What does a well-aligned strategy mean in McKinsey's 7-S model? In general, a sound strategy is the one that is clearly articulated, is long-term, helps to achieve competitive advantage and is reinforced by strong vision, mission and values. But it is hard to tell if such strategy is well-aligned with other elements when analysed alone. So the key in 7-S model is not to look at your firm to find the great strategy, structure, systems etc., but to check if it is in sync with other elements. For example, a short-term strategy is usually a poor choice for a firm but if it is in sync with the other 6 elements, then it may provide strong results. Strategy is the firm's alignment of resources and capabilities to "win" in its market.

Structure refers to the way business divisions and units are organised and includes information of who is accountable to whom. Thus, structure is the organisational chart of the company. Moreover, it is one of the most evident and easy to change components of the model. **Structure** includes roles, responsibilities and accountability relationships.

Systems are processes and procedures of the firm, which disclose its daily activities and how decisions are made. Systems represent the sphere of the organisation that influences how business is conducted and it should occupy the attention of executive during organisational change. **Systems** refer to the business and technical infrastructure that employees use on a daily basis to accomplish their aims and goals.

Soft 'S'

Skills refer to the abilities that the firm's employees excel at. Additionally, they encapsulate capabilities and competences. In the process of organisational change, the issue frequently arises of what skills the firm will truly require to reinforce its new strategy or new structure.

Staff represents what type and how many employees a company will require and how these employees will be recruited, trained, motivated and rewarded.

Style represents the way the organisation is managed by top-level executives, how they interact, what actions they take and their symbolic value. Thus, it is the management style of firm's leaders.

Shared Values are at the heart of McKinsey's 7-S model. They are the norms and standards that influence and determine employee behaviour and organisational actions and consequently, constitute the bedrock of every firm.

Organisation of this Book

Supply chain management

An attempt is made to examine how supply chain management concepts can be applied in the private and public sectors and in different industries in a developing country. Also discussed is the impact of effective supply chain management on business performance in a number of countries, focusing particularly on African economies.

Operations management

This section starts with the general underlying concepts and subsequently focuses on how effective operations management can be applied in a developing economy. The subject is further explored with case studies which are presented on how operational excellence can be adopted for superior performance in an emerging economy; firstly, in a manufacturing organisation with total quality management as a bedrock of its strategy, and secondly, in a service firm with quality service delivery as the pivot of its strategy.

Marketing management

Marketing practices are examined from a variety of concepts including market orientation, marketing strategies and activities in a developing economy context and how these different constructs have an impact on organisational performance. Lessons are drawn from findings of different market-based practices in a variety of African countries. Subsequently, a focus is placed on Ghana to draw out implications of the series of findings for business executives.

Services management

How do the effective management of services result in superior performance of service firms and how do manufacturing firms take advantage of services to augment their products, maintain a competitive advantage and superior performance in their respective industries? These are the questions that this chapter attempts to answer within the context of a developing economy. Appiah-Adu's (2016) model of improving business performance is presented in this chapter as a paradigm which firms seeking to excel in their industries would do well to adopt in their efforts to remain competitive over the long term.

Financial management

An effort is made to explore the impact of effective financial management on business performance in a developing economy setting. The existence of appropriate infrastructure to ensure that revenues and costs are properly accounted for is critical in this context. Critical aspects of the firm that need attention in this regard are the planning system, governance framework, financing, accounting, quality management and general management. If these areas are functioning optimally, then they will accomplish the effective value addition needed to propel the business to appropriate levels that will result in the optimal realisation of its goals, objectives, strategies and tactical plans, in other words, achieving success in executing its strategic plan.

Human resource management

It is argued by practitioners and scholars alike that human resources are the best resources an organisation possesses. No wonder it features in both the Porter value chain and McKinsey 7-S Models as critical to strategy development and implementation respectively. Specific areas covered in this arena include workforce planning, talent management, succession planning as well as learning and development. The implications of human resource management for achieving a sustainable competitive advantage and superior business performance are subsequently highlighted.

Systems and technology development

Against the backdrop of Porter's value chain framework the advantage of embracing IT innovation buttressed by a standardised systems development framework for business performance in a developing economy is explored. In this chapter which focuses on systems and technology using industry analysis, it is contended that generating IT value from adopting IT innovation will only guarantee competitive performance for businesses if it is conceived and implemented within the appropriate support systems.

Strategy

An effort is made to explore the impact or effect of strategic management on corporate performance and provides an array of tools to assist business practitioners to adapt their organisations to the business environment in an attempt to achieve their main goals. Strategic management can facilitate sound decision making and unity. Nevertheless, to a certain degree, realisation of corporate strategy is contingent upon on the appropriate conceptual perspective rather than specific tools, since tools in themselves can really become an obstacle to innovative thinking, especially in markets that are extremely unpredictable, and therefore require continual adaptations to achieve best fit between strategy and evolving conditions.

Organisational culture

Corporate culture is concerned with patterns of shared values and beliefs that help individuals understand organisational functioning, and thus, provides them with norms for behaviour in the firm. The significance of corporate culture as an organisational variable is embedded in the fact it serves as a critical element which management might utilise in shaping the direction of their firms due to the influence it has on the way in which organisations adapt to external pressures in the business environment. Corporate culture can serve as a tool to improve productivity and if properly communicated, culture can be used to encourage all employees to subscribe to organisational goals for the improvement of its performance.

Organisational structure

The structure of an organisation serves as one of the fulcrums around which many key activities revolve to facilitate the attainment of a firm's set goals. Consequently, instituting a suitable structure is critical to the effective performance of the firm. It is therefore not surprising that many organisations find it expedient to make structural transformations that are congruent with use of emerging technologies, which call for better horizontal coordination. In this chapter it is contended that there are several internal and external dynamics that determine the most suitable organisational structure to embrace for competitive performance.

References

- Porter, M. (1985). *Competitive advantage: Creating and sustaining superior performance.* New York, NY: Free Press.
- Peters, T. & Waterman, R. (1982). *In Search of Excellence,* New York, NY: Harper & Row

Chapter 2

Effects of the Macro-Economic Environment on Competitive Performance

Mahamudu Bawumia

Abstract

The constant interaction between businesses and their environmental forces confirm that firms do not exist independently of their environment, which implies that favourable conditions will create an enabling environment and positively impact a firm's performance and competitiveness, and an unfavourable environment will impede a firm's progress. This study looks at the different macro-economic environmental forces that impact firm performance. The questions to be investigated are; how do the macro-environmental forces facilitate or hinder firm performance, profitability and overall competitiveness? To achieve the study's objectives and goals, the methodology used in the study was based on a qualitative approach through the administration of electronic questionnaires to participants in diverse private sector organisations. The findings in the study will aid existing and emerging businesses and their senior executives in decision-making and help address some of the major challenges posed by the macro-economic environmental forces to firm performance, growth and competitiveness. The study also has major implications for policy makers in various developing countries in terms of formulating the right corporate governance policies to help streamline and strengthen business management and enhance the performance of developing economy firms operating in their respective sectors.

Keywords: Macro-economic environment; Firm performance; Developing countries.

Introduction

Changes in the global economic system over the last three decades have significantly impacted the global business environment and firms' macro-economic environments in diverse ways. As a result, firms in developing economies are often under pressure to take advantage of the new opportunities created and strive to meet the challenges posed by macro environmental forces. Emeka and Eyuche (2014) define the business environment as the entire "surroundings of a living organism, including natural forces and other living things, which provide conditions for development and growth." In the macro-economic environment, the external stakeholders are people and policies in the organisation's external environment that are affected by it, which in turn, affect a firm's operations and activities. The macro-economic environmental forces usually fall beyond the control of the firm, and their effect on a firm's performance is more pronounced in today's competitive global business environment. The macro-environmental forces that could positively or negatively impact decisions managers make to achieve sustainability and competitiveness include; the different threats that are posed by a firm's competitive forces in the industry in which it operates, general external forces such as government policies, economic forces, socio-cultural forces, demographic forces, technological factors, legal forces in terms of rules and regulatory frameworks, and policies pursued by international organisations and regional trade agreements (RTAs) or regional economic integration (REIs) in a firm's macro-environment. These forces surrounding a firm are discussed below.

The Competitive Environment–Industry Analysis

The immediate environment surrounding a firm's macro-environment comprises competitors, suppliers, distributors, customers and strategic allies. Competitors are people or organisations that compete with a firm in an industry for goods or services and resources such as talented employees and customers. A firm's macro environment is influenced by competitive forces such as the industry environment. The structure of an industry often affects the firm's performance and competitiveness. Michael Porter discussed the five competitive forces that may require managers to formulate competitive strategies to achieve sustainable competitive advantage (Porter, 1998). Linking the five forces model to firm strategy, Rothaermel (2015) also argued that the five forces model is a framework for identifying the forces that determine industry profitability and help managers shape their firms' competitive strategy by analysing the level of competition within an industry and a firm's strategy development.

The central focus in defining a firm's competitive strategy is the intensity of rivalry among competing firms in an industry, which has significant impact on firm performance and competitiveness. For most industries, the intensity of competitive rivalry is the major determinant of the competitiveness in the industry. Competition in an industry is intense when there are direct competitors. Industry growth is slow and product/service is not easily

16

differentiated. Another competitive challenge is the threat of new entrants that is, the risk that potentially new firms could enter into an industry to reduce a firm's profit potential, leading to lower prices, which could compel existing firms to spend more to create greater value in order to satisfy existing customers.

A number of challenges are posed in the industry's macro-environment due to the threat of substitute products and services, and the availability of complement products and services. The existence of products outside of the realm of the common product boundaries and the propensity of customers to switch to alternatives which fulfil the needs of current customers from outside the industry adversely affect firm profitability and performance. Substitutes also limit the price that industry competitors can charge for their products and services. The power of substitutes is high when price performance has an attractive trade-off and buyers' switching cost is low. The threat of substitute products could be linked to the production of counterfeit goods in certain countries that benefit the home countries of the goods' origin, but hurt the firms that produce the real product by lowering the prices of the fake/imitated goods and taking away a chunk of original firms' market or customers and profit. Also, complements are products, services or competencies that add value when used together with the original product offering such as toothbrush and toothpaste. Providing customers with a good or service that leads them to value the firm's offering more, especially when those products are combined with other products gives a firm advantage over its competitors.

Another major competitive challenge that impacts the profit potential of firms in an industry within the macro-economic context is the bargaining power of buyers or customers who pay for the firm's products and services, also described as the market of outputs. Customers are highly important to every organisation because a firm's success or failure is driven by customer experience, satisfaction and retention. In their attempts to satisfy, retain and attract existing and potential customers, managers and firms develop different customer relationship management strategies to respond more effectively to customers' needs and concerns. The ability of customers to put the firm under pressure affects a firm's sensitivity to price changes, with significant effect on firm profitability. When powerful buyers demand lower prices through price discounts, higher product quality or better services, it leads to higher cost to firms since firms get limited revenue, which inadvertently reduces a firm's profit potential as buyers capture part of the economic value created. The power of buyers is high if they have many alternatives or buy in large quantities, and their power is low if they act independently or are dispersed.

Some of the potential factors for increased buyer power are, buyer concentration to firm concentration ratio (demand and supply); the degree of dependency on existing channels of distribution; the bargaining leverage, especially in industries with high fixed costs; buyer information availability; availability of existing substitute products; buyer price sensitivity and differential advantage or uniqueness of a firm's products and services; and buyer switching costs relative to firm switching costs which could force down prices dramatically, as well as the level of customer value analysis, and the total volume of trading.

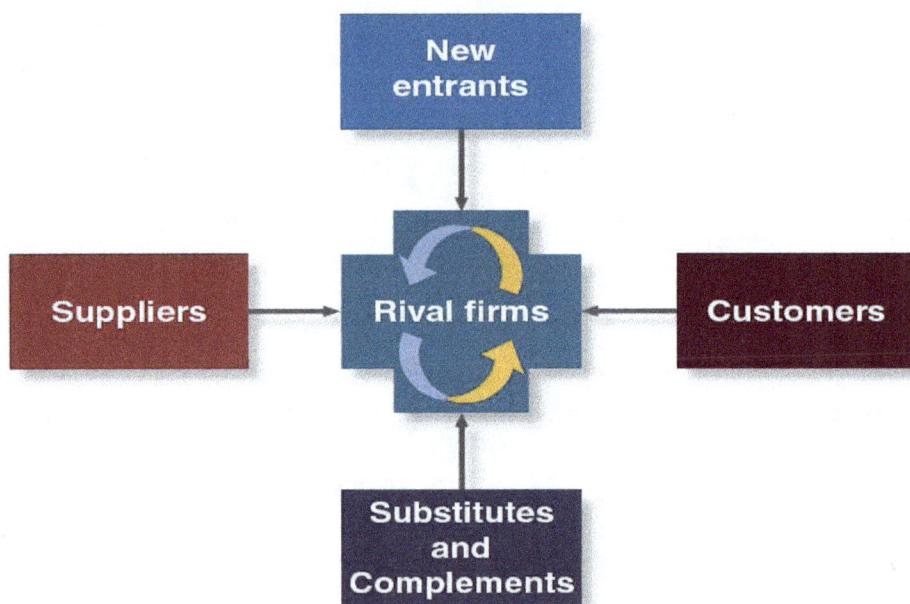

Figure 2.1: Five Forces model and its implications on firm performance and competitiveness in an industry.

Source: Porter (1998); and Rothaermel (2015)

In addition, suppliers and distributors also play key roles in firms' macro-environment. Suppliers or the market of inputs that provide raw materials, services, equipment, labour and other inputs needed for production can be a source of power over the firm when there are few substitutes, and in situations where a firm's switching costs or fixed costs is high. Powerful suppliers can demand higher prices for their inputs and capture a large part of the economic value created. Signs of powerful suppliers are where the supplier industry is concentrated and does not depend heavily on the incumbent's industry. Incumbent firms face high switching costs, where suppliers' products are differentiated, or where there are limited substitutes and suppliers' products have credible forward integration threats.

Distributors also help firms to sell or deliver their goods and services to customers in the supply chain, but can also pose a major challenge to firm profitability. In supply chain management, managing the network of facilities and people (suppliers & distributors) that obtain materials outside the firm to transform them into finished products, and distribute them to customers more effectively is key to organisational success and competitiveness. Figure 1 below explains Porter's Five Forces model and its implications on firm performance and competitiveness in an industry.

The General Forces in the Macro Environment

Moving from the competitive forces in the macro-economic environment, the study also examined forces in the general environment that influence firm performance in the global business environment, and particularly in developing economies. Since changes in the global economic system and the macro-economic environment affect businesses in countries across the globe and developing countries are no exception, the general environmental forces identified in this study that greatly influence firm performance in developing countries are grouped into five forces, which are discussed below using the PESTEL analysis:

Political Forces

The political system and policies a government pursues in a country and its ideological orientation have direct impact on business performance and competitiveness. A country's ideological orientation in terms of whether the government pursues socialism based on the command economy system, or capitalism in terms of the free market system or a mixed economy system by combining aspects of both capitalism and socialism greatly impacts a government's economic policy and affect businesses operating in that country. In free-market economies with democratic systems, governments pursue the free-market system by liberalising their markets and deregulating their trade policies to create the enabling environment for businesses to thrive and be competitive. Very often, in democratic settings where businesses are regulated by laws, rules, regulations and the government's corporate governance policy is administered based on due process, businesses are able to operate freely without unnecessary state interference. Conversely, in command economies where investments, production and the distribution of goods and services are directly controlled by the state or where private businesses are regulated through decrees, firms have little control over the factors of production. Businesses that operate in politically unstable regions or command economies stand the risk of being nationalised by the state on the pretext of opposition to the government, tax-evasion, breaking the business regulations designed and implemented by an authoritarian regime.

A country's political environment and government policy have a strong influence on business performance and growth, and the economy in general. Spencer and Gomez (2003) in their studies on how political environments affect firm growth, concluded that government intervention in the market, corruption in government and predictability of government policies have a significant influence on how businesses perform. Change in government can also affect businesses in many ways. Even in a democratic system where government policy is sharply skewed towards partisanship, this could deprive well-performing and genuine business the necessary support needed from the state to enhance their productivity and competitiveness. For example, while Ghana and many other countries in Africa's economic development continue to suffer from extreme partisanship, the industrial growth of countries in Asia, especially the "Asian Tigers'" (Hong Kong South Korea, Taiwan, Singapore and China) accelerated economic development and rapid industrialisation was devoid of partisanship.

Hence, the popularly termed "carrot and stick" strategies used by governments in these countries applied equally to all businesses regardless of their party affiliation. In addition, forceful removal of political leadership could for instance lead to rioting, chaos, anarchy, looting and uncertainty in the business environment. For example, attempts to forcibly change ruling governments in Ivory Coast, Liberia and other countries on the African continent led to chaos and the spread of civil wars. The political economy of a country also has significant impact on the rate or level of economic progress in that country with significant impact on business development and expansion because innovation and entrepreneurship are the engines of growth, and require a market economy and strong property rights since absence of state interference help firms to thrive and be competitive.

Economic Forces

The economic environmental forces consist of the general economic conditions and trends that may affect a firm's performance, its strategy and/or activities. Economic forces dramatically affect managers' ability to function effectively and influence their strategic choices. These include inflation (increase in levels of goods and services affect firms and erosion in consumers' purchasing power), interest rates (high interest rate means high cost of borrowing and low interest rate implies low cost of borrowing for firms). Interest rate and inflation rate affect the availability and cost of capital, business expansion opportunities, prices, costs, and consumer demand for goods and services. In times of high unemployment, firms may pay less for labour, and therefore reduce their labour costs. Nonetheless, where there are more job applicants or high unemployment rate, there are fewer customers with money to spend, which affect consumers' purchasing power parity as many people are not able to afford even the basic needs in life. The level of taxation in a country may also affect firms' profitability and financial performance.

The availability of natural resources or raw materials for production could impact businesses positively or negatively based on whether there is abundance or scarcity of resources respectively. In terms of productivity growth, rising productivity leads to higher profits, and lower inflation and high stock prices and vice versa. Increase in taxes to service debt especially when the economy has slowed down may distort the market, and affect productivity. Domestic borrowing to service government debts could result in serious financial difficulties such as high interest rates, which has the potential of crowding out private investments. For developing countries, offshore borrowing should be considered carefully because debts owed in foreign currencies expose the business environment to the risk of exchange rate depreciations.

The macro-economic environment contributes significantly to an economy's productivity in terms of increase in its gross domestic product (GDP). A stable macro-economic environment creates the necessary conditions to increase business productivity, performance and competitiveness, and serves as the basis for sustainable economic development because it promotes savings, domestic investments and direct foreign investments into the country, and contributes towards increasing its exports, leading to a favourable trade balance. The growth rate in many countries, together with other factors or variables could determine whether the country is advancing economically, is in recession or retrogressing economically. Sluggish growth rate in an economy due to economic recession or economic downturn could negatively impact the performance and competitiveness of businesses operating in that country in diverse ways. Although the average growth rate in Africa is about 3%, Todaro and Smith (2009), attribute weak economic performance and lack of competitiveness on the part of African businesses to the continent's unstable macro-economic environment. The World Economic Forum's Global Competitiveness Report (2006-2007) also noted that without macroeconomic stability productivity is adversely disturbed. While macro-economic stability in terms of fiscal reforms is necessary for a state to advance and rejuvenate its economy, leading to economic development, the promotion and pursuit of a reasonably fair corporate taxation policy that helps to raise revenues for the state, and at the same time takes into consideration the interests and concerns of businesses, is crucial for the competitiveness and survival of businesses.

In highlighting some of the factors that constitute an unstable macro-economic environment, Haghighi, Sameti, and Isfahani (2012) identified instability in inflation, unhealthy fiscal policies, instability in real exchange rate and exchange relationships. While some theorists argue that theoretically, the effect of inflation on growth is inconclusive and ambiguous, there is ample evidence from various studies that economically, low and stable inflation in a business environment promotes demand for goods and services in an economy and that higher inflation threatens economic growth and stability of the economy (Walter, 1993). Besides creating uncertainty in the market, unstable inflation also alters government revenue and individual liabilities, since tax rates are usually adjusted by inflation average. Though other studies have argued that there is a nonlinear relationship between inflation and growth, the conclusion has indicated that inflation is only positive to a threshold, after which it becomes "significantly negative." Other economic forces which influence firms are the role of financial institutions in business development and expansion, the stability and value of a country's domestic currency, and its exchange rate value.

This study argues that pegging a country's currency too high or too low may not be good for investments and the import/export trade. Whereas valuing the domestic currency at a lower rate may help attract more importers into industrialised countries with large manufacturing and export sectors, and help their export market, high value of currency in non-industrialised developing economies may help importers since the high value of currency in their home countries reduces their import cost and their costs in the exchange rate market. Secondly, high value of currency and stability of the local currency may boost direct foreign investments into developing economies because foreign investors may benefit from a more stable currency and exchange rate system. It is also prudent for countries that are engaged in the export of raw materials to maintain high currency value to increase their earnings from exports and reduce their expenditure on imports. Furthermore, the level of certainty in public finance and stability of the economy have influence on the macro-economic environment, which in turn impacts businesses in diverse ways, because while a high level of certainty in public finance promotes investments and productivity, uncertainty may cause investors to hold back investments in new projects and new business ventures.

Socio-cultural environment

Socio-cultural forces are based on influences and trends originating in a country or society or a culture's human relationships and values that may affect businesses. Societal trends regarding how people think and behave have major implications for management of the labour force, customers, corporate social actions and managers strategic decisions about products/services and markets. As Adeleke, Oyenuga and Ogundele (2003) noted, the socio-cultural environment consists of elements, conditions and influences which shape the behaviour of an individual as a whole, and highly important in formulating business strategies. Changing lifestyles and interests in health have for example, led to increasing consumption of certain goods and services and the decline of others. In terms of social networking in contemporary times, many people use social media such as Facebook, Twitter, WhatsApp, Google etc. to find information about products and communicate their satisfaction and dissatisfaction in their shopping experience about products and services to firms, and even their friends online.

Modern businesses have taken advantage of the existence of the Internet and online networks such as social media to communicate information about their products and services to customers. These social media are changing long-standing patterns of communication in the global business environment. Additionally, the mass media is another social force in facilitating business/customer relationships and creating customers' awareness about products and services. For example, in Ghana, the activities of the media support the roles of government and its regulatory agencies such as the Food and Drugs Authority to create consumer awareness to avoid exposure to defective products or unhealthy foods and medicines. The media also holds the government and its regulatory institutions accountable to monitor firms' activities so that they do not take undue advantage of customers' lack of access to information and/or ignorance about product contents. By pressuring firms to promote ethical and sustainable production practices and corporate social responsibility, the media impacts firm performance, accountability and responsibility to their clients in diverse ways. To promote openness and transparency in their activities, and to avoid media backlash, managers in some firms take the initiative to communicate defective products honestly and frequently through the media and collaborate with government agencies to find immediate and ideal solutions.

Technological Forces

The development of modern technology has led to the introduction of new developments in methods for transforming resources into goods and services. Since the 1980s, most business transformations have depended on technology and firms use information and communication technology (ICT) to cut cost and make more profits. Changes in ICT, particularly the internet, continue to influence and inform managerial decision-making, products, labour, markets and competitiveness. It greatly contributes towards realising firms' corporate and global strategies and especially business strategies through cost reduction, to improve the quality of products and services, and innovation of products and services for growth and competitiveness.

As technology evolves, new industries, markets and competitive niches develop in many countries and regions across the globe. The introduction of the Internet has also facilitated e-business and e-commerce to a great extent and proactive firms have taken advantage of these e-strategies to gain and sustain competitive advantage in the industries in which they operate (Kotler, 2009; Strauss, El-Ansary & Frost, 2003; Weill, Peter & Vitale, 2001). The introduction of ICT has for instance changed the way business is carried out in our world today.

Technology has changed production methods, marketing and distribution. With technology, local businesses are able to compete globally with associated challenges. It is therefore important that businesses are able to strategise to cope with the global environment in order to remain competitive. The technological environment is so dynamic that businesses need to continuously adjust to changing global business trends in order to survive, and businesses that are unable to cope with the pace of progress in technology usually fade out of the market and go bankrupt or are compelled to merge with or be acquired by other organisations in order to avoid going bankrupt.

Ecological Forces

In addition to the above, other macro-environmental forces that could significantly impact businesses growth and performance in many countries are ecological forces. Changes in the global economic system due to globalisation, technological innovation and increasing competition among businesses have drawn serious attention to the impact of business activities on the ecology. Issues such as climate change, global warming, pollution of the environment, environmental degradation and sustainability, as well as the protection of biodiversity and ecosystems have come to the fore in international conferences and international trade agreements and treaties. These issues have been increasingly emphasised by the multilateral institutions including the International Monetary Fund (IMF), World Bank, World Trade Organisation (WTO), United Nations (UN) and other global governance institutions. The resultant effect is that these contemporary issues now tend to have a great impact on business operations and competitiveness.

Since the launch of the Bruntland Commission Report on Sustainable Development in 1987 which outlined the need to preserve the environment for future generations, policies of the multilateral organisations and many national governments have focused on the need for businesses to promote ethical practices, corporate social responsibility, green management, green manufacturing etc. to contribute towards protecting the natural environment. Besides, the resurgence of Regional Economic Integration (REIs) bodies or Regional Trade Agreements (RTAs) such as the European Union (EU), the African Union (AU), the North American Free Trade Agreement (NAFTA), Brazil, Russia, India, China and South Africa (BRICS), including regional banks like the African Development Bank, Asian Development Bank etc. have not only facilitated business development and expansion, but have also had significant impacts on businesses in various regions in terms of promoting environmental sustainability in countries across the globe.

Legal Forces

In terms of the legal framework, the local and national regulatory bodies such as government ministries, departments, agencies, boards and commissions that establish rules and regulations and specify, prescribe or proscribe the conditions under which firms operate their business activities immensely impact business efficiency and effectiveness in diverse ways. These bodies ensure business compliance to national statutory laws (based on rules, regulations in the Constitutional, administrative and legal system) and local government by-laws. For example, in Ghana, the Food and Drugs Authority ensures product safety and quality, and set standards of operation for firms, among other mandates. In the same vein, the Securities and Exchange Commission regulates investment firms and issues in the Ghana Stock Exchange. Other regulatory bodies such as the Energy Commission, Forestry Commission, Lands Commission, Minerals Commission etc. play similar regulatory roles in specific industries and the economy as a whole.

While these institutions exist in most developing countries, and the roles they play have significant impact on the effectiveness of government policy, the challenge is how effective do the regulatory institutions play these roles to ensure strict firm compliance? Other legal factors such as laws protecting customers, labour laws, environmental laws, competition laws, as well as health and safety regulations could all affect organisations in the macro-environment. A government's corporate governance policy and the existence or absence of tax and business courts to deal effectively with business issues could also impact business operations within a country positively or negatively. In other words, countries with stable political environments and well-established legal systems are more likely to attract investors than countries experiencing political upheavals and/or with compromised legal systems.

Conclusions and Implications

In summary, it could be argued that while changes in the global economic system and the numerous macro-economic environmental forces have brought a great deal of positive developments to businesses in developing countries, they also pose major challenges to business survival, profitability, performance and competitiveness. As a result, managers in firms need to decide on the relative importance of the various forces to their firms, and focus on identifying factors in the macro-environment that are most likely to change and which ones will have greater impact on their firms. One way of doing this is to rank the likelihood of a change occurring in any of the macro-environmental factors and rate the impact of the change on their firms.

To address the competitive forces that threaten the survival and competitiveness of their firms, managers must be aware of their firm's competitors and learn from their competitors' best practices to improve upon the quality of their goods and services and to enable them enhance their firms' competitive strategies. It is also imperative that managers constantly analyse the forces in the general environment in order to take advantage of the opportunities they present and be able to deal more effectively with the threats they pose to their firms. Managers wishing to gain and sustain competitive advantage need to develop different scenarios to look at future conditions in the best-case and worst-case scenarios in order to be able to deal more effectively with potential problems, threats and opportunities available to their firms (Kinicki & Williams, 2010; Robbins & Coulter, 2013; Hill & McShane, 2015). These forward-looking business strategies can be achieved by forecasting or predicting how variables in the macro-economic environment of the firm will change, whether in a negative or positive direction. For firms and managers to influence their macro-environments, there is a need for different firms from different geographical regions to work together to manage the external environment since the macro-environmental issues facing businesses are many and varied.

Since the macro environment is usually beyond the influence or control of the internal dynamics of the organisation, it is imperative that managers develop more effective strategies to help mitigate the impact of the environmental effects on their operations by designing and administering appropriate strategies to manage the macroeconomic environment, using strategic tools that could help them understand their businesses' position, potential threats and opportunities, market growth or decline, and direction for operation. The study therefore concludes with the view that managers in organisations need to employ four interdependent strategies – technology, competitiveness, efficiency and effectiveness to help them address the macro-economic environmental forces and compete more effectively in the global business environment.

References

- Adeleke, A., Oyenuga, O. & Ogundele, O. (2003). *Business policy and strategy*. Mushin, Lagos: Concept Publication Limited.

- Emeka, N. & Eyuche, A. (2014). Environmental factors and organisational performance in Nigeria (A case study of Juhel Company). *World Engineering and Applied Sciences Journal* 5(3), 75-84.

- Haghighi, H., Sameti, M. & Isfahani, R. (2012). The effect of macroeconomic instability on economic growth in Iran. *Research in Applied Economics* 4 (3), 39-61.

- Hill, C. & McShane, S. (2015). *Principles of management* (Africa Edition). London, UK & New York, USA: McGraw-Hill.

- Kinicki, A. & Williams, B (2010). *Management*. Boston, MA: McGraw-Hill.

- Kotler, P. (2009). Defining marketing for the 21st century. In *Marketing management* by Kotler and   Keller, Englewood Cliffs, NJ: Prentice Hall

- Porter, M. (1998). Competitive strategy: Techniques for analyzing industries and competitors. New York, NY: Free Press.

- Robbins, S. & Coulter, M. (2013). *Management*. London, UK: Pearson Education

- Rothaermel, F. (2015). *Strategic Management: Concepts & Cases,* 2nd Edition. Boston/New York, USA: McGraw Hill.

- Spencer, J. & Gomez, C. (2003). How political environments affect the growth of firms: Evidence from small and large enterprises in Latin America. George Washington University: Center for Latin American issues.

- Strauss, J., El-Ansary, A. & Frost, F. (2003). *E-marketing*. Newark, NJ. Prentice Hall.

- The World Economic Forum's Global Competitiveness Report (2006-2007).

- Todaro, M. & Smith, S. (2009). *Economic development*. London, UK: Pearson Educational Limited.

- Walter, J. (1993). *Economics*. Hauppauge, NY: Barron's Educational Services.

- Weill, P. & Vitale, M. (2001). *Place to Space: Migrating to E-business Models*. Boston, MA: Harvard Business School Press.

Chapter 3
Supply Chain Management and Competitive Performance
Douglas Boateng

Abstract

This chapter seeks to promote a general understanding of supply chain management and its inextricable link to competitive performance, service delivery, product quality and overall economic growth in Africa. It highlights the differences between, among other things, supply chain management, logistics and procurement, and explores the influence of these areas on organisational performance. Numerous industrial and scholarly reports (especially from Europe, Asia and the Americas) continue to provide evidence that the successful implementation of supply chain management can assist local and international businesses (profit and non-profit/public and private) to extend their market reach and achieve sustainable customer-driven service delivery quality. It has also been seen to assist with product innovation and new product (tangible/intangible) development. In addition to this, supply chain management has been recognised for its ability to assist countries in realising long-term socio-economic growth and development. An understanding of supply chain management is therefore considered critical for achieving sustainable business growth, service quality, product innovation, international trade, and overall competitive performance in Africa. This chapter not only expounds on the potential impact of supply chain management in African countries, but also endeavours to fix the terminological mix-up often found on the continent between supply chain management, logistics, and procurement.

Keywords: *Supply chain management; Procurement, International trade, Logistics, Africa, Quality, Service delivery, Competitive performance.*

Introduction

According to various World Bank reports (2006, 2007) a variety of selected countries on the African continent have witnessed unprecedented socio-economic growth and infrastructural development in the last decade; the rate of which has never before been experienced anywhere in post-independent Africa. Yet, many of those who had hoped that such positive developments would bring with it relative socio-economic liberation and improvements are becoming increasingly bitter towards their respective governments due to among other things, a continued lack of perceived quality of service delivery, youth unemployment, corruption in selected spheres of the economy, and disillusionment with targeted, affirmative empowerment policies. In addition, local businesses, especially medium to large scale enterprises that were hoping to extend their market reach – thus contributing to much needed double-digit growth and sustainable job creation on the continent – have not been as successful as initially expected (Boateng, 2009a).

Despite these disappointments, today's global competitive environment pushes public and private sector organisations to continue to seek newer markets and lower-cost sources of production, raw materials, and human capital. This emergence of new markets and supply sources is driving African organisations with international ambitions to find innovative and cost-effective ways to extend their networks and value chain reach. While more and more organisations are increasingly adopting supply chain management as a tool for competitive advantage, one of the most pervasive paradoxes of the above mentioned constraints on business growth and the government service delivery conundrum has been the unfortunate desire of many such organisations to drive supply chain improvements via procurement and the use of technological platforms (Boateng, 2009b). As a result, SCM managers in both local and international organisations are not always given the latitude to develop and implement long-term strategies that will drive sustainable supply chain performance and related competitive performance on the continent.

Following a brief discussion on the terminological mix-up between supply chain management, logistics, and procurement that are often found on the African continent, this chapter seeks to explore the role of supply chain management in market reach and competitive performance, as well as the strategic importance of supply chain management in Africa.

Defining Supply Chain Management (SCM)

Supply chain management (SCM) is the seamless management of all the interlinked value-adding activities that goods and services encounter while they move through a value chain *en route* to the ultimate customer. The supply chain is made up of suppliers, manufacturing centres, warehouses, distribution centres, retail outlets, raw materials, in progress inventory, and finished products. In a broader context, a supply chain encompasses not only the internal value-adding processes, but also the various tangible and intangible inputs from external suppliers and customers (Boateng, 2009a; 2009b). In short, supply chain management has been defined as "a set of approaches utilised to efficiently integrate suppliers, manufacturers, warehouses, and stores, so that merchandise is produced and distributed at the right quantities, to the right locations, and at the right time, in order to minimise system wide costs while satisfying service level requirements" (Simchi-Levi, 2003, p.1).

Competition in today's global market, as well as increases in customer demand have led many organisations to invest significant time, energy and money in their supply chains. Advances in information and communication technologies have also encouraged businesses to constantly update and improve their supply chain management techniques. Simchi-Levi at al. (2003, p.1) explain the typical supply chain as follows: "raw materials are procured and items are produced at one or more factories, shipped to warehouses for intermediate storage, and then shipped to retailers or customers." As such, in order to limit costs and ensure service delivery, quality supply chain strategies need to take interactions at all levels of the supply chain into account.

In their highly acclaimed article, 'The Seven Principles of Supply Chain Management' Anderson et al., discuss the principles of effective supply chain management. Viewing supply chain management as a strategic variable, they insist that managers involved in the supply chain process need to understand two core elements of the supply chain environment. Firstly, they need to "think about the supply chain as a whole - all the links involved in managing the flow of products, services, and information from their suppliers' suppliers to their customers' customers (that is, channel customers, such as distributors and retailers)." Secondly, they need to "pursue tangible outcomes - focused on revenue growth, asset utilization, and cost" (Anderson et al., 2007, p.3). In this regard, they maintain that successful supply chain management is determined by "how well activities coordinate across the supply chain to create value for customers, while increasing the profitability of every link in the chain" (Anderson et al., 2007, p.4).

In relation to this, Li et al (2006) assert that supply chain management has a dual purpose. Firstly, it aims "to improve the performance of an individual organisation," and secondly, it aims to "improve the performance of the whole supply chain" (Li et al., 2006, p.107). Consequently, they insist that the goal of supply chain management "is to integrate both information and material flows seamlessly across the supply chain as an effective competitive weapon" (2006, p.107).

In order for supply chain management to be used as a so called 'competitive weapon' Simchi-Levi et al. (2003) insist that three critical abilities are needed. Firstly, organisations need to have the "ability to match supply chain strategies with product characteristics;" secondly, they need the "ability to replace traditional supply chain strategies, in which each facility or party in the chain makes decisions with little regard to their impact on other supply chain partners, [with] … those that yield a globally optimised supply chain;" and thirdly, they should possess the "ability to effectively manage uncertainty and risk" (Levi et al., 2003, p. 11).

While supply chain management is increasingly being recognised as an important element of organisational performance and success, some confusion surrounding the term remains. Although many practitioners still consider the concepts of supply chain management, procurement and logistics as interchangeable terms, various academics and seasoned industry professionals have, over the last 20 years, developed succinct distinctions between these three functions (Boateng, 1997; Christopher, 1992; Lambert, 1992; Sterling, 1985; Trent, 2004). Indeed, extensive research in Europe, Asia, America and Africa (largely industrial verticals in South Africa), seems to indicate an emerging consensus that provides clear differences between these ideas, and between supply chain management and logistics management in particular (Boateng, 2009a,; Ellram & Cooper, 1993; Jacoby, 2009; Lambert, 2006; Stevens, 1989; Tan et al., 2002).

As mentioned above, *supply chain management* involves the management of all the interlinked activities within a value-adding chain. These include, but are not limited to, planning, procurement, manufacturing/production distribution, and customer service. Also included are all the value-adding linkages outside of an organisation (Boateng, 2009c). *Logistics management* is one of the elements in a supply chain. In line with the views of the Chartered

Institute of Logistics and Transport (CILT), the largest and oldest body of professionals who engage in the logistics and supply chain field, as well as the Council on Supply Chain Management Professionals (CSCMP), a US-based international body of professionals who are engaged in activities that are related to supply chain management, logistics is described as one of the mega processes within a supply chain. Logistics is responsible for the planning, implementation and control of the efficient and effective inward and outward flow and storage of goods, services, and related information between a point of origin and a point of need (Boateng, 2009c). As such, logistics management is primarily focused on the actual movement and storage of products within the supply value chain.

In comparison to supply chain management and logistics, *procurement* is one of the sub-processes of supply chain management. Procurement focuses primarily on the sourcing and purchasing of goods and services within the supply value chain. According to the Chartered Institute of Purchasing and Supply (CIPS) and CSCMP guidelines, procurement can be described as one of the mega-processes within a supply chain that plans, implements, and controls the efficient and effective sourcing and purchasing of goods, be it tangible or intangible (Banfield, 1999). Strategic sourcing is part of the procurement process that assists an organisation to optimise the total cost of ownership (Boateng, 2010).

Based on the above descriptions it is clear that although connected, supply chain management, logistics, and procurement, function at three separate levels on a supply chain, and as such cannot be grouped together as one 'logistics' concept or activity.

SCM: Key to Extending Market Reach and Competitive Performance

It is an accepted fact that companies which continue to innovatively apply supply chain management techniques have achieved significant cost savings, improved customer service, market share, and bottom-line financial performance. Quantifiable benefits have included a reduction in total product cost of 10% to 25%, a reduction in product inventory of between 12% to 30%, improved customer satisfaction, increased competitiveness in global markets, and the development of a more collaborative relationship with both suppliers and customers. In a number of cases, this has translated into millions of dollars of overall earnings. Supported by the relevant infrastructure, it offers practical solutions for meeting customers' needs in a manner that will result in an increase in long-term shareholder value (Jacoby, 2009).

Over the past 30 years numerous publications have provided clear evidence that supply chain management can assist companies to profitably extend their market reach well beyond their borders. Toyota, Cargill, Shell, HP, Coca Cola, Merck & Co, Nike, MacDonald's, SAB, Honda and Nissan are all classic examples of companies that have benefited from the effective use of supply chain strategies to reach out to their global customers. In Africa, companies including SAB, Pick 'n Pay, BHP, MTN, Sasol and Bidvest, have also made significant strides in applying supply chain management to improve bottom-line performance and results. For these organisations, the challenge is to maintain customer service across rapidly changing markets, supply chain partners, and distribution channels.

The Strategic Importance of Supply Chain Management in Africa

According to the IMF, sub-Saharan Africa's growth performance in the last three years has been the best in the last three decades. Selected countries have, over the last 10 years, seen significant economic growth, with South Africa, Nigeria and relatively smaller countries like Ghana virtually doubling their respective nominal GDP to US$349.8 billion (World Bank, 2014), US$568.5 billion (World Bank, 2014); and US$38.65 billion respectively (World Bank, 2014). This growth can mainly be attributed to the commodity boom and to improvements in supply chain management. All public and private sector organisations, irrespective of size, ownership or listing, invariably make use of some elements of supply chain management in their day-to-day business activities. According to Frazelle (2002), in 1996 the global expenditure for logistics was well in excess of US$3.5 trillion. This represented almost 20% of the world's GDP. Over the last 30 years, most companies have, on average, spent between 5% and 20% of total revenues on logistics and selected supply chain related activities (Bowersox & Calantone, 1998; Bowersox et al., 1999; Hausman et al., 2005). Using a 10% percentage baseline, one can confidently postulate that in 2006 global logistics expenditure was in excess of US$4.8 trillion.

Nonetheless, it has been argued that African countries, for example, South Africa, Nigeria, Kenya, Egypt and Ghana, can do much better if there is a more *coordinated and action-oriented* effort between governments and the private sector in relation to infrastructure development. In particular, the coordination will necessitate more innovative, multi-sectoral approaches to resolving inter-country and intra-country linkages. To date, it is logistically easier to transport goods from the Americas, Europe and the Middle East to selected parts of Africa than from

South Africa. This is primarily because there is still very limited value-adding activities and links between South Africa and other parts of the continent and Asia.

As a result, the percentage of logistics spend in Africa is relatively higher than global statistics due to, among other things, limited infrastructure and continental-wide service providers (Hausman et al., 2005). According to the International Monetary Fund (IMF), in 2006, Africa's GDP was in excess of US$1 trillion, with South Africa accounting for about 25%. Using 9% as a baseline percentage spend; one can confidently and conservatively estimate that the total African logistics expenditure at that time was worth well in excess of US$90 billion.

Despite the continuation of the above -mentioned logistical complications, growing expenditure in the area of supply chain management has led to it becoming an increasingly hot topic in the boardrooms of a number of top companies on the African continent. Indeed, with the ever increasing need for organisations to go in search of newer, more competitive markets, the stereotype of supply chain management as a relatively insignificant part of business strategy is quickly evaporating. Today, both public and private executives are openly discussing supply chain management for a number of reasons. Some of these reasons include:

- emerging technologies have made it possible for effective communication to take place between supply chain partners;
- new paradigms have developed on the continent, which has made it easier for businesses to harness the necessary resources;
- the rapid development of employees is making it easier for supply chain members to assume responsibility and make decisions for mutual benefit;
- the global need for Africa's raw materials;
- an increasingly borderless business world;
- the increasingly sophisticated and global customer;
- the internet, mobile phones, and electronic and mobile commerce;
- the global financial crisis and the limited financial kitty;
- the gradual shift in economic power from the West to the East;

- the need for accountability and transparency; and

- the increase in eco-sensitive and socially responsible supply chains.

Superseding all of this is the intense competition for complex and ever-demanding local and global customers (Jacoby, 2009, pp.42-49). Since "competition is no longer between organisations, but among supply chains," effective supply chain management is increasingly becoming recognised as "a potentially valuable way of securing competitive advantage and improving organisational performance" (Li et al., p.107).

Key Issues for Business Executives to Consider in Strategic Evaluation of Supply Chains

Rethinking and reconfiguring a supply chain requires a fundamental paradigm shift, vis-à-vis, how all the process activities and associated steps contribute to the total value chain costs and satisfaction of a need. Businesses can no longer look at these value-adding activities as separate puzzle pieces. Rather, they should institute a culture that ensures the seamless integration of all functions of research and development, sourcing, production, and distribution, among others (Boateng, 2009c).

As Lambert and Stock (2001) and Christopher (1992) quite rightly point out, the interconnected supply chain functions must be:

- viewed as one complete pipeline process and not as several distinct functions, for example, forecasting, purchasing, transportation and customer service.
- best in its class, vis-à-vis, time compression, total cost reduction, customer satisfaction linkages across multiple channels, businesses and geographies.
- adaptive and agile.
- socially responsive.

Christopher (1992) Lambert (2006), and Lambert and Stock (2001) go on to succinctly summarise the critical success factors in supply chain management. These, they assert, include, but are not limited to, a lowering of the total delivered costs and lead times; improved trading partner relationships and value; improved inventory performance – cost and velocity; improved transportation performance – cost, speed and service; lower break-even costs and times; increased revenues; increased flexibility/visibility/responsiveness;

timely information exchange, and improved customer service; an environmentally friendly and socially responsive value chain, and improved shareholder value.

While these factors are seen as critical to supply chain success, additional elements need to be taken into account. For example, strategic, tactical and operational levels of the supply chain also need to be thought-out and considered. Indeed, Simchi-Levi et al (2003) highlight the importance of being able to differentiate between these three levels for organisational supply chain success. At a strategic level, supply chain managers need to make decisions that have a long-lasting effect on an organisation. Some of these decisions may be related to "product design, what to make internally and what to outsource, supplier selection, and strategic partnering as well as decisions on the number, location, and capacity of warehouses and manufacturing plants and the flow of material through the logistics network" (2003. p, 12). At the tactical level managers need to make short-term decisions that are largely updated or renewed "anywhere between once every quarter and once every year. These include purchasing and production decisions, inventory policies, and transportation strategies" etc. (2003, p.12). Finally, at the operational level managers are required to make day-to-day decisions, including "scheduling, lead time quotations, routing, and truck loading," among other things (2003, p.12). All of these levels of the supply chain need to be taken into consideration when evaluating and implementing strategies for supply chain success.

As mentioned earlier, Anderson et al (2007) discuss seven fundamental principles for effective, competitive, and successful supply chain management processes. These principles provide supply chain managers, executives, and decision makers with additional benchmarks for the implementation of effective, efficient, and competitive supply chain strategies. These principles include:

- Principle 1: Segment customers based on the service needs of distinct groups and adapt the supply chain to serve these segments profitably.
- Principle 2: Customise the logistics network to the service requirements and profitability of customer segments.
- Principle 3: Listen to market signals and align demand planning accordingly across the supply chain, ensuring consistent forecasts and optimal resource allocation.

- Principle 4: Differentiate product closer to the customer and speed conversion across the supply chain.

- Principle 5: Manage sources of supply strategically to reduce the total cost of owning materials and services.

- Principle 6: Develop a supply chain-wide technology strategy that supports multiple levels of decision making and gives a clear view of the flow of products, services, and information.

- Principle 7: Adopt channel-spanning performance measures to gauge collective success in reaching the end-user effectively and efficiently (Anderson et al., 2007, pp. 4 – 7).

While these principles offer organisations with a sound starting point for the implementation of supply chain related activities, supply chain managers and executives also need to recognise the complexity of supply chains and invest time and effort in the development of a well thought-out plan before implementation can begin. This plan should specify "funding, leadership, and expected financial results" and will help to "forestall conflicts over priorities and keep … management focused and committed to realizing the benefits" (Anderson et al., 2007, p.8).

As mentioned earlier, supply chain management is without a doubt inextricably linked to economic growth. There is a direct correlation between Europe's, the Americas' and now Asia's economic growth and supply chain management. Notably, all of these regions are able to cost-effectively value add and efficiently manage the inflows and outflows of goods and services, both locally and internationally. In order for Africa to achieve double-digit growth and create much needed jobs, companies must be able to compete with their counterparts globally through lean, agile and responsive supply chains (Boateng, 2009c). It is therefore important for executives and policy makers to understand the critical role that supply chain management plays in organisational growth and success. In particular, executives need to promote and embrace some of the key critical success factors of supply chain management.

References

- Anderson, D., Britt, F. & Favre, D. (2007). *The 7 Principles of Supply Chain Management. Supply Chain Management Review.*

- Banfield, E. (1999). *Harnessing value in the supply chain.* New York, NY: Wiley & Sons.

- Boateng, D. (1997). R*e-configuring an international pharma-chemical customer service policy through Delphi and process mapping.* (Unpublished doctoral dissertation). University of Warwick, UK.

- Boateng, D. 2008. Can Africa's senior executives continue to relatively underrate the strategic importance of supply chain management (SCM) and logistics in today's rapidly changing business world? Institute of Directors, South Africa, Part 2

- Boateng, D. (2009a.) *Achieving middle income status through supply chain management. A case in point for Ghana.*

- Boateng, D. (2009b). *The changing role of procurement in managing a supply chain network.* Paper presented at the Smart Procurement and Supply Chain Conference.

- Boateng, D. (2009c). *Fundamentals of supply chain management. Executive insight working book series and study school material.* (2nd ed). Midrand: SBL UNISA.

- Boateng, D. (2010). *Africa gearing up for supply chain productivity and operational improvements.* Retrieved from http://www.iomnet.org.uk/News/IOM-News/July-2010/Africa-gearing-up-for-supply-chain-productivity-and-operational- improvements-0.aspx.

- Bowersox, D.J. & Calantone, R.J. (1998). Executive insights: global logistics. *Journal of International Marketing,* 6(4), 83–93.

- Bowersox, D. J., Closs, D. J. & Stank, T. P. (Eds.). (1999). *21st century logistics: Making supply chain Integration a reality.* Oak Brook, IL: Council of Logistics Management.

- Christopher, M. (1992). *Logistics and supply chain management.* London: FT Press.

- Ellram, L.M. & Cooper, M.C. (1993). The relationship between supply chain management and keiretsu. *International Journal of Logistics Management,* 4(2), 1–10.

- Frazelle, E. (2002). *Supply chain strategy: The logistics of supply chain management.* New York, NY: McGraw-Hill.

- Hausman, H.L., Warren, H. & Subramanian, L.U. (2005). *Global Logistics Indicators, Supply Chain Metrics, and Bilateral Trade Patterns.* Washington, DC: World Bank.

- Jacoby, D. (2009). *Guide to Supply Chain Management.* New York: Bloomberg Press.

- Lambert, D.M. (1992). Developing a customer focused logistics strategy. *International Journal of Physical Distribution and Logistics Management*, 22(6), 12–19.

- Lambert, D.M. (2006). *Supply Chain Management Processes, Partnerships and Performance.* Sarasota: SCMI.

- Lambert, D. M. & Stock, J. R. (2001). *Strategic logistics management.* (4th ed). Homewood, IL: McGraw Hill.

- Li, S., Ragu-Nathan, B., Ragu-Nathan, T.S. & Rao, S.S. (2006). The impact of supply chain management practices on competitive advantage and organisational performance. *Omega International Journal of Management Science,* 34, 107– 24.

- Simchi-Levi, D., Kaminsky, P. & Simchi-Levi, E. (2003). Designing and managing the supply chain: Concepts, strategies, and case studies. London: McGraw Hill.

- Sterling, J. U. (1985). *Integrating customer service and marketing strategies in a channel of distribution: an empirical study.* (Unpublished PhD dissertation). Michigan State University, Michigan.

- Stevens, G. (1989). Integrating the supply chain. *International Journal of Physical Distribution and Logistics Management*, 9(8), 3–8.

- Tan, K., Lyman, S.B. & Wisner, J.D. (2002). Supply chain management: A strategic perspective. *International Journal of Operations and Production Management*, 22(5/6), 614–631.

- Trent, R.J. (2004). What everyone needs to know about SCM. *Supply Chain Management Review*, 8(2), 52–59.

- World Bank. (2006) World Bank and IMF Report on Africa. 2006. Washington, DC.

- World Bank (2007). World Bank and IMF Report on Africa. 2007. Washington, DC.

- World Bank. (2014). *South Africa.* Retrieved from http://www.worldbank.org/en/country/southafrica.

- World Bank (2014). *Data: Nigeria.* Retrieved from http://data.worldbank.org/country/nigeria.

- Word Bank. (2014). *Ghana.* Retrieved from http://www.worldbank.org/en/country/ghana.

Chapter 4

Supply Chain Management and Competitive Performance:
A Cross Industry Analysis in Ghana

Theophilus Maloreh-Nyamekye

Abstract

Supply chain management (SCM) is arguably the single most important concept applied in the production and distribution of goods, works, and services from producers to the final consumers. Despite this role, supply chain management is among the key neglected areas with very few publications in developing countries, especially in Ghana. In this chapter, a cross industry analysis of supply chain management is provided on three selected industries in Ghana to enhance readers' understanding of the application of the concept in a variety of contexts. Beginning with a definition of the concept, the chapter analyses the competitive performance of supply chains (SC) and its benefits in the SCM process. The Input-Process-Output Model was used to assess the SC performance of health, pharmaceutical and oil sectors in Ghana. Taking each of the sectors separately, the author identifies the important elements at each of the three stages of the model and explains how these elements function individually and collectively to ensure the success of the process. The chapter brings to the fore key issues of supply chain management for the understanding of policymakers, industrialists and the academic community in Ghana and other African countries.

Keywords: Supply chain management; Supply chain; Competitive performance; Health sector; Pharmaceutical sector; Oil sector.

Introduction

In this chapter the author compares three industries, namely health, pharmaceutical and the oil sectors using input, process and output framework. Key elements are identified in each sector, followed by similarities and differences leading to a set of conclusions. The chapter begins with the definition of supply chain management as a concept in order to set the stage for discussion. This is followed by a benchmarking/cross-industry analysis of supply chain performance with regard to the Ghanaian context of the above-named sectors, resulting in appropriate conclusions. It is hoped that this chapter will provide much food for thought for its readers from diverse backgrounds.

Supply Chain Management

Supply chain management is an important concept in the production and distribution of products and services. It involves all the interconnected processes of making goods, services and works available to the final consumer. Several definitions of supply chain management have been offered by both academicians and practitioners. Notable among the definitions are those by Slack et al (2001) and Kulkarni and Sharma (2004). According to Slack et al (2001), supply chain management is "the management of the interconnection of organisations which relate to each other through upstream and downstream linkages between different processes that produce value in the form of products and services to the ultimate consumer." On the other hand, Kulkarni and Sharma (2004) define supply chain management as "a network of chain of facilities and distribution options that execute the process of the obtainment of products, the transformation of these products into intermediate and finished goods, and the distribution of these finished goods to customers"

Their definitions have widened the scope of the subject matter to include even production of services. The definitions imply the process of transforming obtained facilities (including raw materials) to goods desired by customers (finished goods); and finally, the processes that are involved in transferring the finished goods to the final consumer through value creation along the supply chain from upstream. According to Slack and associates the objective of supply chain management is to satisfy customers effectively and efficiently. For this to be fulfilled one needs to recognize the roles or activities of key actors in the production process in the supply chain network (Kulkarni and Sharma, 2004). Thus the final process (the distribution process) involves several actors and activities. Some of these actors include wholesalers, retailers, distributors, etc.; while the activities include transportation, inventory management, storage, issuing to user departments, and to the disposal of unserviceable goods (GHS, 2010). Thus, both definitions highlight the essence of linkages or network of organisations or actors in the supply chain, without whom the expectations of customers cannot be realised.

Kulkarni and Sharma (2004) notes that implementing supply chain management is a long drawn process that requires restructuring of not only internal organisational activities but also demands a relook at the relationships the company shares with its suppliers, distributors and all others who participate in the value creation process in order to remain competitive. This is true with the health, pharmaceutical and oil and gas firms in Ghana, if headway is to be made regarding supply chain performance related to customer satisfaction. Hitherto, attention has shifted from manufacturers to customers (Kulkarni and Sharma, 2004), all in a bid to enhance business agility and competitive advantage (Christopher, 1998).

Benchmarking/Cross Industry Analysis

Cross industry analysis is an important activity for the success of organisations in doing business. In more specific terms, it has been referred to as competitive benchmarking (Christopher, 1998). Competitive benchmarking is "the measurement of company's products/services processes and practices against the standards of competitors and other recognised leading companies" (Christopher, 1998:103).

There are three main dimensions of competitive benchmarking. These are customer perception, comparing leading companies, and competitors comparing inputs and processes to output. Benchmarking was first adopted by Xerox (and other few companies) in manufacturing activities to focus on quality. It helped the organisation and top management to gain competitive advantage in the sector. As a result, Xerox directed that all cost units should adopt benchmarking. By 1981 benchmarking was adopted almost by all leading companies worldwide.

Although, it is good to compare with competitors because of such reasons as achieving performance (which cannot be obtained by looking at only competitors), difficulties in obtaining all important information from competitors, and achieving competitive advantage by outperforming rather than matching efforts with competitors, makes it more advisable to expand our horizon beyond competitors to more selective performing industries. This helps to appreciate the extent to which these industries are doing. It was for this reason that the above-named sectors have been selected as they offer interesting food for thought for government, policy makers, industrialists, bilateral and multilateral organisations, and the academic community.

Benefits of Cross Industry Analysis

The following serve as benefits of cross industry analysis:

1. It helps to determine the extent to which a particular supply chain has been able to achieve its objectives.

2. It helps to put in place specific metrics to measure the extent to which an organisation achieves its short and long term objectives.

3. It gives reflection on financial performance of an organisation.

4. It gives feedback on customer satisfaction.

To become a victor in the Supply Chain Business (SCB) process, a firm needs Supply Chain Excellence (SCE) which is a means of achieving an end with the obvious aim of winning the market (Kulkarni and Sharma, 2004). It involves having the weapons that are required to win the market.

Dimensions of Supply Chain Excellence (SCE)

For successful benchmarking, the SCE must have four dimensions which include market, collaborative, operational and strategic dimensions (Kulkarni and Sharma, 2004)

The Market Dimension: Represents all the forces that govern the market (both end user and the sources of raw materials). These forces include political, economic, sociocultural, technological, as well as legal factors.

The Collaborative Dimension: Refers to "work done jointly with others" (Kulkarni and Sharma, 2004:55). Collaboration here refers to the internal organs of the firm (e.g. departments) and externals (e.g. suppliers, government, creditors, etc.) working together to achieve the purpose of the organisation. It is based on both relationships and values. Relationships here refer to building relationships with key departments of a firm; while values are the monetary rewards for the relationships.

The Operational Dimension: Refers to all processes involved in transforming the raw materials to the goods/services desired by the user. This process should be smooth and free of errors. It should also be 'green' (i.e. it should focus on waste reduction or minimization). This has even become more important with the advent of Sustainable Development Goals (SDGs), which require organisations to reduce their carbon dioxide footprint as part of their corporate social responsibility.

The Strategic Dimension is an action plan that drives the whole process. Generically, the strategic dimension is the executive of the whole process - the actual responsibility for achieving competitive advantage which is the ultimate aim of benchmarking. Benchmarking can only be achieved accurately when we measure performance of the organisation we want to compare ourselves to, measure our own performance and finally compare the results. To measure is the same as making an attempt to know how an organisation responds to the needs of customers and customers' ability to pay.

Input-Process-Output Model of measuring competitive performance

There are several models for measuring competitive performance. For instance there is the Key Performance Indicator approach to measuring (Logistics Management, 2006 cited in Coyle et al. 2013) and the Supply Chain Operations and Reference (SCOR) (Supply Chain Council, 2007 cited in Chopra and Meindl, 2007) model. A notable one is the Input-Process-Output Model. The model assumes that to measure performance, we must measure the inputs the organisation obtains, the process they pass through to get finished goods and the outputs related to the outcome (Kulkarni and Sharma, 2004).

Inputs: These are resources that an organisation uses to produce goods and services or works. They include human, financial, or material resources. To measure the inputs of an organisation, we must also measure all activities that link with these inputs. That is why the model assumes that measuring includes evaluating suppliers.

Processes: These are all the activities an organisation engages in converting inputs into outputs. The outputs should be customer desired. They should satisfy a need. Examples of such processes are manufacturing, storekeeping, packaging, patient care, etc. At this stage, we measure how efficient the activities are.

Outputs: Outputs are the "tools or indicators to count the services and goods produced by an organisation" (Kulkarni and Sharma, 2004). In measuring, we must consider both the units produced and the distribution performance.

Figure 4.1 below shows a diagrammatic representation of the Input-Process-Output Model.

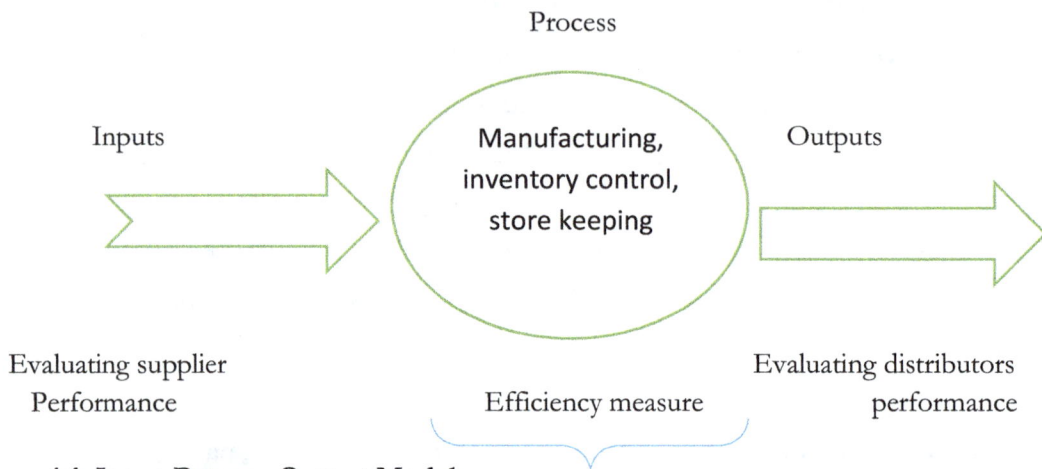

Process

Inputs

Manufacturing,
inventory control,
store keeping

Outputs

Evaluating supplier
Performance

Efficiency measure

Evaluating distributors
performance

Figure 4.1: Input-Process-Output Model
Source: Kulkarni and Sharma (2004)

In this chapter, the supply chain management performance of selected organisations in different industries in Ghana is assessed based on this model.

Supply Chain Structure of the Health Sector

The supply chain structure of the Ghanaian Health Sector is a three-tier system made up of the Central Medical Stores (CMS), ten Regional Medical Stores (RMSs) and the user facilities. The system operates as follows.

The Ministry of Health procures drugs and supplies from suppliers who could be local or international. These supplies are received by the CMS located in Accra, the nation's capital. From the CMS, the health commodities are distributed to a network of RMSs (which are managed by the respective Regional Health Administrations (RHAs) within the Ghana Health Service (GHS) at the various regional capitals in the country. Each facility then receives their supply from their respective RMS (GHS 2010).

There are few exceptional cases. These facilities include the teaching hospitals (i.e. Korle-Bu, Komfo-Anokye, Tamale and the Cape Coast Teaching Hospitals) and regional hospitals which may receive their supply directly from the CMS or suppliers from the open market.

Again, a facility may receive supplies from private suppliers if such supplies are not available at the CMS and/or RMS.

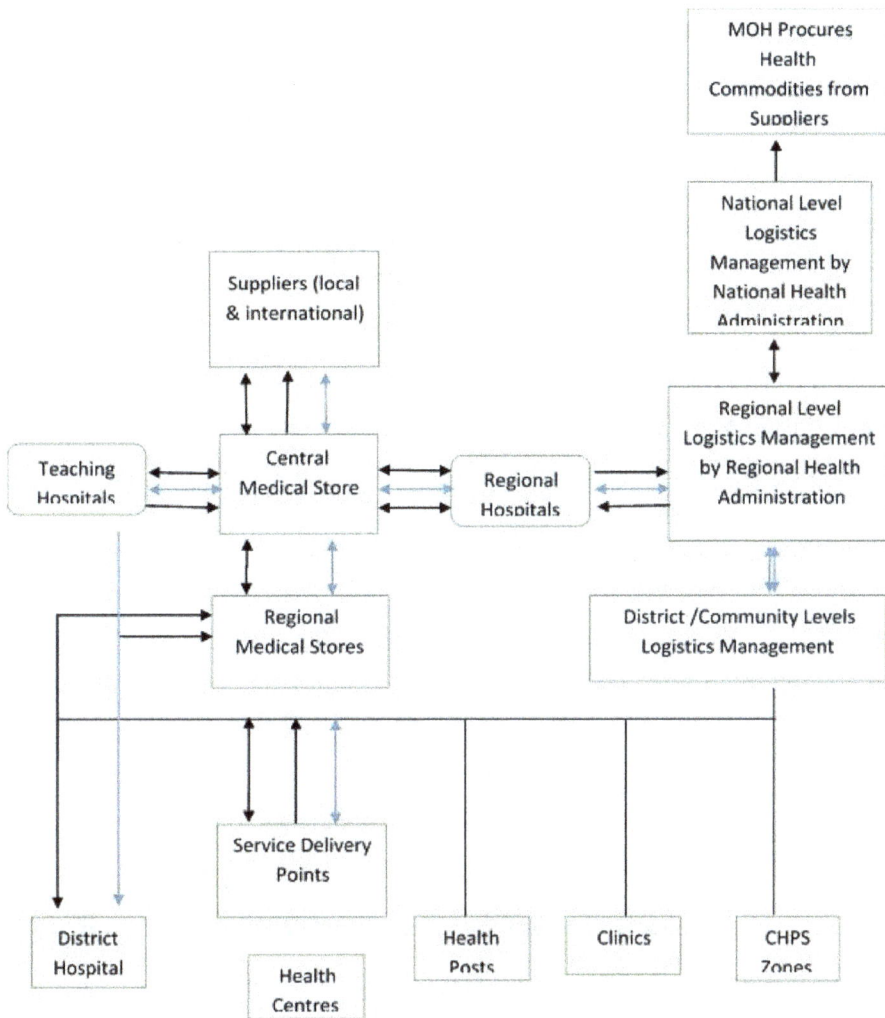

Figure 4.2: The Structure of Supply Chain of the Ghanaian Health Sector

Source: Frimpong Manso et al (2013)

Procurement is therefore decentralised to the health facilities. Budget Management Centres (BMCs) procure directly from the private sector (this is not allowed officially) or the public sector. Before procuring from the private sector, the BMCs are supposed to seek non-availability certificate of that particular drug from the CMS, which is mostly adhered to. Reasons that are normally cited for this practice include better quality and low price (Selah, 2013).

To a large extent, the private sector is less developed and its use in the supply chain is limited. However, there are efforts to acknowledge and accommodate the role of the private sector in the supply chain (Ballou-Aares et al. 2008). At the apex are the private sector suppliers and Catholic Distribution Centre (CDC) and at the bottom are mission service delivery points, private dispensaries and non-mission sector delivery points.

The private sector suppliers procure from either local or foreign manufacturers. They may then resell to all the actors in the supply chain except the mission service delivery points. On the other hand, the CDC procures drugs from either the CMS or local and international manufacturers, and then sells them to the mission service delivery points (mission hospitals). The mission hospitals have to strictly receive their supplies from the CDC. Nearly 60-70 percent of their products are procured from International Dispensary Association (IDA) (McCabe, 2009).

Elements in the Ghanaian Health Sector Supply Chain

There are several elements along the supply chain of the health sector in Ghana. These elements are different in structure but their functions complement each other in our quest to provide quality health care to the Ghanaian population.

Input stage

At the input stage, elements are spread across the various tiers in the supply chain. There are institutions that can be found in the third-tier of the supply chain and others that are outside the main tiers of the supply chain. The main institutions at the input stage are discussed below.

Ministry of Health (MoH)/Ghana Health Service (GHS): The MoH is the government arm of the Ghanaian health sector. The Ministry was established to oversee all activities of the health sector from input to process and to make sure the people are provided with accessible health service. MoH delegates functions to other actors like the Ghana Health Service, teaching hospitals, regional hospitals, district hospitals, among others. The ministry is solely in charge of formulating policies in the health sector. The GHS procures healthcare commodities from either local or foreign manufacturers/wholesalers. They also determine price of healthcare products; but largely prices of health commodities are determined by market forces.

Teaching Hospitals (THs): Currently, there are four (4) teaching hospitals in Ghana which are located in Tamale, Kumasi, Accra and Cape Coast. At the input level, the teaching hospitals perform two main functions. The teaching hospitals have autonomy to procure their own supplies. They are also learning centres for the medical, nursing, and allied health training schools across the country.

Regional Hospitals (RHs): There are ten (10) regional hospitals in Ghana. The regional hospitals are located at the regionals capitals. At the input stage of the supply chain process, the regional hospitals procure supplies. However, this can only be done when a non-availability certificate is issued from the CMS and RMS.

Catholic Distribution Centre (CDC): The Catholic Distribution Centre is the central warehouse for all the mission health facilities in Ghana (Ballou-Aares et al., 2008). The centre is based in Accra. It procures a large percentage of their supplies from IDA. They also procure from the CMS and other local and international manufacturers. The centre then distributes to the mission service delivery points/mission hospitals.

Process stage

The process stage of the Ghanaian health sector consists of the major elements in the tier one and tier two of the health care industry's supply chain. These elements include a CMS and ten regional medical stores (RMSs). The main activities of these elements are inventory control, transportation, storage, etc.

Central Medical Store: The CMS is the central storage for all healthcare products. Consignments procured by the MoH are stored here. Beside storage, the CMS also performs a distribution function by distributing to RMSs, THs and other private organisations.

Regional Medical Stores: The RMSs are located in each of the regions and are controlled by the regional health administration. The main activities of the RMSs involve receiving health commodities from the CMS, storing them, and distributing them to the health facilities in the regions.

Output stage

It is at the output stage that actual healthcare delivery occurs. At this stage, there are far more elements than any of the stages in the supply chain. All the elements here are in the third tier of the supply chain. The elements are discussed briefly below.

Teaching Hospitals (THs): The final service delivery point itself is 3-tiered. THs are at the apex of health service delivery. At the output stage, the main function of the THs is the provision of specialised care. Patients are expected to be referred from the lower level delivery centres through the district and regional hospitals before getting to the teaching hospitals.

Regional Hospitals (RHs): At the output level, the role of the RHs is different from the role played at the input stage. At this stage, the main role the RHs play is service delivery. The regional hospitals are the final referral points for the district hospitals and other lower level health facilities in the region.

District Hospitals (DHs): These are located in the districts mostly the district capitals. Their main function is to provide health care delivery to people in the district. They also refer cases beyond their capacity to the regional hospitals. Cases that community health facilities are not able to handle are referred to the district hospitals.

CHAG facilities: These are located throughout the country based on choice, and experience, in serving such communities and christian operation of service to the poor, marginalised and disadvantaged. The main function of the CHAG facilities is to deliver health care service to clients.

Other delivery centres: Besides the actors mentioned above, there are other actors in the supply chain of health service delivery in Ghana. These are mainly quasi-government private health care institutions. Among the quasi-public health care institutions are university hospitals (e.g., University of Ghana, Cape Coast University and Kwame Nkrumah University of Science and Technology); the military hospitals (e.g., 37 Military Hospital); police hospitals (e.g., Accra Police Hospital), prisons clinics and the Airport Clinic. Examples of private hospitals are Nyaho Medical Centre, Trinity Hospital and Twumasi Hospital, all located in Accra.

Supply Chain Structure of the Pharmaceutical Sector

A related sector of health sector is the pharmaceutical sector. The total market value of pharmaceuticals was updated last time in 2008 to be US$300 million. The supply chain of the pharmaceutical sector refers to the supply and distribution of medicines (McCabe, 2009). After the collapse of CareShop, the main supply chain model in the country's pharmaceutical sector is the pharmacy chains model which exists side by side with the cooperatives. The use of e-procurement is also emerging but having difficulty in finding its feet due to challenges like the smallness in size of many retail outlets.

The supply chain of pharmaceuticals in Ghana is 4-tiered which includes product manufacturing, flow of goods into the country, flow of goods within the country and retailing of medicines. According to McCabe (2009), in terms of the product manufacturing, there are about 32 pharmaceutical manufacturers in Ghana (of which 22 are active), with almost 10 of them being inactive. Some of the prominent ones are Danadams, Ernest Chemists, Tobinco Pharmacy, LaGray and Kinapharma. The manufacturers take care of about 30% of the country's needs with most of their products being basic over the counter (OTC) products and few specialised ones such as Kama Group manufacturers' syrups, and Danadams Antiretroviral (ARV) drugs with several companies producing anti-malarial drugs. A mechanism has been put in place to protect these manufacturers by banning import of all 44 drugs produced locally and exempting 66 of the 200 basic materials used for producing these drugs (McCabe, 2009).

The importation, flow and distribution channel of pharmaceuticals in Ghana is said to be much more fragmented and chaotic (McCabe, 2009). In most cases, importers possess additional one, two or all three statuses as wholesalers, pharmaceutical manufacturers, or pharmacists. In Ghana importers/ wholesalers are about 60. Wholesalers are about 166. Importers who do not double as wholesalers may import for one-stop-shop wholesalers. Wholesalers are often agent(s) who mostly do not have exclusive rights to distribute for the company. The agents then sell to user facilities such as chemical stores and health facilities. This is where the chaos is: agents may double as manufacturers or wholesalers. Wholesalers may double as importers, triple as manufacturers, quadruple as distributors and even go further to retail pharmacies.

The supply chain is represented in Figure 4.3 below.

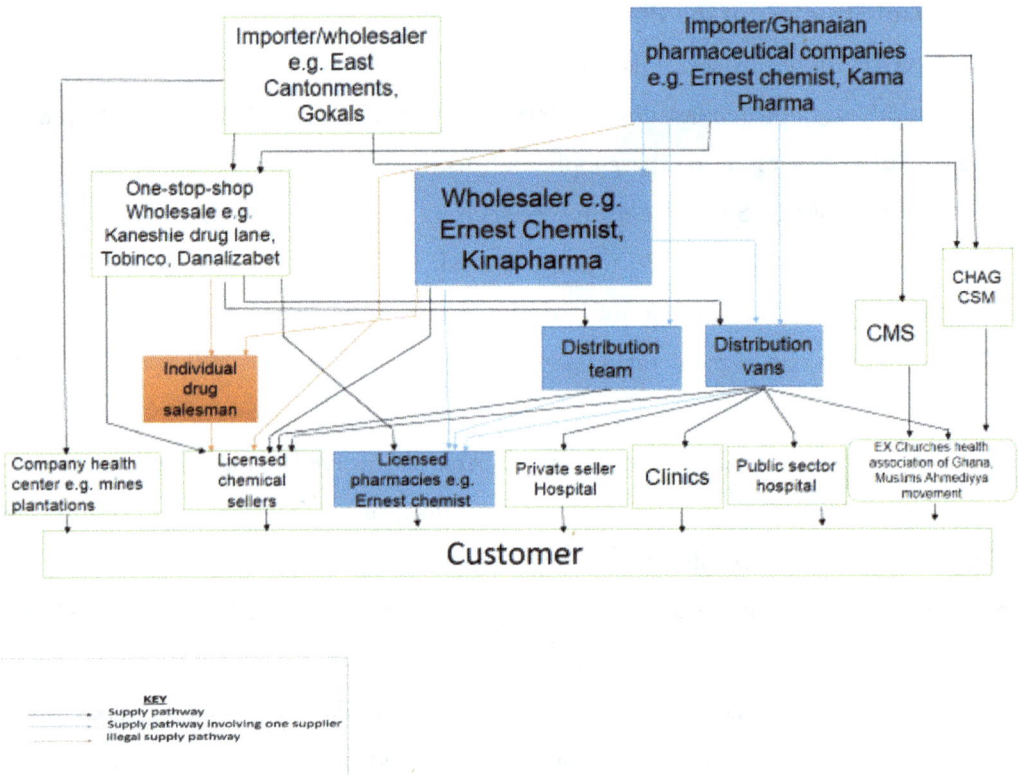

Figure 4.3: The Supply Chain of the Ghanaian Pharmaceutical Sector
Source: Adopted from: McCabe (2009)

In most cases, any of the channels could start retailing outlets and graduate to any of the upper levels by applying for a license. In terms of retailing, license is needed. Pharmaceutical retailers in Ghana number about 12,127. These include 700 licensed pharmacies, 11,159 chemical sellers and 328 who double as retailers (McCabe, 2009).

Elements in the supply chain of the pharmaceutical sector in Ghana

The following are the elements of the supply chain of the pharmaceutical industry in Ghana.

Input stage

Importers: These are entities that procure health commodities from international wholesalers or manufacturers. The government of Ghana through the MoH and the CMS performs this function. There are also private importers.

Manufacturers: There are Ghanaian companies that produce medical and non-medical consumables. The main function of the manufacturers is that they turn raw materials into finished goods. They also import raw materials for the production of their commodities.

Process stage

Wholesalers: The wholesalers are mainly private entities. Wholesalers procure pharmaceuticals and supplies from manufacturers/importers and provide sale and delivery of medicines to public regional medical stores and hospitals, as well as to faith-based or mission health facilities, such as the Catholic Health Services and the Presbyterian Health Services.

One-stop-shop wholesale: These are wholesale companies that do not sell just one product but a variety of products (McCabe, 2009). Their functions are the same as traditional wholesalers except that the one-stop-wholesale shops have variety.

CMS: The Central Medical Stores' main function is to receive pharmaceuticals and supplies that have been procured (either imported or from local manufacturers) by the government, store and distribute them to the RMS, CDC, and other facilities.

CHAG CDC: The Catholic Distribution Centre is the central warehouse for the mission sector. The CDC is located in Accra. Its main function is to procure health commodities primarily from the IDA and CMS. Information from Health Access Network indicates that the CDC procures 60-70 percent of its supplies from IDA. The CDC also stores and distributes commodities to CHAG health delivery centres.

Individual Drug Salesmen: The individual drug sales are the main agents on the illegal supply chain pathway according to the model by McCabe (2009). Their main functions include procurement of pharmaceuticals, brief storage and sales to final health delivery facilities. They usually procure their supplies from one-stop wholesalers or traditional wholesalers, and in turn distribute to licensed chemical sellers and pharmacies.

Distribution Teams/Vans. The distribution teams/vans are usually of main wholesaler or importer/wholesaler companies. Their main function is distribution. As can be seen from the supply chain model by McCabe (2009), the teams get their supplies from mother companies and do door step delivery to all forms of final healthcare delivery centres.

Output Stage

At the output stage, the final delivery of health service occurs. The actors here include all forms of agents of healthcare delivery to the final customer. Notable among these agents are:

— Company health centres

— Licensed chemical sellers/pharmacies

— Private sector hospitals/clinics

— Public sector hospitals/clinics

— CHAG facilities (MoH, 2015)

Supply Chain Structure of the Oil Sector

According to Amponsah and Opei (2014), the global petroleum industry includes "exploration, extracting, refining, transporting and marketing petroleum products". These processes put together are usually divided into three which include upstream activities, midstream activities and downstream activities.

While the upstream activities include exploration and production of crude oil, the midstream activities include storage, marketing and transportation of the "crude oil, natural gas, natural gas liquids (NGLs, mainly ethane, propane and butane) and sulphur" (p.2). Going to the downstream sector, activities there include refining the crude oil, petrochemical plants and distributing oil products (which includes wholesale and retail outlets). According to Amponsah and Opei (2014), the midstream is usually collapsed to be part of the downstream. As a result, we have the upstream and the downstream petroleum sectors.

Two bodies among others discussed in this chapter are those that play key roles in the two sectors above. First is the Ghana National Petroleum Corporation (GNPC) which was formerly a regulator of the upstream sector but is currently a commercial player and Ghana's national oil company (not long after Ghana produced its first oil in December 2010, a Petroleum Commission was established in 2011 to regulate upstream activities). The second entity highlighted is the National Petroleum Authority (NPA) and is in charge of downstream activities.

As oil exploration gathered momentum in Ghana during the early 2000s, exploration rights were sold to Kosmos Energy and Tullow Oil in 2004. In 2007, these two companies and their partners discovered oil in commercial quantities in Ghana at the Jubilee Field (Kastning, 2011). Today, there are four main entities in charge of upstream oil activities (exploration and production) in the country. These are the GNPC, Kosmos Energy, Tullow Oil and Gas and EO Group. As Ghana's oil company, GNPC is a government entity that plays a critical role in the upstream sector. The current shareholding structure of the Jubilee Unit Area after some of the pioneering companies had off-loaded their shares is as follows: GNPC (13.64%); Tullow (35.48%); Kosmos (24.08%); Anadarko (24.08%); Petro SA (2.73%).

A recent study by Amponsah and Opei (2014) has revealed that the downstream supply chain of oil in Ghana involves (a) importation of crude products (which are stored at the Tema Oil Refinery to be refined) and (b) refined oil products. Both product types are shipped to the Bulk Oil Storage and Transportation (BOST) facilities. The shipment is mostly mainly done through pipelines. From these facilities, the products are distributed to the various Oil Marketing Companies before finally to the retail outlets.

There are also Bulk Distribution Companies (BDCs) and Oil Trading Companies (OTCs) which also import oil (crude or refined). The BDCs and OTCs will then sell to either OMCs which will then sell to retailers or Bulk Consumers (BCs) or they sell direct to BCs. The BCs may include companies in the mining industry, marine industry, aviation industry, etc. According to Amponsah and Opei (2014), there are various players whose actions or inactions impact the efficiency, agility and sustainability of the supply chain. Figure 4 below is a diagrammatic representation of the supply chain of oil in Ghana taking into consideration the downstream.

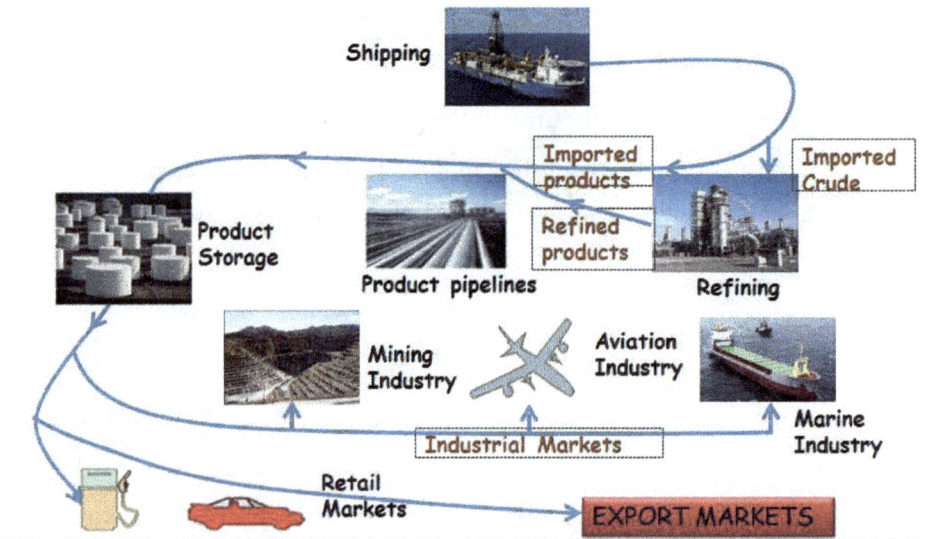

Figure 4.4: Ghana's Downstream Crude and Products Supply Chain
Source: Amponsah and Opei (2014)

Elements in the Supply Chain in the Ghana Oil and Gas Sector

The oil sector supply chain has relatively fewer elements as compared to elements in other sectors. The elements are spread across input, process and output stages of the chain. The oil and gas sector is formalized such that, the activities of the elements in each of the stages are controlled by a government established institution.

Input stage

Ministry of Petroleum (MoP): The Ministry of Petroleum was formally part of the

Ministry of Energy and Petroleum. The ministry provides a representation by the government in the oil and gas sector. The main function of the ministry is the formulation, implementation, monitoring and evaluation of policies in the energy sector (Ministry of Petroleum, 2015). The ministry is the sole agency established by the government to have a general oversight of the sector. Other functions include; reviewing and approving decommissioning plans and production programmes and issuing of regulations on safety, environment, economic impact, and community relations (Heller & Heuty, 2010).

Ghana Petroleum Commission (GPA): It was established in 2011. The main function of the GPA is to regulate upstream oil activities in Ghana. Specifically, its functions include regulating activities in the upstream sector and working with the Ministry of Energy (Petroleum) on formulation of policies for the upstream sector.

Ghana National Petroleum Corporation (GNPC): It was established in 1985. Till 2011, its main function was to regulate upstream oil activities in Ghana and work with the Ministry of Energy to formulate policies and regulate importation activities in the upstream sector. GNPC was also involved in exploration and production of oil. Currently its focus is only on the latter.

Bulk Distribution Companies (BDCs) and Oil Trading Companies (OTCs): BDCs and OTCs are entities that have been licensed to procure and import crude oil (Amponsah and Opei, 2014).

Process stage

National Petroleum Authority (NPA): Is a statutory body established to control the activities of oil at the downstream level. Its functions are related to the functions of GNPC except that the NPA is limited to downstream. The NPA was established in 2005. It plays a role in both the process and the output stages. At the process stage, the functions of the NPA include price regulation (Amponsah and Opei, 2014), market regulations, licensing of oil marketing companies, and procurement of oil for the nation (Energy Commission, 2006).

Bulk Distribution Companies (BDCs): At the process stage, BDCs have licenses from NPA to provide bulk distribution of oil products. In addition, they store and sell particularly to OMCs and to bulk consumers.

Oil Marketing Companies (OMCs): The activities of oil marketing companies cut across both process and output stages of the supply chain. However, in each of these stages, they play different roles. They include companies owned by both government and non-government. Their main function at this stage is distributing and transporting oil to sale centres (Energy Commission, 2006). Since most of the companies have their own sale outlets, they also store the oil briefly at the centres.

Bulk Oil Storage and Transportation Company (BOST): Is also an actor at the process stage. The main activities of BOST are storage and transportation of oil inland. The strategic management of oil to prevent shortage is in the hands of BOST. To do this, the company is expected to keep a strategic stock of three weeks of national demand.

Tema Oil Refinery (TOR): The activities of TOR are limited to only the process stage of the oil supply chain. TOR is the body that was established to take charge of refining crude oil (either imported or produced locally) except for consignments going to the Takoradi Thermal Power Plant for power production (Energy Commission, 2006; Amponsah and Opei, 2014). TOR is also responsible for storage of the refined oil though it is not the only body responsible for storage.

Output stage

NPA: The functions and activities of the NPA at the output stage are similar to the functions and activities at the process stage. For instance, at the output stage, the NPA regulates the retail price of oil products.

OMCs: The main function of the OMCs at the output stage is the distribution/sale of oil to customers.

Summary and Conclusions

After expatiating the concept of supply chain, the chapter goes on to examine benchmarking and its associated benefits. The Input-Process-Output model was used to examine the supply chain performance across selected industries namely, health, pharmaceutical and oil in Ghana. Special attention was paid to the actors in each of the supply chains (see Table 1).

Every supply chain has a network of challenges that hinders the flow of goods, services, supplies and works from the producer to the final consumer. For a supply chain management to be effective, it must be able to develop counter strategies to neutralise the effects of these challenges or at least minimise them to the barest minimum.

The indicators used to measure the effects of supply chain performance in the health care industry apart from its ability to overcome problems in the system are geographic and financial access, availability, affordability, and quality (Ballou-Aares et al, 2008). Research indicates that there is wider geographic access to healthcare, apart from few areas in the northern sector of Ghana. In terms of availability, the supply chain performance is said to be poor. This is because, availability from CMS and RMSs is described as poor, while at the SDPS, and it has best been described as mediocre. It is only the private sector that has been rated good (Ballou-Aares et al, 2008). The Ministry of Health and the Ghana Health Service were however, quite quick in developing a health commodity management procedure manual to address the weaknesses in the public health sector supply chain (GHS, 2010). What is yet to be seen is the positive impact of the use of manual by stakeholders. This requires further investigation. Because of the introduction of the National Health Insurance Scheme (NHIS) and its exemptions for the indigents, children and the aged, healthcare is said to be affordable in Ghana. The quality of healthcare products and services has generally been good. However, there are cases of ineffective antimalarial drugs, uncertified local drug manufacturers etc. (Ballou-Aares et al, 2008).

In the pharmaceutical industry, it has been observed that there are weak incentives to conduct quality testing. This has oftentimes led to the compromising of quality. Other weaknesses in the supply chain include lack of regional provider distribution points to improve and schedule delivery system, lack of incentive to reduce prices of medicines and maintain environmental safety standards. It has also been observed that suppliers do not select medicines with greater public need (Anum, et al, 2010). These weaknesses have questioned the affordability, access, quality and availability indicators of the supply chain. However, it does not mean that the system does not do anything right.

Table 4.1: Summary of elements in supply chain of Ghana's health, pharmaceutical and oil industries

	Stage	Element	Function
Health	Input	Ministry of Health	Policies & procure supplies
		Teaching hospitals	Procure supplies
		Regional hospitals	
		CDCs	
	Process	CMS	Inventory, storage, distribution
		10RMSs	Inventory, storage, distribution
	Output	Teaching hospitals	Service delivery
		Regional hospitals	
		Quasi government hospitals	
		District hospitals	
		CHAG facilities	
		Private dispensaries	
		Private service delivery points	
Pharmaceutical	Input	Importers	Importation of pharmaceuticals
		Manufacturers	Manufacturing
	Process	CMS	Distribution and storage
		CDC	
		One-stop-shop wholesale & traditional wholesalers	
		Individual drug salesmen	
		Distribution teams/vans	Distribution , door step delivery
	Output	Company health centres	Sale of pharmaceuticals and supplies to final consumer
		Licensed chemical sellers/pharmacies	
		Private sector hospitals/clinics	
		Public sector hospitals/clinics	
		CHAG facilities	
		Company health centres	
		Licensed chemical sellers/pharmacies	
Oil	Input	Ministry of Petroleum	Oversight, policy formulation
		Petroleum Commission	Regulate upstream activities
		GNPC	Oil exploration and production
		BDCs	Importation of oil (crude & refined)
		OTCs	
	Process	NPA	Regulate activities like pricing
		OMCs	Storage and distribution
		BOST	
		TOR	Refinery and storage
	Output	NPA	Regulate activities like pricing
		OMCs	Sale of oil to consumers

For instance, Anum, et al (2010) in their abstract, note that pharmaceutical actors....

> ...*have a strong incentive to trade in registered medicines, maintain good storage practices, implement best procurement practices, improve efficiency in inventory management, maintain responsible financial practices, maintain good corporate image and select medicines that give better public health outcomes.*

A close look at the rights and wrongs in the supply chain of the pharmaceutical sector gives a signal that, things to help increase profits are done right while those with cost implications are neglected.

The supply chain of the Oil sector has not received favorable comments from the literature. This means there is much to be done to ensure its improvement of the discovery of production of commercial quantity of oil in Ghana. For instance, a study by Amponsah and Opei (2004) indicates that government interference in the activities of the actors is the cause of these challenges. As an example, government is not able to pay, causing indebtedness to most actors. Besides, there is inadequate infrastructure. In addition, TOR is not able to refine crude oil regularly. These and other challenges have impacted on an effective and efficient supply chain process.

As Ghana aspires to become an upper-middle income country, there is the need to recognize the essence of competitive performance of firms, whether in the public or private sector. Companies along the supply chain must not see themselves as competitors (adversaries) but as collaborators whose common goal is to satisfy the customer effectively and efficiently. Competition should rather exist between different supply chain networks to encourage the superior management of different supply chains, thereby creating superior value for the final consumer. For this to be achieved government must create an enabling environment for businesses not only to thrive, but also to flourish.

References

- Anum, P., Mankartah, G. & Anaman, K. (2010). *Assessment of pharmaceutical wholesale market in Ghana.* Accra: Meta Ghana.
- Amponsah, R. & Opei, F. (2014).Ghana's downstream petroleum sector: An assessment of key supply chain challenges and prospects for growth. *International Journal of Petroleum*

and Oil Exploration Research ISSN: 2163-4372, 1 (1), 001-007. Available online at www.internationalscholarsjournals.org.

- Ballou-Aares, D., Freitas, A., Kopczak, L., Kraiselburd, S., Laverty, M., Macharia, E. & Yadav, P. (2008). Private sector role in health supply chains: Review of the role and potential for private sector engagement in developing country health supply chains. *Dalberg Global Development Advisors and MIT-Zaragoza International Logistics Program.*

- Chopra, S. & Meindle, P. (2007). *Supply chain management: Strategy, planning and operation.* (3rd ed.). Upper Saddle River, NJ: Prentice Hall.

- Christopher, M. (1998). *Logistics and supply chain management: Strategies for reducing cost and improving service* (2nd ed.). London, UK: Financial Times Professional Limited.

- Coyle, J., Langley Jr., C., Novack, R. & Gibson, B. (2013). *Managing supply chain management: A logistics approach.* (9th ed). UK: South-Western Cengage Learning.

- Energy Commission. (2006). *Strategic national energy plan* 2006-2020. Main Report, July.

- Frimpong Manso, J., Annan, J. & Anane, S. (2013). Assessment of logistics management in Ghana Health Service. *International Journal of Business and Social Research*, 3 (8), 75-87.

- Ghana Health Service (2010). *Logistics management of public sector health commodities in Ghana: Standard operating procedures manual (Regional medical stores to service delivery points).* Accra: Ministry of Health/Ghana Health Service.

- Heller, P. & Heuty, A. (2010). Accountability mechanisms in Ghana's 2010 proposed oil legislation. *Ghana Policy Journal*, 4, 50-67.

- Kastning, T. (2011). *Basic overview of Ghana's emerging oil industry.* Available online on *library.fes.de/pdf-files/bueros/ghana/10490.pdf.*

- Kulkarni, S. & Sharma, A. (2004). *Supply chain management: Creating for faster turnaround.* New Delhi: Teta McGraw-Hill.

- MacCabe, A. (2009). *Private sector pharmaceutical supply and distribution chains: Ghana, Mali and Malawi.* World Bank.

- Ministry of Petroleum (2015). *Brief background.* Available online on http://www.energymin.gov.gh.

- MOH (2015). *Holistic assessment of the health sector programme of work 2014. Pre-summit draft 2.* MOH: Accra, Ghana.

- Selah, K. (2013). *The health sector in Ghana: A comprehensive assessment.* Washington, DC: World Bank.

- Slack, N., Chambers, S. & Johnston, R. (2001). *Operations management* (3rd ed.). Harlow: FT/Prentice Hall.

Chapter 5

Operations Management and Business Performance

Alex Addae-Korankye

Abstract

This chapter examines the relationship between operations management and business performance. It commences with the exploration of the concept and functions of operations management in an organisation. To understand the subject of business performance, the notion of competitive advantage is investigated with a focus on three of Michael Porter's fundamental pillars required for a firm to gain a competitive edge in the market. These are Porter's five competitive forces, his three generic strategies and the firm's value chain required to deliver customer value and satisfaction. Next, the chapter explores the association between operations management and business performance, and in this regard, examines this relationship in the context of a developing economy. This chapter concludes with implications of its findings for policy makers, business executives and also advances critical areas for future research by scholars in the field of operations management.

Keywords: *Operations management; Business performance; Competitive advantage; Total quality management; Manufacturing Services.*

Introduction

In today's global market place success and even survival depends on an organisation's ability to improve everything it does, otherwise it will be competed out of business or at best market share and hence profit will dwindle. That is why in recent years a great deal of debate about competitive advantage has taken the centre stage in organisations. Businesses and organisations are therefore seeking ways of gaining competitive advantage through many means. One of the means through which organisations achieve competitive advantage is operations management. Organisations add value through a series of processes, including research and new product development, manufacturing and service activities (Thompson 1997). However to create and sustain competitive advantage from this value, organisations need the help of their suppliers and distributors, as well as manufacturing infrastructure. This chapter focuses on how businesses/organisations can gain competitive advantage through operations management. The areas covered include but are not limited to: the concept of operations management; the notion of competitive advantage; the relationship between operations management and competitive advantage/business performance; the implications of the findings of this chapter for policy makers as well as business executives, and future research directions to scholars.

The Concept of Operations Management

Operations constitute that part of a business organisation that is responsible for producing goods and services (Stevenson, 2009). He went on further to define goods as physical/tangible items that include raw materials, parts, subassemblies such as motherboards that go into computers, and final products or finished products such as cell phones and automobiles. Services on the other hand are activities which provide some combination of time, location, form, and psychological value. The function of operations is therefore the conversion or transformation of inputs into output. Inputs include land, labour, capital, information; whilst outputs are the goods and services.

Inputs =>Transformation/conversion process=> Output

Operations management involves the design, planning and control of the production function, and the decision which relates to the use of materials, people and machines (Thompson, 1997). It is the management of systems or processes that create goods and/or provide services. Operations management has been recognised as an important factor in a country's economic growth. The traditional view of manufacturing management is the concept of production management with the focus on economic efficiency in manufacturing. Later the new name operations management was identified, as the service sector became more prominent. Rapid changes in technology have provided numerous opportunities and posed challenges, which have resulted in enhancement of manufacturing capabilities through new materials, facilities, techniques and procedures. Hence, managing a service system has become a major challenge in the global competitive environment. It has been a key element in the improvement of productivity in business around the world. Operations Management leads the way for organisations to achieve their goals with minimum effort.

Functions of Operations Management

The operations function includes many interrelated activities such as forecasting, capacity planning, scheduling, managing inventories, assuring quality, motivating employees, deciding where to locate facilities, and so on (Stevenson, 2009). Using an airline company to illustrate the functions or scope of operations management, the airline company should forecast such things as weather and landing conditions, seat demand for flights, and the growth in air travel. The second function is capacity planning. The airline company should maintain cash flow and ensure a reasonable profit. Thirdly, the company should decide on facilities and layout. This is necessary to achieve effective use of workers and equipment. Another very important function is scheduling of planes for flights and routine maintenance; scheduling of pilots and flight attendants; and scheduling of ground crews, counter staff, and baggage handlers. Managing inventories is another function with the provision of items such as food and beverages, first-aid equipment, in-flight magazines, pillows and blankets, and life preservers. For quality assurance in flying and maintenance operations, the emphasis is on safety; and more importantly in dealing with customers at ticket counters, check-ins, telephone and electronic reservations, while for curb service quality assurance stresses efficiency and courtesy. Another function is motivating and training all employees. Last but not least is locating facilities. This will depend on the manager's preference or decision on the cities/towns to provide the services regarding where to locate maintenance facilities, and where to locate major and minor hubs.

It must be noted that operations functions in the airline industry will not be exactly the same as other industries; for example, block manufacturing, furniture manufacturing, food and beverage industry, bicycle manufacturing industry and many more. Again there is a difference between a service provider and a producer of goods. However, in terms of their operations functions they have certain things in common; for instance both involve motivating and training of employees, ordering supplies, and ensuring that quality standards are met. Operations functions also include the following: purchasing, industrial engineering, distribution, and maintenance.

Purchasing has the duty for the procurement of materials, supplies, and equipment. To purchase the right quantity with the right specification, at the right time, at the right price is a highly important function of operations department of an organisation. Additionally, purchasing involves receiving and inspecting the items. Industrial engineering which is considered as part of operations is concerned with scheduling, performance standards, work methods, quality control, and material handling. Thirdly, distribution is also considered as part of operations. It involves the shipping or transferring the goods to warehouses, retail outlets, or the final customers. Maintenance which is another function of operations management is responsible for the general upkeep and repair of equipment, buildings and grounds, heating and air conditioning, removing toxic waste, parking and perhaps security.

The Concept of Competitive Advantage

There is continuing interest in the study of the forces that impact on an organisation, particularly those that can be harnessed to create competitive advantage. Whether a firm has a competitive advantage depends on the business system that it has developed to relate to its business environment. A business system is a configuration of resources (inputs), activities (throughput), and product/services offerings (output) intended to create value to its customers (Wit & Meyer, 2004). The ideas or models of competitive advantage which emerged during the period from 1979 to mid-1980s (Porter, 1988) were based on the idea that competitive advantage came from the ability to earn a return on investment (ROI) that was better than the average for the industry (Thurlby, 1998). Porter (1980) contends that effective strategic management is the positioning of an organisation, relative to its competitors, in such a way that it outperforms them. Marketing, operations, and personnel, in fact all aspect of the business, are capable of providing a competitive edge; an advantage which leads to superior performance for profit-oriented firms. Again it needs to be noted that one of the fundamental missions of strategic management is to investigate and explain differences in performance among firms. The reigning incumbent explanation for the heterogeneity of firm performance is based on the concept of competitive advantage.

The fundamental basis of long-run success of a firm is the achievement and maintenance of a sustainable competitive advantage. Indeed, understanding which resources and firm behaviours lead to sustainable competitive advantage is considered to be the fundamental issue in marketing strategy (Varadarajan and Jayachandran, 1999). A competitive advantage can result either from implementing a value-creating strategy not simultaneously being employed by current or prospective competitors or through superior execution of the same strategy as competitors (Bharadwaj, Varadarajan, and Fahy, 1993). The competitive advantage is sustained when other firms are unable to duplicate the benefits of this strategy (Barney 1991).

Porter's Five Competitive Forces

Michael Porter, a renowned authority on competitive strategy, believes that a firm is most concerned with the intensity of competition within its industry. The level of this intensity is determined by basic competitive forces namely the threat/ bargaining power of buyers, the threat (bargaining power) of supplies, the threat of new entrants, the threats of substitute products and services, and rivalry among existing firms (industry competitors). The collective strength of these forces determines the ultimate potential profit in the industry; where potential profit is measured in terms of long-run return on invested capital.

Threat of new entrants

New entrants to an industry typically bring to it new capacity, a desire to gain market share, and substantial resources. They are therefore a threat to an established firm. The threat to entry depends on the presence of entry barriers and the reaction that can be expected from existing competitors. An entry barrier is an obstruction that makes it difficult for a firm to enter an industry. For example, no new domestic automobile company has been successful in the United States since the 1930s because of the high capital requirements to build production facilities and to develop a dealer distribution network (Wheelen & Hunger, 2006). These entry barriers include: economies of scale; product differentiation; capital requirements; switching costs; access to distribution channels; cost disadvantages independent of size; and, government policy.

Rivalry among existing firms

The intensity of rivalry, which is the most obvious of the five forces in an industry, helps to determine the extent to which the value created by an industry will be dissipated through head-to-head competition. The most valuable contribution of Porter's "five forces" framework may be its suggestion that rivalry, while important, is only one of several forces that determine industry attractiveness. In most industries, firms are mutually dependent. A competitive move by one firm can be expected to have a noticeable impact or effect on its competitors and thus may cause retaliation or counter efforts. Intense rivalry is related to the presence of many factors including: number of competitors; rate of industry growth; product or service characteristics; amount of fixed costs; capacity; height of exit barriers; and, diversity of rivals.

Threat of substitutes

The threat substitute products pose to an industry's profitability depends on the relative price-to-performance ratios of the different types of products or services to which customers can turn to satisfy the same level of need. The threat of substitute is also affected by switching costs; that is costs in areas such as retraining, retooling and redesigning that are incurred when a customer switches to a different type of product or service. It also involves:

- Product-to-product substitution(email for mail, fax); is based on substitution of need;
- Generic substitution(video suppliers compete with travel companies);
- Substitution that relates to something that people can do without(cigarettes, alcohol)

Bargaining power of buyers

Buyers affect an industry through their ability to force down prices, bargain for higher quality or more services, and play competitors against each other. A buyer or group of buyers is powerful if some of the following factors hold true:

- A buyer purchases a large proportion of the seller's product or service;
- A buyer has the potential to integrate backward by producing the product itself;
- Alternative suppliers are plentiful because a product is standard or undifferentiated (for example motorists can choose among many gas stations);
- Changing suppliers costs very little (for example office supplies are easy to find);
- The purchased product represents a high percentage of a buyer's costs, thus providing an incentive to shop around for a lower price;
- A buyer earns low profits and thus very sensitive to costs and service differences;
- The purchased product is unimportant to the final quality or price of a buyer's product or service and thus can be easily substituted without affecting the final product adversely.

Bargaining power of suppliers

Supplier power is a mirror image of buyer power. Suppliers can affect or influence an industry through their ability to raise prices, or reduce the quality of purchased goods and services. The analysis of supplier power typically focuses first on the relative size and concentration of suppliers relative to industry participants and second, on the degree of differentiation in the inputs supplied. The ability to charge customers different prices in line with differences in the value created for each of those buyers usually indicates that the market is characterised by high supplier power and at the same time by low buyer power (Porter, 1988). A supplier or supplier group is powerful if some of the following factors exist:

- Where switching costs are high e.g., switching from one internet provider to another;

- High power of brands;

- Possibility of forward integration of suppliers;

- Fragmentation of customers with a limited bargaining power.

It must be noted that the nature of competition in an industry is strongly influenced by the above five forces. The implication is that the stronger the power of buyers, and suppliers, and the stronger the threat of substitutes, potential entrants, the greater the intensity of the competition.

A sixth force has been suggested, which is seen as an extension of Michael Porter's five forces model. The sixth force is the relative power of other stakeholders. The other stakeholders may include complementors (those who produce complementary goods/product); the government, the public, employees, and shareholders. Depending on the particular industry, and organisation, it may have one or a combination of the above as a sixth force.

Porter's Generic Strategies

To achieve a sustainable competitive advantage in an industry, a firms needs to implement strategies or a strategy. According to Porter (1985), there are three generic strategies that a firm can implement to achieve competitive advantage; these are cost leadership, differentiation, and focus.

Cost leadership

Cost leadership is defined as the low cost producer in an industry. A low cost producer must find and exploit all sources of cost advantages through organisation-specific competencies driving down cost though the value chain (Johnson and Scholes, 1997). In other words the firms/companies that attempt to become the lowest-cost producers in an industry can be said to be using cost leadership strategy. The company with the lowest costs would earn the highest products in the event when the competing products are essentially undifferentiated and selling at a standard market price. Firms that follow this strategy place much emphasis on cost reduction in every activity in the value chain. It needs to be noted that a company might be a cost leader but does not necessarily imply that the firm's products will be sold at the lowest price. It can be a cost leader in an industry but charge an average price for its products and reinvest the extra profits (Lynch, 2003). The risks of being a cost leader is that at certain times the firm employs this strategy at the expense of other vital factors, and because of its focus on cost reduction may lose vision on why it follows that strategy.

Differentiation

A firm following a differentiation strategy seeks to be unique in terms of dimensions widely valued by buyers, and which is also different from its competitors. The aim is to achieve a higher market share than its competitors (Johnson and Scholes, 1997). They contend that this strategy might be achieved through uniqueness or improvements in products, and also marketing-based approaches. When a company differentiates its products, it is often able to charge a premium price for its products or services in the market. In other words companies that efficiently and successfully differentiate their products from their competitors attract a premium price. Some general examples of differentiation include better service levels to customers, better product performance, i.e., quality products, etc. It must be emphasised that firms following differentiation strategy most of the time would incur extra costs. For example the firm must incur extra cost to embark on extensive advertising, purchase high quality raw materials, and employing high calibre experts, amongst others.

Focus

Porter initially saw focus as a third generic strategy but later viewed it as a moderator of the two strategies: cost leadership and differentiation. According to Pearson(1999) companies employ this strategy by focusing on areas in a market where the intensity of competition is low. Organisations, firms, or companies can make use of the focus strategy by focusing on a specific niche in the market and offering specialised products for that market. This is why Lynch (2003) referred to this strategy as niche strategy. Competitive strategy therefore can be achieved by focusing on a firm's target segment. In other words, this strategy focuses on a segment of the market; identifies the needs of the segment and serves the segment extremely well. When this is done competitive advantage will be achieved.

It must be noted that this strategy cannot be implemented in isolation. A company may use focus in addition to differentiation or cost leadership strategy hence we have differentiation focus, and cost leadership focus. Cost focus is a low-cost competitive strategy that focuses on a particular group, geographical market, or a segment of the market and attempts to serve only that niche, to the exclusion of others. Differentiation focus like the cost focus, concentrates on a particular buyer group, product line segment, or geographical market, and ensures that it becomes unique in the eyes of the buyers (Wheelen and Hunger, 2006).

The Concept of the Value Chain

The value chain approach was developed by Michael Porter in the 1980s in his book 'Competitive Advantage: Creating and Sustaining Superior Performance' (Porter, 1985). Value chain refers to the various activities involved in the production of goods and services within an organisation/firm/company. According to Porter (1990), value chain is an interdependent system or network of activities connected by linkages. When the system is managed carefully and efficiently, the linkages can be a vital source of competitive advantage. These activities are grouped under primary activities and support activities.

Primary activities:

- Inbound Logistics: These activities are concerned with receiving the materials from suppliers, storing these inputs to the product/services. This includes material handling, stock control, etc.

- Operations: These are the activities that transform the inputs into outputs (goods and services). It includes machining, packaging, assembling, testing etc.

- Outbound Logistics: These are activities concerned with distributing the final product and /or services to the customers. It includes collecting, storing and distributing the final product to the customers/consumers.

- Marketing and Sales: This comprises analysis of the needs and wants of customers, and is responsible for creating awareness among the target audience of the firm about the products and services. This includes sales administration, advertising, sales promotion, selling, etc.

- Services: These include all those activities that enhance or maintain the value of a product/service; for instance, pre-installation or service before and after sales; installation, repair, training and spares.

Support activities:

- Procurement, human resources management, technology development, and infrastructure.

When a firm performs the above activities efficiently it achieves competitive advantage either through cost leadership or differentiation strategy. In other words, to achieve competitive advantage either through differentiation or cost leadership, a company should efficiently perform the activities in the value chain efficiently and effectively.

Operations Management and Business Performance

Operations management is responsible for providing the right goods or services ready at the right time, produced at the right quality, and also at the right cost to ensure that profits are earned. Hill (1991) contends that operations management can contribute to the achievement of competitive advantage and corporate objectives in the following ways, but it should be stressed that the importance of each factor for any organisation depends upon the key success factors.

- *Capacity and capability*: Can the organisation produce and provide the goods and services demanded? We must consider dependability and quality.

- *Dependability* is the ability to meet delivery, cost targets and promises, and as a result of just-in-time systems, it is becoming increasingly important.

- *Quality* issues include the ability to maintain a reliable and consistent product quality, the quality of customer services both before and after sales, and the speed of delivery offered and achieved. It is important to understand which quality issues and measures customers regard as more crucial and in order to achieve these.

Organisations must identify and distinguish between order qualifiers (things they have to be able to do in order to compete in a market) and order winners (distinctive skills and activities that create competitive advantage). When one competitor opens a competitive gap, say with an innovation, and this is attractive to customers, it becomes an order qualifier for rivals. The lead competitor must then search for a new competitive advantage to sustain its lead.

- *Efficiency*: The effectiveness of the production process, essentially costs, is determined by such measures as cost per unit produced and profit or turnover per employee.

- *Adaptability*: We must consider the flexibility in the short-term to respond to changes in demand, and strategies for investing in the future through innovation, research and development. In some industries product life cycles are shortening, and this emphasises the need for adaptability and a willingness and readiness to change in line with demand.

Stevenson (2009) also believes that operations management has a major influence on competitiveness through product and service design, cost, location, quality, response time, flexibility, inventory and supply chain management, and services.

- *Product and service design* should reflect joint efforts of many areas to achieve a match between financial resources, operations capabilities, supply chain capabilities, and consumer wants and needs. Special characteristics or features of a product or service can be a key factor in consumer buying decisions. Other key factors include *innovation*, and the *time-to-market* for new products and services.

- *Cost* of an organisation's output is a key variable that affects pricing decisions and profits. Cost-reduction efforts are generally on-going in business organisations. Productivity is an important determinant of cost. Organisations with higher productivity rates than their competitors have a competitive cost advantage. A company can outsource a portion of its operations to achieve lower cost, higher productivity or better quality.

- *Location* can be important in terms of costs and convenience for customers. Location near inputs can result in lower inputs costs. Location near markets can result in lower transportation costs and quicker delivery times. Convenient location is particularly important in the retail sector.

- *Quality* refers to materials, workmanship, design, and service. Consumers judge quality in terms of how well they think a product or service will satisfy its intended purpose. Customers are generally willing to pay more for a product or service if they perceive that the product or service has a higher quality than that of a competitor.

- *Quick response* can be a competitive advantage. One way is quickly bringing new or improved products and services to the markets. Another is being able to deliver existing products or services to customers after they are ordered, and still another is quickly handling customers' complaints.

- *Flexibility* is ability to respond to changes. Changes must relate to alterations in design features of a product or service, or to the volume demanded by customers, or the mix of products and services offered by an organisation. High flexibility can be a competitive advantage in a changeable environment.

- *Inventory management* can be a competitive advantage by effectively matching supplies of goods with demand.

- *Supply chain management* involves coordinating internal and external operations (buyers and suppliers) to achieve timely and cost-effective delivery of goods throughout the system.

- *Service* might involve after-sales activities customers perceive as value-added, such as delivery, setup, warranty work, and technical support. Or it might involve extra attention while work is in progress, such as courtesy, keeping the customer informed, and attention to details. Service quality can be a key differentiator and it is one that is often sustainable. Moreover, businesses rated highly by their customers for service quality tend to be more profitable, and grow faster, than businesses that are not highly rated.

- *Managers and workers* are the people at the heart and soul of organisations, and if they are competent and motivated, they can provide a distinct competitive advantage edge by their skills and the ideas they create. One often overlooked skill is answering the telephone. How complaint calls or requests or information are handled can be a negative or a positive. If the person answering is rude or not helpful, that can produce a negative image. Conversely, if calls are handled promptly and cheerfully, that can produce a positive image and potentially, a competitive advantage.

Geuens (2010) contends that competitive advantage in operations is normally defined around four major concepts: cost leadership, short throughput, flexibility, and reliability.

- Cost leadership does not mean a company should be the cheapest in the market; it rather means giving the best price for the right kind of product/services. It can be achieved when the company is able to maintain the right cost for the right product. An important way to get cost under control is the measurement of production performance, based on production feedback captured by a production control system.

- *Short throughput* (delivery times) are not only important in cost reduction; reducing the time between order intake and delivery to customers will help a company in eliminating waste and getting procedures under control. A good planning process, both in the long term and the short-term, starts with the definition of demand. It is important for a company to know that there might be different types of demand and that they all need their own approach. There is a clear link between the kind of service a company can give to its customers, the average utilization of the production facilities and variability of demand (or the possibility to predict demand). It needs to be understood that a company cannot promise a 24 hour delivery to all customers, never have stock-outs and at the same time run an efficient shop where all machines are constantly planned for 100%.

- *Flexibility* does not mean that anything is possible, at no cost. The results would be chaos, and would create lots of hidden costs. It is important to understand the cost of flexibility at each point in the logistics process. The basic idea is to be very flexible up to a certain point, and then be very inflexible in order to guarantee reliability and keep costs under control.

- *Reliability* has to do both with the product and the process. A company's customers must be sure that they can get the correct quantity and quality of their product at the expected time, and in a consistent way. A production control system shows the operators all information required to produce the correct product. Using online visualisation helps to avoid a situation where people work with outdated product specs or drawings. In order to deliver spotless quality to your customers, a good production control system should come with embedded quality tracking system, which asks operators to perform quality checks and follow up the results.

Operations Management and Business Performance in Ghana

In developing economies and particularly with regard to organisations operating in Ghana, not much work has been done to ascertain the impact of operations management on business performance. This is the case for both firms operating in the manufacturing and service sectors. Agyapong and Muntaka (2012) conducted a study on strategic planning and performance of businesses in Ghana and concluded among others that there is a direct and positive correlation between strategic planning and business performance among Ghanaian firms. However, according to the study, this relationship is insignificant with larger firms but positively significant for micro and small businesses. In other words, the positive relationship between strategic planning and business performance is stronger for micro and small firms in Ghana.

This may be so possibly because many large firms sometimes enjoy a market advantage which smaller firms do not and regardless of the effectiveness or otherwise of their strategic plans. Therefore, smaller firms may have to take strategic planning more seriously, adhere more closely and monitor their plans more effectively in order to compete successfully in the same marketplace where they sometimes compete for the patronage of the same customers that their larger competitors vie for. While this may be the case in the current business environment, managers of large firms should not expect the picture to stay the same in the future, as technology and market demands continue to change. As these changes transform the marketplace in which businesses operate, smaller firms which use technology to enhance their business operations are likely to become more agile and their ability to compete with larger organisations will be enhanced. In the near future and beyond, it is expected that large organisations would need stronger strategic planning skills and they would have to be more effective in the area of operations management to compete with smaller firms as the latter become more nimble and position themselves to make faster decisions in order to take advantage of opportunities that are presented in the business environment.

Another study was conducted in Ghana by Addae-Korankye (2013) on total quality management and competitive advantage. This study revealed that implementation of total quality management improves service quality, increases clientele base, market share. There is reduction in operational and overall unit cost of production and consequently increase in profitability. The implication is that the implementation of total quality management practices improves business performance and hence is a source of achieving competitive advantage. Given the inextricable positive link between total quality management and operations management, it may be concluded from this study that in the Ghanaian context, there is likely to be a positive association between effective operations management and business performance.

While the findings of this study are quite revealing, the respective relationships between total quality managements and the various performance measures are regarded as one of correlation and not causation. Longitudinal research would have to be undertaken to establish causal relationships between total quality management and the customer, market, as well as financial based performance indicators employed in this study. Nevertheless, in the interim, business practitioners would do well to take the principles of effective operational excellence seriously. In this respect, an approach which executives and managers could adopt or adapt to suit the needs of their firms is the model proposed by Kwapong (2015) which identifies eight steps to operational excellence, namely:

1. Identifying market and customers
2. Defining strategic priorities
3. Assembling customer requirements and success criteria
4. Setting up tracking dashboard
5. Identifying key processes that support deliverables and priorities
6. Standardise processes and set expectations for standards
7. Review complaints, review dashboard, review strategy and goals
8. Review customer feedback analysis

Conclusions

A firm must seek to understand the nature of its competitive environment if it is to be successful in achieving its objectives and establishing appropriate strategies. If a firm fully understands the Porter's five forces, and particularly appreciates which one is most important, it will be in a stronger position to defend itself against any threats and influence the forces with its strategy. Moreover, if a firm understands the impact of operations management on achieving competitive advantage and business performance, it will always seek to improve the quality of the processes in the production of goods and services in order to gain competitive advantage. The situation is fluid, and the nature and relative power of the forces will change. Consequently, the need to monitor and stay aware is continuous.

Implications for Policy Makers and Business Executives

Today's competitive business world calls for a diligent search for appropriate strategies to outperform one's competitors consistently and also achieve a sustainable competitive advantage. Porter's generic strategies framework suggests that a company can maximise performance by striving to be a cost leader, by differentiating its products from its competitors or by focusing on a segment of the market. It is therefore important for policy makers and business executives to search for sources of competitive advantage and business performance. When operations management activities are performed efficiently, they can help a firm to achieve a sustainable competitive advantage. This calls for identification of a company's core competences and use them to their advantage. When policy makers or business executives diligently differentiate themselves from their competitors, and /or become cost leaders, that respond effectively to competitive forces in their business environments, profit will be maximised and their firms will be well positioned to achieve and maintain a competitive advantage.

Implications for Researchers

There are many obstacles to further theory development for the operations management and competitive advantage constructs. First, researchers lack a robust operational definition for sustainable competitive advantage and operations management. Without this, we cannot measure either construct, nor can we begin to empirically understand their antecedents and consequences. Current theory has not developed a mutually agreeable method of assessing whether a sustainable competitive advantage has been achieved by a firm or not. For example, should market based or financial related performance indicators such as market share or profitability be used to determine if a sustainable competitive advantage has been achieved? If such performance indicators are used, how can they be empirically linked as the result of a sustainable competitive advantage rather than other factors? These are just a few measurement issues that need to be addressed in order to develop further theory related to sustainable competitive advantage based on an empirically acceptable methodology. The outcomes of such efforts could then be tested empirically, and subsequently, the findings emanating from these studies can be shared with business practitioners to guide them in decisions relating to the management of the operations with a view to gaining a sustainable competitive advantage and maintaining higher levels of performance.

References

- Addae-Korankye, A. (2013). Total quality management as a source of competitive advantage: A comparative study of manufacturing and service firms in Ghana. *International Journal of Asian Social Sciences*, 3 (6), 1293-1305.

- Agyapong, A. & Muntaka, S. (2012). Strategic planning and performance of businesses in Ghana. A comparative study of micro, small and large firms. *International Business and Economic Research Journal*, 11 (11), 1261-1268.

- Barney, J. (1991). Firm resources and sustained competitive advantage. *Journal of Management*, 17 (1), 99-120.

- Bharadwaj, S., Varadarajan, P. & Fahy, J. (1993). Sustainable competitive advantage in service industries: A conceptual model and research propositions. *Journal of Marketing*, 57 (October), 83-99.

- De Wit, B. & Meyer, R. (2004). *Strategy: Process, content, context* (3rd ed). London, UK: International Thomson Press.

- Geuens, J. (2010). Competitive advantage through operations management: Information system for the corrugated packing industry. Technical Article.

- Hill, T. (1991). *Production/Operations management* (2nd ed). London, UK: Prentice-Hall

- Johnson, G. & Scholes, K. (1997). *Exploring corporate strategy. Text and cases* (4th ed). London, UK: Prentice Hall.

- Kwapong, V. (2015). OAK: *Business principles of Strategic and operational excellence*. Port Charlotte, FL, USA: Book-Brokers Publishing Ltd.

- Lynch, R. (2003). *Corporate strategy* (3rd ed). London, UK: Prentice Hall.

- Pearson, G. (1999). *Strategic thinking, understanding and practice*. Upper Saddle River, NJ: Prentice Hall.

- Porter, M. (1990). *The Competitive advantage of nations*. New York, NY: Free Press.

- Porter, M. (1988). *Competitive Strategy: Techniques for analysing industries and competitors*. New York, NY: Free Press.

- Porter, M. (1985). *Competitive advantage: Creating and sustaining superior performance*. New York, NY: Free Press.

- Stevenson, W. (2009). *Operations management* (10th ed). New York, NY: McGraw-Hill.

- Thompson, J. (1997). *Strategic management: Awareness and change* (3rd ed). London, UK: International Thomson Business Press.

- Thurlby, B. (1998). Competitive forces are also subject to change. *Management Decision*, 36 (1), 19-24.

- Varadarajan, P. & Jayachandran, S. (1999). Marketing strategy: An assessment of the state of the field and outlook. *Journal of the Academy of Marketing Science*, 27 (2), 120-143.

- Wheelen, T. & Hunger, J. (2006). *Strategic management and business policy* (10th ed). London, UK: Pearson-Prentice Hall.

Chapter 6

Operational Excellence for Superior Performance

Vincent Kwapong & Hene Aku Kwapong

Abstract

In the current age of rapid globalisation, companies large and small, face increasingly competitive market pressure as national boundaries become insignificant on trade matters. To survive and compete in their markets, companies need to deliver consistent superior performance to their customers and shareholders. Operations excellence presents a tried and true pathway to achieving that goal. In this chapter, we review how basic elements of operations excellence can allow companies both in the manufacturing and service sectors to deliver outstanding performance without significant outlay of capital. Specifically, we examine two examples from developing economies that applied three such elements around; an engaged workforce, defined standardised processes, together with a spirit of innovation to dominate their markets.

Keywords: Operations; Excellence; Performance; People; Process; Product; Service.

Introduction

Why do some companies consistently outperform their competitors in their industries, while others in same industry struggle to maintain even a consistent average performance? This is the fundamental question that companies struggle to develop answers to. In this chapter we examine the key common levers that dominant companies in different industries from service delivery to manufacturing employ to achieve superior performance. The basis of this model stems from over 25 years work experience with companies large and small, fast growing and matured; in financial services, construction, and manufacturing, healthcare and technology development. Fundamentally, all businesses employ the 3Ps in their operations to deliver value to their customers:

- Processes
- People
- Products

How well these 3Ps are deployed, coordinated, and improved upon on a continuous basis determines the firm's ability to consistently stay ahead of the competition in their performance. Within the last two decades, the world has seen emerging economy companies go from being trifling players in their respective economies to becoming global players dominant in their industries. While the list of such companies is extensive, clear examples abound in the automotive, transportation, manufacturing, and communications sector, among others. You have the Samsungs and LGs of Korea to the Huaweis and the ZTEs of China in mobile telecommunications. In the automotive world, Hyundai Motors and Kia Motors have gone from a low cost imitator of Japanese car brands to a leader in both the luxury and mass automotive markets. As a matter of fact and within the last decade Kia Motors has gone from not having any vehicles on the luxury map of J.D. Power and Associates (a company that tracks initial build quality of new vehicles) in 2006 to taking the number one spot on new luxury vehicle rankings in 2016. It's best showing a decade ago in 2006 was at number 25. In the next few paragraphs we will examine the prerequisites that enable companies in both developed and developing economies to achieve this level of operational excellence. In order to achieve sustained superior performance, a solid foundation in operational excellence needs to be in place. The key characteristics of the 3Ps will be described in the following sections.

Processes

From an academic definition perspective, a process is a sequence of interdependent and linked procedures which, at every stage, consume one or more resources (employee time, energy, machines, money, etc.) to convert inputs (data, material, parts, etc.) into outputs. These outputs may feed into other processes or end up being the final value-offering goal or deliverable. Businesses use processes to assure that they consistently deliver value to meet customer expectations. That means delivering products and services that meet with customers' expectations of price, quality and performance. In order to achieve these results, processes must conform to a basic set of process excellence criteria. A process generally supports operational excellence if it meets the criteria outlined below.

1. Process has a defined owner
2. Process is mapped
3. Process is not contributing to any low customer feedback

4. Process metrics are continuously monitored to identify improvement opportunities

5. Systematic process exists to continuously improve standard work

6. Process success is not dependent on workarounds/heroics

7. Process performance to meet customer requirements is predictable

8. Process performance consistently meets customer expectations

Process excellence also means an established business rhythm that is understood by all stakeholders including employees around:

- **Daily routines** - what happens from the beginning of a work day to closing time.

- **Everything in its right place** - all business tools, data and equipment are situated in their right places.

- **Area ownership and responsibilities** - Responsibilities for work areas are defined and communicated.

- **Clear signage** for all to see and follow.

- **Design and maintain for capacity** - workplace systems are designed with intended capacity in mind and maintained accordingly.

Stefan Thomke provides us with provoking thoughts on how these key attributes are crucial even in a low capital-intensive business operation in his 2012 paper titled "Mumbai's Models of Service Excellence" in the Harvard Business Review. These principles are reinforced in his 2014 article titled "Food for Thought: What Makes Mumbai's Dabbawalas Successful" in a follow up article published in the Economic Times on 22 August 2014. In these articles, Thomke illustrated how service excellence allows a business to thrive even in environmentally challenging situations. Indeed, he argues that these business principles and levers can be instituted without resorting to capital-intensive programs.

To recap his story, he talks about Mumbai's *dabbawalas,* who deliver meals prepared in customers' homes to their offices and then return the empty *dabbas* (metal lunchboxes) the same day. Each day, about 5000 dabbawalas transport more than 130,000 lunch boxes throughout Mumbai, the world's fourth-most-populous city. That entails conducting upwards of 260,000 transactions in six hours each day, six days a week, fifty-weeks a year with barely a miss. Service record is phenomenal. Amazingly, the dabbawalas - who largely manage themselves - have achieved a high level of performance at very low cost, in an eco-friendly manner, without the use of any elaborate electronic or software scheduling system. The service is legendary for its reliability.

The dabbawalas in essence employ the 3Ps of Process, People and Product (Thomke illustrates these as organisation, management, process, and culture). They employ these to achieve the singular goal of achieving on-time delivery of their goods (the lunch boxes) while preserving its integrity.

In his paper, Stefan described how the dabbawalas use the Mumbai Suburban Railway to synchronise their operation and maintain steady rhythm. Office workers in India generally do not regularly eat out - because of the expense, a preference for home-cooked food, and the poor quality of the few office cafeterias that exist. Instead they will have their lunches prepared at home and delivered by the dabbawalas after the morning rush hour. On any given day, the lunch boxes or dabba, as they are known change hands several times as they progress through the delivery route. In the morning a worker picks it up from the customer's home and takes it (along with other dabbas) to the nearest train station, where it is sorted and put onto a wooden crate according to its destination. It is then taken by train to the station closest to its destination. There, it is sorted again and assigned to another worker, who delivers it to the right office before lunchtime. In the afternoon the process runs in reverse, and the dabba is returned to the customer's home.

To perform their work most efficiently, the dabbawalas have organised themselves into teams of about 200 units consisting roughly of 25 people each. These small groups maintain local autonomy. With a relatively flat organisational structure they are able to provide a low-cost delivery service.

The railway system sets the pace and rhythm of work. The daily schedule of the train determines when certain tasks need to be done and the amount of time allowed for completion of each task. For instance, workers have 40 seconds to load the crates of dabbas onto a train at major stations and just 20 seconds at interim stops. In essence, these constitute the process steps and their individual cycle times. Combined, they result in an overall throughput (the amount of material moved through the process steps successively in a given time period) that meets the customer's requirement for timely delivery.

The tight schedule helps synchronise everyone and imposes discipline in an environment that might otherwise be chaotic. In addition, it provides clear feedback when performance slips. If a worker is late dropping off his dabbas at a station, his delinquency is immediately obvious to everyone, and alternative arrangements then have to be made for transporting his dabbas on another train. Problems cannot be swept under the rug and must be dealt with promptly.

Many service businesses lack a built-in mechanism like a railway. But they can adopt a system that confers similar benefits. This determines the rhythm that drives everything and exposes deviations from the norm. The dabbawalas essentially manage themselves with respect to hiring, logistics, customer acquisition and retention, and conflict resolution. This helps them operate efficiently and keep costs low and the quality of service high. For the dabbawalas, having the right process in place means more than simply implementing efficient work flows. It also entails just about everything in the organisation, including the way information is managed, the use of built-in buffers, and a strict adherence to standards.

To convey information, the dabbawalas rely on a system of very basic symbols. The lid of a dabba has three key markings on it. The first is a large, bold number in the center, which indicates the neighbourhood where the dabba must be delivered. The second is a group of characters on the edge of the lid: a number for the dabbawala who will make the delivery, an alphabetical code (two or three letters) for the office building, and a number indicating the floor. The third - a combination of colour and shape, and in some instances, a motif - indicates the station of origin. Customers supply small bags for carrying their dabbas, and the variation in the bags' shapes and colours helps workers remember which dabba belongs to which customer.

The coding system contains just enough information for people to know where to deliver the dabbas, but it does not allow for full addresses. The dabbawalas, who run the same route for years, do not need all those details, and inserting them would clutter the lid, slow the sorting process, and possibly lead to errors. This insight is applicable in many other contexts. People operate in a visual world. Whether you run an airline, hotels, or a university, how and what information is conveyed can make a huge difference. Less is often more because it can reduce confusion.

Even with an efficient coding system, workers still have a tiny margin of error for certain tasks. The allotted time for picking up a dabba at a house, for example, might be only 30 to 60 seconds, and any number of minor delays could easily have a cascading effect that slows thousands of deliveries. So, to stay on schedule, each group has two or three extra workers who fill in wherever they are needed, and all members are cross-trained in different activities: collecting, sorting, transporting, finance, and customer relations. This approach is not unlike the Japanese Toyota Production System or a lean manufacturing system that employs kanban and buffering inventories to control production.

This minimises variations that might throw a wrench into the works. The dabbas, for instance, are all roughly the same size and cylindrical shape. To encourage customers to conform, containers incur an additional fee when, say, they are so large that they require special handling. Unusual containers that interfere with the delivery operation are simply not accepted. This uniformity allows the dabbas to be packed quickly onto crates, which are also a standard size so that they can be efficiently loaded onto trains.

The dabbawalas strictly observe certain rules. For instance, they do not eat until they have completed all their deliveries. Workers are fined or fired for repeated mistakes and negligence. Customers are also expected to abide by the process. Those who are repeatedly late in having their dabbas ready for pickup and do not respond to warnings are dropped. The system empowers frontline workers to take action - just as Toyota does in its manufacturing plants, where workers who spot problems can pull an "andon cord" to halt a production line so that they can be addressed immediately.

The individual pillars help explain certain aspects of the success of the dabbawalas. However, to truly understand how they do what they do, you must look at the whole and consider the ways in which the pillars reinforce one another. Take the coding system. It is simple and visual, which allows a semi-literate workforce to sort dabbas quickly. That allows the use of a hub-and-spoke organisation in which railway stations serve as hubs and the need for centralised management is minimal. This is an important lesson for executives who mistakenly think they can alter just one pillar without taking into account the impact on the other three. The dabbawalas show that with the right system, an organisation does not need extraordinary talent to achieve extraordinary performance.

The basic levers of operations excellence described in the example of the service operations of the dabbawalas also play a role in manufacturing settings. This is illustrated by an experience we encountered in the early 2000's at a mosquito coil manufacturing plant.

In 2002, a global consumer product manufacturing company we were working with made items ranging from household cleaning products to consumer chemicals; from bug repellents to deodorant, and everything in between. One of the things the company did from time to time to drive continuous improvement was to look at competitive products as a way of benchmarking how our own products were performing in the marketplace. Benchmarking typically included everything from product design, product costs, product performance and so forth. We would also look at customer satisfaction data and analyse complaints to identify areas of opportunity for improvement.

One of our product family lines happened to be insect repellent; including mosquitoes, ants and other bugs. Some of our products at this point were being sourced as private labelled products made by a third party for us. The third party supplier manufactured them to an agreed specification for us to sell under our brand. The contract with the supplier was coming up for renewal so we also had a decision to make around how we sourced the product going forward; from making our own product, retaining the private labelled product, or acquiring a company with a similar product portfolio.

Our benchmarking process typically entailed procuring competitive products, testing performance, quality and estimating costs in order to assess our competitiveness. This activity was part of our business process for product line management. As part of our overall global product management program, we were also looking at opportunities to manufacture locally in Africa. All of these came together in due course to prompt us to consider a short-term engagement with a local company in Africa (we have decided to leave the specific country and city out to maintain anonymity for the company in question, although it has since been acquired by another company). As part of this effort we spent quite a bit of time with a mosquito coil manufacturing company in Africa and the result was an eye-opener for us.

History of the Company

The company was founded by an entrepreneur who had initially started out as a trader of petty items including electronics and clothing. He lived in a large city but would travel occasionally to visit his extended families in a very small town. He had noticed during these visits that the locals would burn a particular type of plant material to ward of mosquitoes so he proceeded to investigate further and subsequently came across an opportunity to set up a local mosquito coil manufacturing company with an investment from an international economic development partner.

Their Process

The company initially had started production importing all of its raw materials, including the active ingredients but had recently found a local manufacturer of a substitute raw material for the active ingredient. A significant investment in process development research had been made with this substitution, and in the process they realised additional benefits in identifying other local substitutes for the rest of the ingredients. Additional product SKU's were added to offer multiple price points to customers (mostly based on the "burn-time" of the coil). With a bit of marketing, sales were beginning to grow. So much so that when the rainy season started, a second shift had to be added to keep up with demand.

The plant's operation is fairly straightforward. On a typical production run, the production starts out at the mixing department where workers mix the raw materials which are procured in powder form and include wood powder, a binder, the active ingredient (usually insecticide based) and fragrance. In the right ratios, the mix is kneaded with water and extruded into sheets. The sheet is allowed to cure before being fed into a stamping machine where it is cut out into coils and loaded onto drying trays. The loaded trays are then transferred into a drying oven where final curing occurs. The oven curing time varies anywhere from 8 hours to 16 hours depending on the load. At the end of the curing cycle the trays with the coils are retrieved from the oven. The cured coiled products are then paired with metal stands from one of their suppliers and packaged into boxes for distribution and sales to customers.

Typically, a good manufacturing process has a well-defined process flow. Each sub-process has operating set points for machinery, along with standard operating procedures that are well documented. Supported by a good preventive maintenance schedule, the operation will use a well-run production planning process to review production process performance and develop action plans to drive continuous improvement to achieve business targets. All of these were in place at the start of the operation.

Through their initial marketing effort and as their sales picked up, they began to show up on our radar for competitive assessment. We eventually decided to add them as we benchmarked a number of products from different countries that competed with us on the market. We were surprised to discover that their products in our testing performed significantly better than our products at similar price points. Our products at this point were being sourced as private labelled products made by a third party for us. With the third party's contract coming up for renewal, we also had a decision to make around making our own product, retaining their product, or acquiring a company with similar product portfolio. We entered into an agreement to begin an assessment of this company with the view to either becoming partners or acquiring them outright. As consultants, we were charged with leading this effort.

Benchmarking is used by major companies as a means of assessing their competitiveness in the market place. At a recent event in early 2016, Google's CEO was pictured on multiple occasions using an Apple I-phone, the key competitor to Google's Android phones. When a reporter queried him it, his response was "how else can you assess your performance in the marketplace if you are not evaluating the competition"? Benchmarking is a continuous, focused process of measuring and comparing a company's products, services or processes against industry leaders to assist the corporation in becoming Best-In-Class.

As we looked a bit more at the product performance data it became apparent that of their 3 different product lots (from different manufacturing dates) that were tested, one lot was particularly consistent in burning for long hours with little variation in the overall burn time. Additionally, products from the same lot were highly effective at repelling mosquitoes. As an aside, the company that did the testing has an entomology laboratory with just about every known household insect and pest, including all the different cockroaches, ants, spiders, and everything in between that typically annoy humans in our homes! Products from the remaining lots had significant variation in performance – to the point that some of them had structure integrity issues and broke apart with minimal handling; others burnt out very quickly and a few met the minimum burn time specification on the packaging. We decided to gather additional data by reaching out to customers that have made purchases of mosquito coils in the recent past to gather market feedback. These data confirmed our findings and revealed that some customers were becoming upset with the performance of their coil purchases specifically, the brand made by this company. So what happened? How is it that this company is able to produce a batch (or lot) of products that perform so well with minimal variation in performance and yet will make products that do not meet their own published performance standards?

Since we now had a relationship with the coil manufacturing, we took the our benchmarking report, with the test data, market feedback analysis and all to our new partners, meeting with the Production Manager and the Quality Manager to review the findings. That is when we found out about all the recent changes that had happened at the company.

As it turned out, when demand picked up and the company needed to ramp up production, they decided to add a night shift. Although, day shift workers reported to their shifts in the morning via their own mode of transportation, the company went out of its way to secure two company-owned mini-buses to pick up the night shift workers and drop them off at the beginning and at the end of their shifts. This was done in part because the company was having difficulty finding workers that were willing to work at night. Moreover, armed robbery, random murders and mugging were prevalent. So this service provided the security and peace of mind assurance for workers to sign on to do the night shift. Management supervision of the night shift was minimal as none of the management supervisors wanted to be there at that time of the day. That meant once the night shift workers completed their training, they were typically on their own. They had their quota and they were expected to meet them in order to get monthly bonuses that were offered as incentives for each shift.

Both the Operations Manager and the Quality Manager after reviewing the data at our initial meeting concluded the night shift was producing and letting out the low performing products. They had come to this conclusion in part as they shared that the night shift typically had a higher count of products that they were rejecting (each shift was responsible for its own quality checks). They were therefore going to meet with the night shift and develop a plan of action. A couple of days after our meeting on the benchmark data, we got a call from the Production Manager. It looked like he had also had some documentation issues at the plant - production lots that were made on the night shifts had been mislabelled as well. As we asked him to explain how they came to find out, we realised that we were was coming up with more questions than he had answers for. We asked if we could spend some time on his production floor, to which he readily and happily accepted. He thought it would be an excellent opportunity for him to give us a closer overview of the production process. As consultants, we took him up on it and went a step further to arrange a few days with the day shift and an equal number of days with the night shift. What we found out ended up being an eye-opener.

Without prolonging the rest of the details, we will summarise the observations. It turned out the night shift was producing the better quality product with the higher performance and lower variability. Because the company-provided bus service, shifts were starting right on time compared to the day shift. A common problem with the day shift involved workers arriving late and offering all sorts of excuses, sometimes not even showing up. In contrast, everybody on the night shift was there at the same time to start the shift. It also seemed that workers apparently found it a bit more difficult to take off from work when the bus was coming to their homes. Absenteeism was virtually non-existent on the night shift. Workers were also required to complete all their chores before they could board the bus to go home. All these related factors meant the night shift had longer productive hours during their shift versus the day shift, resulting in more production units. The time spent on the bus and the fact that they could not go out to eat lunch meant the night shift workers had built up a camaraderie that was clearly missing on the day shift.

Training was another interesting difference between the night and day shift. Apparently, while workers on the day shift typically receive classroom and on-the-job training, the night-shift had to make do with self-directed video-taped training (which they watch on their own in the training room) plus on the job-training. With a skeleton crew and limited training support, they had all taken the time to review all the training videos (which they did during production or equipment downtime). This had led to the night shift being cross-trained and able to support each other to manage production flow.

The entire production had been synchronised to the bus schedule, which meant all production activities and processes start and stop time were set relative to that schedule, inherently producing repeatable process runs across the operations. In contrast, the day shift had supervisors who would routinely inspect in-process materials to determine if they were ready for the next process steps. In so doing we noticed different processing times from one supervisor to another and sometimes even with the same supervisor.

There were few issues that affected both shifts and caused significant productivity issues. Instead of doing routine maintenance, the plant tended to run the manufacturing equipment until it broke down resulting in real costs due to unreliability. This is a hidden and normally unmeasured cost that results in breakdowns, reduced asset performance (speed, quality), waste, rework, unnecessary production downtimes, etc. It is recommended best practice that these avoidable costs are measured and are taken into account in maintenance decisions. In this way the 'direct' costs of maintenance can be regarded as an investment, with the return coming through avoiding, or reducing, the costs of unreliability.

The day shift tended to believe management was in charge and they were to do as directed with limited examples of initiative taking being observed. The night shift on the other hand, felt they were on their own and had been entrusted to deliver to the shift targets. They displayed a sense of full ownership and accountability in the performance of their production processes. In essence the lack of intrusion from senior management, the autonomy they had, coupled with the accountability to deliver to production shift targets had led the night team to exhibit all the key attributes of a self-managed high performing team.

Effective organisational strategy requires accountability to be assigned to a specific team or individual role. Accountability is a specific duty of performance and should be linked to one or more measures of achievement, reported at the point where accountability has been assigned. Accountability cannot be assigned without necessary authority, which means sufficient freedom of independent decision-making and action to enable complete fulfillment of assigned accountabilities. Individuals and teams should be fully self-sufficient in terms of the skills and resources required for satisfactory achievement of the goals for which they are held to account. These skills and resources must be comprehensively defined once specific goals and accountabilities have been defined.

Once we shared these discrepancies between the two shifts with the production and quality managers, they decided to constitute a team comprising members from both shifts to standardise all production activities across the board. They changed the bus schedule to allow for shift exchange communications meetings, where the leaders from prior shift would meet and review status of key production activities and review issues that needed to be addressed. The day shift also got the benefit of the bus, resulting in significant reduction in tardiness and absenteeism. Importantly, the role of "people", a sense of engagement coupled with mechanisms to drive continuous innovation is fundamental to achieving superior performance with operations excellence.

In all, the team aligned production shifts to one single set of processes that included; production planning and reviews, standardised operating procedures and set points for all processes, clear ownerships for all key processes, and clear performance metrics. They also instituted a new business process to periodically collect feedback from customers on their products and competitors' products. These efforts which lasted a couple of months resulted in significant improvement in production, higher product quality, and to their surprise better performance in the product's burn-time. The ultimate reward came in much later when they received a lucrative acquisition offer. In the next sections, we will further examine other key elements of operational excellence that were crucial in the case studies described.

People

At the end of a meeting, most leaders know how to recap next steps and determine who is accountable for each. As prescribed in the commonly used responsibility models such as the Responsible, Accountable, Consulted and Informed (RACI) matrix, among others – accountability should fall to one (and only one) person per item, even if the work involved requires input and contributions from others. The reason for this is to minimise any confusion around who has the ultimate responsibility or ownership. Every key business process, activity or project needs to have an OAK as described in the book "OAK -

Business Principles of Strategic and Operational Excellence" by Vincent Kwapong (2015). This is the person who is defined accountable for a key process, activity or project.

The level of accountability can vary. On one end of the spectrum is the *issue owner*. In this role the accountable person has complete control over an issue or decision. A full team may be assigned to help, but the issue owner can make the decision however they choose. On the other end of the spectrum is the *team coordinator*. In this role the accountable person is an equal member of the team with the added responsibility of logistics, such as scheduling and defining the agenda. They are responsible for ensuring that there is a discussion but not for the outcome, and they have no more authority than anyone else in the "room". If the team cannot come to an agreement, they cannot force closure — they must escalate the decision up a level. In the middle is the *tiebreaker*. In this role the accountable person does not have the absolute authority of an issue owner, but they are more than just a coordinator. They are responsible for helping the team reach a decision, and in the absence of consensus they should make the final call.

The RACI template is a tool that allows an organisation to define accountability across key processes, or major projects. The following definitions are utilised in the model (see Figure 1 - RACI matrix for Mumbai dabbawala's operation).

RACI Analysis

- Responsibility 'R' - the individual(s) who actually completes the task, the doer.
- Accountability 'A' - the individual who is ultimately responsible. Includes yes or no and veto power.
- Consult 'C' - the individual(s) to be consulted prior to a final decision or action. This incorporates two-way communication.
- Inform 'I' - the individual(s) who needs to be informed after a decision or action is taken. This incorporates one-way communication.

Responsibility, Accountability, Consult & Information (RACI) matrix

Processes	dabbawala	muqaddams (supervisor)	managing committee
		ROLES	
Receive new orders			
Prospect for new customers	R		
Record new customers and orders	R	A	I
Morning Deliveries			
Pick up daily orders	R		
Deliver orders to stations	R		
Sort orders at station	R	A	
Transport orders on prescribed trains	R		
Sort orders at arrival stations by final destination	R	A	
Assign orders for final delivery to workplace	R		
Afternoon Deliveries			
Pick up dabba from workplace	R		
Deliver dabba to station	R		
Sort returning dabba at station	R	A	
Transport by train	R		
Sort dabba at staion	R	A	
Deliver to customers home	R		

RACI analysis

● Responsibility 'R' - the individual(s) who actually completes the task, the doer.

● Accountability 'A' - the individual who is ultimately responsible. Includes yes or no and veto power.

● Consult 'C' - the individual(s) to be consulted prior to a final decision or action. This incorporates two-way communication.

● Inform 'I' - the individual(s) who needs to be informed after a decision or action is taken. This incorporates one-way communication.

Figure 6.1 - RACI matrix for Mumbai dabbawala's operation

Engagement

Having an engaged workforce is just as important as having employees with the right skills. So what do we mean by "engaged workforce"? For this discussion we will offer the following:

- *Employee Engagement - the productive use of one's talents, ideas and energy.*
- *One's talents - the capabilities we have lodged within our knowledge, experiences, skills, and abilities which equip us to perform.*
- *Ideas and energy - our ideas and energy that help drive our desire to perform.*

In order to have an engaged workforce, employees need to feel connected, empowered and equipped with the skills needed to complete their assigned tasks. This means that the business leadership must find ways to involve employees so they understand the organisation's growth strategies, and how important their work is towards the attainment of the defined strategic goals. Employees must know that the work they do makes a difference to customers and their communities every day. When employees feel that that their leaders value them, they tend to be passionate about helping the organisation's customers win and the business grow.

Product Innovation

Products (or services) offered by the business embodies the values that customers pay for. In as much as a business is able to deliver products and services that customers are willing to pay for at a profit, competition in the marketplace means no company can afford to stay complacent when it comes to product innovation. Product innovation is the engine for organic growth. A company that is not growing is bound to shrivel in the marketplace due to competition. Innovation is term-based, with a shelf-life. Competitive dynamics in the marketplace means that all the cool new technologies from yesteryears will be outdated or obsolete this year. Innovation happens in the future which means we need to have mechanisms for introducing new products and services that we think customers will pay for. While the products and services of today bring in revenues in the current period, continuously innovating to deliver products that customers want in the shortest possible time at the right price ensures that a company can continue to achieve superior performance in the marketplace.

Now that we have outlined the prerequisites, how does one go about achieving operational excellence? This journey is one that has no end point; nonetheless, we are going to look at it as a sequence of steps.

OPS Excellence Plan of Action

1. Understand who your customers are:

Understanding who your customers are is the first step to knowing your customer and what their needs are. After all, customers will pay you for products and services that they see value in. You would want to involve your customers in your effort to determine what they want and what they value. If you don't know what they want - ask them, do not guess. Once you think you have ascertained what they want, validate your findings with customers.

2. Understand customer metrics

Once you know who your customers are, and know what they want, you need to define mechanisms for assessing how well you are delivering to those expectations. What they want is the output of your business operations - product attributes and specifications, measure of quality and measures of delivery. These metrics will determine your success in meeting your customers' needs and expectations over time. Generally, if you deliver to your customers' expectations and the metrics that have been determined, you should be able to expect good customer and market feedback scores from your marketplace.

3. Understand business needs

It is imperative that the overall business strategy be considered as part of figuring out how customer needs would be met, from available budget, personnel resources available, supply chain strategy, etc. The strategy defines direction and aligns the efforts of every individual in the organisation toward a common destination and purpose. It identifies specific goals for how the business will serve its customers, employees and shareholders. Ideally, it should integrate a set of goals that are important for meeting the needs of customers. Those goals should be balanced and represent all the stakeholder interests of the group including customer value and satisfaction; leadership, culture and environment; product, process and business results. These will guide your choices in selecting and prioritising initiatives to improve business operations.

4.   Identify your deliverables to your stakeholders

Your plan of action will always entail commitments and deliverables that need to be fulfilled in the operations of the organisation. Take items off as they are completed and add items to the plate as they are identified. Each item should however, always have a clear point of "Accountability" and the appropriate timeline.

5.   Understand the health of your processes

Understanding the health of your business processes is fundamental to your ability to prioritise and allocate limited resources to improve your operations. This means all key processes need to be identified. Using the process excellence criteria described earlier, you can identify the processes that present weak links in your overall operations and develop action plans to mitigate them. It is necessary to validate the importance and quality of processes with customers. Understanding the composition and capability of a process is a prerequisite for improving it.

6.   Apply appropriate continuous improvement tool

You must not stand still in your quest to deliver value to your customers. You can employ various productivity improvement tools such as found in lean six sigma to drive improvements. A lean six sigma programme employs elements of two different well established quality initiatives to improve business performance. The Lean part of the program focuses on improving "flow" throughout the business operation with the goal of minimising or eliminating non-value added activities that inherently add cost but do not generate revenue. Eight types of waste are specifically targeted under this initiative:

- **Overproduction**: Making more than what the customer needs (and will pay for).
- **Inventory**: When inventory is created, it must be moved, tracked, stored, and managed.
- **Defects**: Defective products waste time in the form of detection, sorting, repair, and replacement.
- **Over-processing**: Created when we do more than required to transform raw materials into acceptable product.
- **Motion**: Movements beyond that required to transform product. Includes staging, stacking, and searching for tools and materials.

- **Waiting Time**: The idle time of manpower and machines.
- **Transportation**: Moving material from one point to another.
- **Talent**: The exclusion of the use of our people's knowledge.

The fundamental principle of lean is to provide the highest quality, lowest cost products and services in the shortest cycle time possible, and provide them just in time to customers.

The Six Sigma part on the other hand focuses on improving the quality of the output of a process by identifying and removing the causes of defects from the process and reducing variability in processes. Several principles of Six Sigma derive from age-old quality principles, and then Motorola (now part of Google) trademarked Six Sigma in 1993. The basic steps of Six Sigma are defined around the DMAIC principles (this process is repeated until the desired quality level is obtained):

- **Define** the system, the voice of the customer and their requirements, and the project goals.
- **Measure** key aspects of the current process and collect relevant data; calculate the 'as-is' Process Capability.
- **Analyse** the data to investigate and verify cause-and-effect relationships. Determine what the relationships are, and attempt to ensure that all factors have been considered. Seek out causes of variation and root cause of the defect under investigation.
- **Improve** or optimise the current process based upon data analysis using techniques such as design of experiments, poka yoke or mistake proofing, and standard work to create a new, future state process (or what the process ought to be).
- **Control** the future state process to ensure that any deviations from the target are corrected before they result in defects. Implement control systems such as statistical process control, production boards, visual workplaces, and continuously monitor the process.

Summary

In conclusion, globalisation today has resulted in the blurring of country borders when it comes to the business landscape. That means companies in emerging economies need to be able identify and apply to their organisation the enabling principles of operations excellence that drive superior performance. By leveraging the 3 key levers of process excellence, engaged workers, and continuous innovation within the context of their local environments, companies can position themselves to deliver superior performance to their stakeholders.

References

- Kwapong, V. (2015). *Business principles of strategic and operational excellence*. Port Charlotte, FL: Book-Broker Publishers.

- Thomke, S. (2012). Mumbai's models of service excellence. *Harvard Business Review* 90 (11) (November), 121-126.

- Thomke, S. (2014). Food for thought: What makes Mumbai's dabbawalas successful. *The Economic Times*, 22 August.

Chapter 7

Marketing and Organisational Performance

Kwaku Appiah-Adu

Abstract

For more than half a century, leading advocates of marketing have argued that sound marketing is a key to competitive success. This study examines the extent to which marketing practices impact business performance, and the competitive environment influences on the market orientation-performance relationships in a developing economy. Based on studies of firms that adapted successfully to the changes engendered by economic liberalisation through effective implementation of marketing practices tailored towards economic reforms, the results indicate that in a developing economy environment, foreign firms' marketing practices tend to exert a greater effect on performance than those of domestic firms; and that a significant link between market orientation and performance emerges over a longer period compared to industrialised economies.

Keywords: Market orientation, business performance, thematic study, developing economy.

Introduction

The marketing-performance paradigm of marketing theory and practice postulates that effective marketing practices exert a positive impact upon business performance (Levitt, 1960; Jaworski and Kohli, 1993; Ulrich and Smallwood, 2007). An underlying premise is that the environment conditions the effectiveness of marketing principles and, thus, it is hypothesised that the market orientation-performance link may be influenced by environmental factors. Different conceptualisations of marketing practices are explored in the studies reviewed in this paper but essentially are outlined, in conjunction with environmental variables and performance measures.

Although the marketing-performance framework forms the bedrock for the summarised thematic studies presented in this paper, the impact of corporate culture on marketing practice is also considered. Corporate culture has been discussed extensively in the management literature and many definitions have been proposed (Jelinek et al, 1983).

Following an extensive review of the literature, Deshpande and Webster (1989) describe it as a pattern of shared values and beliefs that help individuals to understand organisational functioning and, thus, provide them with norms for behaviour in the firm. Corporate culture is the organisational dimension which ultimately influences behaviour (e.g., marketing practice) and performance (e.g., productivity) of employees. Managers can use corporate culture to shape the future direction of their firm (Schneider and Arnon Reichers, 1983). Corporate culture can serve as a tool to improve productivity and can be used to encourage all employees to subscribe to organisational goals (Wilkins and Ouchi, 1983). Further, it has been found that a strong marketing culture has a positive link with marketing effectiveness (Webster, 1995) and business performance (Deshpande et al, 1993). In this paper, we examine the impact of corporate culture on marketing.

Furthermore, in response to changing business practices in a number of countries which have embarked on economic reform programmes, a distinctive trend has emerged in marketing-related research on liberalised African economies over the last decade. The late 1980s was characterised by a focus on the relevance, incidence and performance of *marketing (mix) activities* in evolving African markets (e.g., Dadzie et al, 1988). The early 1990s saw a flurry of empirical studies on the impact of economic reform policies on the business environments and the *marketing strategies* which the resulting transformation in the marketplace had given rise to (e.g., Steel and Webster, 1992; Okoroafo and Kotabe, 1993; Okoroafo and Torkornoo, 1995; Muuka, 1997). Some of these works were based on single countries (e.g., Okoroafo and Kotabe - Nigeria; Muuka - Zambia) while others used samples from several countries which had embarked on structural adjustment programmes (SAP) in an effort to liberalise their economies (e.g., Okoroafo and Torkornoo - Ghana, Kenya, Nigeria, Uganda, Zambia). The works reported in this paper do not only explore further dimensions of these subjects but also incorporate new areas. Specifically, consideration is given to the significance of *marketing strategies* (Appiah-Adu, 2009).However, this study differs from previous efforts in that it is based on a case approach and, secondly, objective (not subjective) indicators are used to measure performance. In addition, *marketing mix activities* (Appiah-Adu and Singh, 2008) are investigated but a clear attempt is made to conduct a comparative analysis of the practices of foreign and domestic firms. The concept of *market orientation* (Appiah-Adu, 2001) is also examined in the context of a liberalised developing economy (Ghana). Further, the importance of marketing to economic development is investigated (Appiah-Adu and Singh, 2008).

Therefore, the purpose of the study is to examine the extent to which marketing practices contribute to organisational performance, and whether the competitive environment influences the market orientation-performance relationship in a developing economy. More specifically, the objective is to gain an understanding of the link between marketing practices and different performance dimensions of firms in the contexts investigated. In this regard, we provide a discussion of marketing strategies, marketing mix activities amongst foreign and domestic companies, and an assessment of the impact of corporate culture on marketing practice. To provide additional insight into the market orientation-performance link, moderators of the relationship and environmental influences on performance are investigated. Finally, we discuss the implications of the findings for managers and conclusions, suggesting possible future research avenues on the consequences of sound marketing practice for firms in developing economies.

Thematic Studies of the Market Orientation-Performance Link

In developing economies such as Ghana, Kenya, Nigeria and Zambia, the marketing-performance relationship has been explored by investigating the effects of marketing practices (Appiah-Adu and Singh, 2008), marketing dynamics (Lewa, 2008), marketing strategies (Okoroafo and Kotabe, 1993) as well as marketing decisions (Okoroafo and Torkornoo, 1995; Muuka, 1997) on performance. For the purpose of this paper, we selected five studies. A number of the studies in this paper (Studies 2, 4 and 5) were designed to generate primary data among businesses. This is entirely different from industry or government data which are generally of limited value in much competitive research because of the level of aggregation that extends beyond the product or business unit level of most strategic research. Consequently, three of the five studies in this paper focus on data collection, processing and analysis based on primary research. The methodologies used involve a range of approaches. Sample sizes range from three companies used in a case approach (Study 3) to the 78 responses obtained in a survey of large organisations (Study 4). Samples include a cross-section of manufacturing and service organisations (Studies 2 and 5). Most of the empirical studies start with a survey of existing research and in-depth interviews with managers to explore the dimensions of the issues at stake. Hence, a number of face-to-face contacts are made with potential respondents during the exploratory stage. In addition to the primary empirical research and case study, the works include a purely conceptual paper (Study 1).

Summary of the Studies Selected and Their Significance

This section provides a summary of the studies used for this review and the contents here only contextualise the issues under discussion. Details of these papers are published in Appiah-Adu (2009) with some updates in Appiah-Adu (2015). Although the central theme is marketing-performance, a close examination of the articles reveals that they include a key antecedent of marketing practice, namely corporate culture (Study 2), consequences of sound marketing practice (Studies 1, 2, 3, 4, 5) and moderators of the market orientation-performance relationship (Study 5).

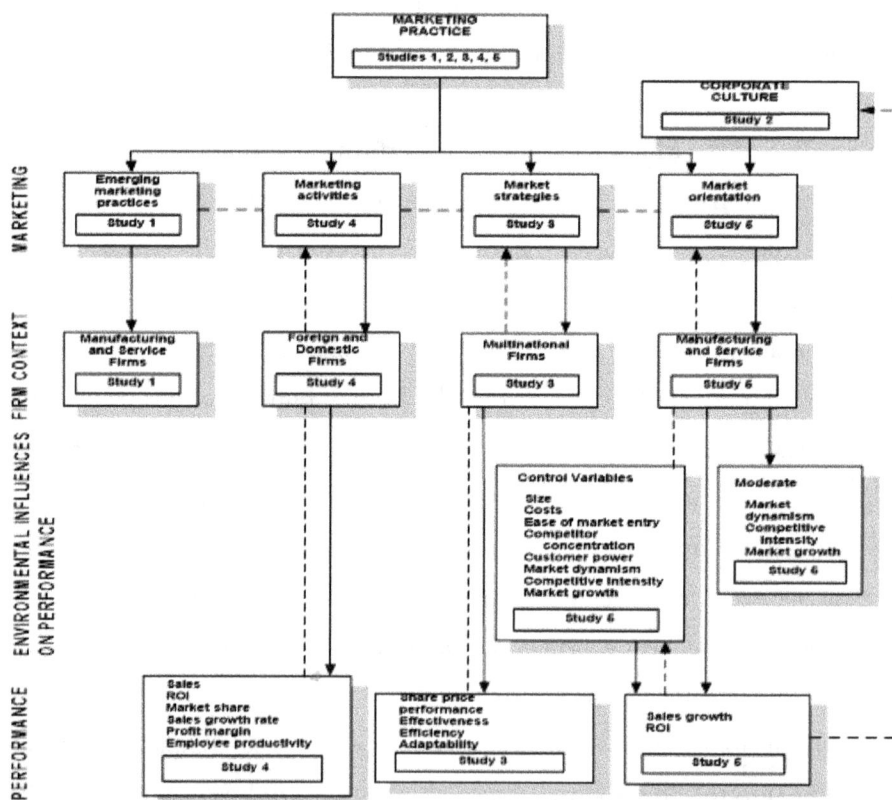

Fig 7.1: Marketing Performance Framework: Developing Economy.

Therefore, the principal propositions derived from the marketing-performance framework which are investigated in the context of developing economies are listed below.

Proposition 1: There is a link between corporate cultural orientation and the effectiveness of marketing practice.

Proposition 2: There is a positive association between market orientation and performance.

Proposition 3: There are internal and external environmental influences on performance such as firm relative size, relative cost, product quality, and customer power, ease/time of market entry, market turbulence, competitive intensity, technological turbulence, and market growth.

Proposition 4: External competitive variables such as market turbulence, market growth, competitive intensity and technological turbulence may moderate the market orientation-performance association.

Proposition 5: In developing economies, the economic reforms taking place will increase the need for and utilisation of marketing strategies among firms tailored to the economic reforms.

Proposition 6: Foreign firms are more likely to be characterised by superior marketing practices compared to domestic firms.

Definitions and Operationalisation of the Variables

Market orientation is operationalised by Kohli and Jaworski (1990) as the implementation of the marketing concept, that is, the organisation-wide generation of market intelligence pertaining to current and future customer needs, dissemination of the intelligence across departments and organisation-wide responsiveness to it. A complementary definition by Narver and Slater (1990) is based on the notion that market orientation comprises three behavioural components - customer and competitor orientations and inter-functional coordination. .

Marketing activities represent decisions relating to five basic marketing functions, namely: product-related functions; pricing-related functions; promotion-related functions; distribution-related functions and customer orientation (McCarthy and Perreault, 1993; Moller, 2006).

Marketing is also described in a strategic context by combining elements of the marketing mix with related areas such as strategic planning, diversification, operational efficiency and organisational rationalisation, and their overall impact on competitive success among selected multinational companies is explored.

Marketing practices refer to the adoption and utilisation of philosophies, strategies and activities associated with the marketing concept. Generally, they represent a broad range of practices, usually defined as constructs which are based on marketing principles. In this paper the focus is on marketing strategies, marketing activities and market orientation.

Environmental variables influence marketing practices and performance. Corporate culture is considered to exert a significant influence on the extent and effectiveness of marketing practice (Deshpande et al, 1993; Webster, 1995). Environmental effects on performance include market turbulence, competitive intensity, market growth, technological turbulence, relative size, relative cost, customer power, ease of market entry and competitor concentration (Slater and Narver, 1994). Furthermore, market turbulence, competitive intensity, market growth and technological turbulence are postulated as moderators of the marketing-competitive success association (Kohli and Jaworski, 1990).

Performance of firms is assessed by adopting a multi-dimensional approach. This includes: financial measures relating to growth, profitability, effectiveness, efficiency; adaptability and innovation success; employee-based measures such as productivity; and, customer-focused measures, namely, customer satisfaction and retention (Walker and Ruekert, 1987; Deng and Dart, 1994; Reichheld, 2006).

Performance Measurement

Different studies have used different frameworks for conceptualising performance; e.g., the goal approach (Etzioni, 1964), systems resource approach (Yutchman and Seashore, 1967) and multiple constituency approach (Thompson, 1967). However, an examination of the marketing strategy literature highlights Walker and Ruekert's (1987) performance paradigm as one of the most influential frameworks endorsed by marketing academics. Based on an exhaustive review of the literature, they conclude that performance can be measured and judged on a number of dimensions with varying relevance and importance: across stakeholder groups (e.g., investors vs. employees vs. customers); and, in relation to whether one takes a long-term or short-term view of the firm's performance. Although there are various ways of measuring adaptability, the most common indicators are the new product success rate (Johne, 1996) in comparison with those of competitors or the percentage of sales attributable to products introduced within a given recent period (often operationally defined as the past five years).

For the purpose of our study, we used a variety of indicators according to their relevance and applicability in each case study in our sample; in this context, conventional measures such as profitability and sales growth, but the comparison of foreign and domestic firms includes employee productivity because of the emphasis on increased efficiency in the new environment. The majority of studies reviewed in this paper adopted the subjective method; firstly, due to the difficulty in obtaining objective indicators from documentary sources; and secondly, because in most cases respondents were unwilling to provide such data which was considered to be confidential. However, Study 3 was based on objective performance measures.

Study 1 - Marketing in a Liberalised Economy: Emerging Trends and Implications for Strategy

This article focuses on fundamental issues relating to marketing in a liberalised developing economy and also serves as an introductory text to all the empirical studies which are subsequently reported in Studies 1 to 5 of this paper. Contents of the article include a review of some of the research themes of the last decade and a half, the introduction of economic reform and structural adjustment programmes in developing economies and the general consequences of liberalisation. A background on Ghana and specific reform policies are provided. In the context of developing economies, the relevance of marketing is highlighted, followed by a discussion on typical marketing practices in a non-reformed developing economy. Next, issues relating to the evolution of marketing systems and marketing organisations are discussed. Moreover, several areas in which sound marketing practices are becoming increasingly significant in Ghana's transitional marketplace are identified and, finally, the implications of the changing environment for business practitioners are addressed. This research contributes to existing knowledge in a number of ways. First, in response to the suggestion by both practitioners and scholars that a major difficulty in the economic development of developing economies stems from the scant attention paid to the problems and opportunities of marketing (Kaynak and Hudanah, 1987), this article explores the role of marketing in developing economies. Second, the article

107

facilitates a comparison of marketing activities in a typical developing economy with the increased significance of marketing decisions in a liberalised economy. Third, the Ghanaian context of the study responds to the need to study the potential impact of structural adjustment programmes on marketing practices and the likely effects on firm performance in individual countries (Okoroafo and Kotabe, 1993). Moreover, since Ghana was one of the first sub-Saharan countries to adopt economic reform, a study based on this country is insightful because of the long-term impact reforms are expected to have had in the marketplace. Fourth, a conceptual relationship of the investigation of marketing approaches and development of marketing applications is developed using Kaynak and Hudanah's (1987) five-stage marketing evolution model based on economic development. An effort is then made to relate firms in Ghana to the five phases of marketing development. Finally, this paper proposes the need to link functional marketing activities to strategic efforts such as planning, operational consolidation and diversification.

Study 2 - Corporate Culture and Market Orientation of Firms in an Emerging Economy

In the context of Ghana, this research investigates the impact of corporate culture on market orientation. The study is based on but extends Deshpande et al's (1993) four classifications of culture proposed by the *competing values* model and tested in Japan in their study. This conceptualisation results in four main types of culture: market; adhocracy; hierarchical; and, clan which are then related to the degree of market orientation among a cross-section of mainly large businesses in Ghana. Referring to Deshpande et al's (1993) model, the clan culture, which stresses tradition, loyalty and internal maintenance, could result in a lack of attention to changing market needs which, in turn, may lead to a low degree of firm market orientation. The adhocracy culture, with its emphasis on entrepreneurship, innovation and risk taking is expected to have a relatively higher degree of market orientation than the clan culture. The hierarchical culture, with its focus on smooth operations and predictability in a bureaucratic organisation is likely to lead to a low level of firm market orientation. On the other hand, the market culture, which is based on differentiation, competitive advantage and market superiority, is expected to exhibit a high level of market orientation. In support of our hypotheses market culture was found to have a significant impact on market orientation, implying that the influence of a market culture might transcend national frontiers. The constituents of a market culture such as competitiveness, productivity, competitive advantage and market superiority reflect a culture that stresses the creation of sustainable superior value for the customer, and fosters behaviours required for a firm to generate and respond to market intelligence. Consistent with expectations, hierarchical organisations were the least market oriented. Hence, in firms which are governed by rules and uniformity, with strategic principles founded on predictability and stable operations, the consequence is an inward looking bureaucratic business that is not customer or market oriented. However, the adhocracy and clan types provided non-significant results. This research contributes to the literature in three respects. First, it addresses a gap in the literature by responding to the call to examine the impact of corporate culture on organisational variables in general (Webster, 1995) and marketing practices in particular (Deshpande and Webster, 1989). Second, it seems to be the first study to provide empirical evidence of the contribution of corporate culture to market orientation in a developing economy and, hence, bridges the gap between the culture, marketing and international business literature. Third, the Ghana context of this study responds to the need to examine the global universality of a competitive corporate culture that might transcend a more consensually oriented national culture and, indeed, the market culture finding confirms Deshpande et al's (1993) conclusions. Theoretically, the findings extend empirical research in two areas. First, the significance of corporate culture to successful market oriented behaviours is reasonably well supported. Moreover, an important research insight is that different types of culture have varying effects on market orientation.

Study 3 - Marketing in Emerging Countries: Evidence from a Liberalised Economy

This article discusses the importance of marketing in the business environment of a liberalised developing nation. It builds on the background information provided in Study 1 and explores further the significance of marketing principles and application in developing economies which have instituted policies to liberalise their economies, with a focus on Ghana, which has been hailed by World Bank and IMF analysts as a successful bright star of the developing world. Several domains in which sound marketing strategies are assuming growing importance in Ghana's evolving marketplace are highlighted. To offer alternative means of gaining additional insight into our understanding of markets, this article uses a case approach to discuss three large multinational companies which have achieved superior performance as a result of improved marketing practices in the new environment. Core marketing-related issues centred on products, pricing, promotion, distribution, customer satisfaction, branding and market research are addressed. Efficiency measures such as

109

rationalisation and operational efficiency as well as strategic planning, innovation and total quality management are also discussed. Performance indicators employed include operating profits, return on assets, net profit before and after tax, market share, sales growth and new product development success. Implications of the changing environment for managers of both foreign and domestic firms are addressed. This study contributes to existing knowledge in a number of ways. First, from a practical viewpoint, it examines the character and importance of those practices enhancing ongoing marketing efforts of selected multinational firms in order to identify distinguishing practices which have provided them with an edge in the marketplace. Second, from a theoretical standpoint, an attempt is made to relate SAP-tailored marketing strategies to business performance. The study fills a void in the literature by responding to calls to explore the influence of marketing strategies on objective dimensions of performance (Okoroafo, 1996). Third, from a methodological perspective, a case approach instead of a mail survey is employed to provide additional insights into the extent of marketing practices of the selected firms. Although it may be argued that multinational companies are destined to do well because of their immense resources, it has been found that in some developing economies, domestic firms have become effective competitors who have managed to steal share from some of these multinational giants such as Unilever Limited, through the utilisation of sound product, pricing and distribution strategies. Fourth, the Ghana study responds to the need for research in different contexts to enhance our confidence in the impact of marketing strategies on performance (Okoroafo and Russow, 1993).

Study 4 - Marketing Activities and Performance of Foreign and Domestic Firms in Ghana

Against the background of reform in Ghana's economy, Study 4 builds on Study 3 by examining empirically the impact of marketing mix activities such as product, pricing, promotion, distribution, market research, customer satisfaction and customer service efforts on performance among predominantly large foreign and domestic manufacturing companies. The study's first hypothesis is based on previous research (Chong, 1973; Okoroafo, 1996) which suggests that foreign firms tend to emphasise customer service, offering superior product and quality package. They have products with recognisable brand names and pursue practices which have been tested and perfected in their home markets. Foreign firms are familiar with competitive marketing activities because of the experience acquired in their home markets. It is therefore hypothesised that on the whole, the marketing activities of foreign firms are likely to be superior to those of domestic firms. Drawing on precepts from previous research in liberalised economies as well as fundamentals of the marketing concept, it is surmised that effective marketing activities will be positively related to performance of foreign and domestic organisations. This research contributes to the literature in three respects. First, it addresses a gap in the literature by responding to calls for research to examine the impact of marketing mix activities on a variety of performance dimensions in liberalised economies (Golden et al, 1995). Second, it provides empirical evidence of the unique contribution of individual marketing mix components to performance in liberalised African economies. Third, the Ghana context of the study complements research efforts in liberalised economies in other African countries (Okoroafo, 1996) and areas such as Central and Eastern Europe (Hooley et al, 1998). Theoretically, the findings extend empirical research in three areas. First, eight of the ten marketing mix activities for both foreign and domestic firms are established as significant determinants of performance in the medium- to long-term, confirming the importance of marketing in developing economies (Dadzie et al, 1988). Second, the overall superiority of foreign firms' marketing activities is upheld (Chong, 1973; Okoroafo, 1996). Finally, a critical research insight is that foreign companies appear to perform better on profitability and efficiency measures compared with domestic firms' higher performance in sales-related measures.

Study 5 - Market Orientation and Performance in a Transition Developing Economy

This study examines the impact of market orientation on performance in a liberalised developing economy. In such economies, market oriented firms are likely to emphasise customer and competitor focused strategies. Marketing operations will take into consideration customer attitudes and benefits. Hence, there will be a focus on understanding customer needs, emphasising customer satisfaction and service, market research and new product development. Such firms will seek to obtain a competitive advantage by discussing and responding rapidly to competitors' actions. Moreover, market oriented firms are likely to ensure that all functions contribute to customer value and are integrated in strategy development. Previous research based on developing economies, report a positive link between market orientation and performance (e.g., Bhuain, 1996, Lewa, 2008). Indeed, a study by Pitt et al, (1996, p.14) concludes that "... this relationship extends to whole companies, in different industries and countries irrespective of culture or level of economic development." Thus, a positive link is hypothesised between market orientation and performance in Ghana's liberalised economy. Sales growth and profitability (ROI) are the two performance indicators of interest in this study. Several control factors are included in the empirical framework due to their recognised effects on performance. These include relative size, relative cost, customer power, ease of market entry, market growth, competitive intensity and market dynamism. To determine the influence of external moderating influences on the market orientation-performance link, an adaptation of Golden et al's (1995) factors in liberalised economies, reflecting Kohli and Jaworski's (1990) measures is utilised. Findings of main effects indicate no direct impact of market orientation on performance. Relative size and relative cost are respectively positively and negatively associated with both sales growth and ROI while market growth is positively associated with sales growth. The moderated regression analysis demonstrates that market orientation has a higher impact on sales growth in environments exhibiting medium to high levels of competitive intensity. Moreover, market orientation has a greater effect on ROI in conditions characterised by low market dynamism. This study contributes to the literature in several ways. First, it addresses a gap in the literature by responding to recent calls for research to develop constructs for measuring market orientation in environment specific situations (Cadogan et al, 1997). Second, it empirically examines the character and importance of those elements constituting a market orientation in a liberalised developing economy. In this context, it appears to be the first study to provide empirical evidence of the link between market orientation and performance in different contingencies by controlling for competitive environmental factors. This study, therefore bridges the gap between the marketing, strategy and international business literature. Third, the Ghanaian context of this study responds to the need to study market orientation in diverse contexts to increase our confidence in the universality and global importance of the concept. Theoretically, the findings extend empirical research in three areas. First, the significance of market orientation to successful organisational outcomes in a developing economy may be limited in the short-term. Second in concert with executive theory (Kohli and Jaworski, 1990; Golden et al, 1995), the study demonstrates that the influence of market orientation on performance varies with the perceived intensity of competition and market dynamism. Third, this initial effort should act as a stimulus for longitudinal research to test for causal links between market orientation and performance.

Managerial Implications

Findings from the studies which lend partial support to the proposition that sound marketing practices do influence performance have implications for managers of liberalised developing economies in general and Ghana in particular. Specifically, the marketing-performance link is stronger over the long-term. Although marketing activities are on the increase, foreign firms are characterised by superior marketing practices compared with their domestic counterparts. This portends long-term anxieties for indigenous firms which need to maintain a competitive edge in order to survive. These results may stem from the fact that domestic managers still do not *fully* appreciate the benefits of certain marketing functions, as evidenced in the extent to which they utilise pricing and promotion tools. This problem could be resolved by providing training on the relevance of all marketing activities to the firm, emphasising customers as the focus of all marketing efforts. Given the highly competitive Ghanaian environment, this issue is quite crucial because effective marketing activities will become increasingly important for survival or maintaining a competitive advantage. In addition to in-company training efforts, there is a pressing need for transfer of marketing knowledge to developing economies. New forms of marketing could also be developed through the modification of Western techniques and adaptation of these tools to suit a country's culture. Both managers and employees can benefit from these transfers through more formal educational procedures which lead to the attainment of academic qualifications. In this context, colleges and tertiary institutions will serve as the primary agents of such transfers and provision of educational funding for these purposes should be seriously considered.

Performance of marketing activities by domestic and foreign executives may provide an indication of the perceived importance of these activities to their firms. However, based on the contention that sound marketing practices result in higher performance over the long-term (Jacobson and Aaker, 1987; Okoroafo and Russow, 1993), it is important for managers to fully understand the benefits associated with marketing activities in order to perform them effectively. This calls for procedures to formalise marketing programmes with an aim of redressing the apparently *ad hoc* approach that generally characterises certain aspects of marketing practice, particularly among indigenous businesses. Regarding investment prospects, the background provided on the economy indicates that numerous opportunities are available to entrepreneurs and foreign investors. Establishing subsidiaries or branches can be cost effective, particularly in countries which have floated their currencies and experienced a sharp drop in value relative to currencies of industrialised nations. Although misplaced policies of the pre-SAP periods do plague the economy, a long-term view can pay dividends.

Conclusions and Research Implications

Considering all the studies reported in this paper, the main conclusion which can be drawn is that (i) corporate culture influences marketing practice; (ii) sound marketing practices impact upon performance; (iii) environmental factors influence the market orientation-performance link. Specifically, the findings on Ghana indicate that the highest and least market oriented firms are characterised by market and hierarchical culture types respectively. Moreover, market leaders in the manufacturing and service sectors appear to be utilising sound marketing and business strategies tailored to the economic reforms taking place as they strive to maintain a competitive edge and superior performance. Comparing domestic and foreign firms, the latter appear to be superior in their application of marketing principles and this is demonstrated in the significant links found between all their marketing activities and performance. Overall, market orientation is found to have a positive and significant impact on short-term sales growth or ROI, when moderated by competitive intensity and market dynamism respectively.

Generally, these findings lend support to the marketing-performance hypothesis. However, much more work is required if we are to appreciate the mechanisms and implications of sound marketing practice in the competitive contexts of developing economies. It is important to explore further the dynamics of marketing practices and of business performance in order to reinforce the universal significance of the marketing discipline, and it is contended that a useful approach to this is to test the marketing-performance framework in diverse contexts.

References

- Appiah-Adu, K. (2001). *Market oriented strategy and corporate performance in an emerging economy*. Accra, Ghana: AlphaPrint Publishers.

- Appiah-Adu, K. & Singh, S. (2008). Current marketing practices in Ghana. In S. Singh (ed) *Business Practices in Emerging and Re-emerging Markets*. New York, NY:

Palgrave Macmillan, 153-165.

- Appiah-Adu, K. (2009). *Market Orientation and Competitive Performance: A Comparison of Firms in Industrialised and Emerging Economies*. Accra, Ghana: Smartline Publishing Limited.

- Appiah-Adu, K. (2015). Marketing and economic development. In K. Appiah-Adu & M. Bawumia (eds). *Key determinants of national development: Historical perspectives & implications for developing economies*. Surrey, UK: Gower Publishing, 335-342.

- Bhuain, S. (1996). Examining market orientation, its antecedents and consequences among Saudi manufacturing companies. Paper presented at the American Marketing Association Conference, San Diego: CA, August.

- Cadogan, J., Diamantopoulos, A. & de Mortanges, C. (1997). Developing a measure of export market orientation: Scale construction and cross-cultural validation. Paper presented at the European Marketing Academy Conference, Warwick, UK 1, 232-251.

- Chong, S. (1973). Comparative marketing practices of foreign and domestic firms in developing countries: A case of Malaysia. *Management International Review* 13 (6), 91-98.

- Dadzie, K., Akaah, I. & Riordan, E. (1988). Incidence of market typologies and pattern of marketing activity performance in selected African nations. *Journal of Global Marketing* 1 (3), 87-107.

- Deng, S. & Dart, J. (1994). Measuring market orientation: A multi-factor, multi-item approach. *Journal of Marketing Management* 10 (8), 725-742.

- Deshpande, R. & Webster, F. (1989). Organisational culture and marketing: Defining the research agenda. *Journal of Marketing* 53 (1), 3-15.

- Deshpande, R., Farley, J. & Webster, F. (1993). Corporate culture, customer orientation and innovativeness in Japanese firms: A quadrad analysis. *Journal of Marketing* 57 (1), 23-37.

- Etzioni, A. (1964). *Modern Organisations*. Englewood Cliffs, NJ: Prentice Hall.

- Golden, P., Doney, P., Johnson, D. & Smith, J. (1995). The dynamics of a market orientation in transition economies: A study of Russian firms. *Journal of International Marketing* 3 (2), 29-49.

- Hooley, G., Cox, T., Fahy, J., Shipley, D., Beracs, J., Snoj, B. & Fonfara, K. (1998).

Market orientation in the transition economies of Central Europe: Tests of Narver and Slater Market Orientation Scales. Paper presented at the European Marketing Academy Conference, Stockholm, Sweden, May.

- Jacobson, R. & Aaker, A. (1987). The strategic role of product quality. *Journal of Marketing* 51 (4), 31-44.

- Jaworski, B. & Kohli, A. (1993). Market orientation: Antecedents and consequences. *Journal of Marketing* 57 (3), 53-70.

- Jelinek, M., Smircich, L. & Hirsch, P. (1983). Introduction: A code of many colours. *Administrative Science Quarterly* 28 (September), 331-338.

- Johne, A. (1996). Succeeding at product development involves more than avoiding failure. *European Management Journal* 14 (2), 176-180.

- Kaynak, E. & Hudanah, B. (1987). Operationalising the relationship between marketing and economic development: some insights from less-developed countries. *European Journal of Marketing* 21 (1), 48-65.

- Kohli, A. & Jaworski, B (1990). Market orientation: The construct, research propositions and managerial implications. *Journal of Marketing* 54 (April), 1-18.

- Levitt, T. (1960). Marketing myopia. *Harvard Business Review* 38 (4), 45-56.

- Lewa, P. (2008). Market liberalisation in emerging economies: Changing business practices. In S. Singh (ed.). *Business Practices in Emerging and Re-emerging Markets.* Palgrave Macmillan, 17-40.

- McCarthy, J. & Perreault, W. (1993). *Basic Marketing.* Homewood, IL: Irwin.

- Möller, K. (2006). Marketing mix discussion - Is the mix misleading us or are we misreading the mix? Comment on the marketing mix revisited: Towards the 21st century marketing by E. Constantinides, *Journal of Marketing Management*, 22 (3/4), 439-450.

- Muuka, G. (1997). Wrong-footing MNCs and local manufacturing: Zambia's 1992-1994 structural adjustment program. *International Business Review* 6 (6), 667-687.

- Narver, J. & Slater, S. (1990). The effect of a market orientation on business profitability. *Journal of Marketing* 54 (October), 20-35.

- Okoroafo, S. & Kotabe, M. (1993). The IMF's structural adjustment program and its impact on firm performance: A case of foreign and domestic firms in Nigeria. *Management International review* 33 (2), 139-156.

- Okoroafo, S. & Russow, L. (1993). Impact of marketing strategy on performance: Empirical evidence from a liberalized developing country. *International Marketing Review* 10 (1), 4-18.

- Okoroafo, S. & Torkornoo, H. (1995). Marketing decisions and performance in economic reform African countries. *Journal of Global Marketing* 8 (3), 85-102.

- Okoroafo, S. (1996). Differences in marketing activities and performance of foreign and domestic manufacturing firms in Nigeria. *Journal of Global Marketing* 9 (4), 109-118.

- Pitt, L., Caruana, A. & Berthon, P. (1996). Market orientation and business performance: Some European evidence. *International Marketing Review* 13 (1), 5-18.

- Reichheld, F. (2006). *The Ultimate Question Driving Good Profits and True Growth.* Boston: Harvard Business School Press, 2006.

- Schneider, B. & Arnon Reichers, E. (1983). On the etiology of climates. *Personnel Psychology* 36 (1), 19-39.

- Slater, S. & Narver, J. (1994). Does competitive environment moderate the market orientation performance relationship? *Journal of Marketing* 58 (January), 46-55.

- Steel, W. & Webster, L. (1992). How small enterprises in Ghana have responded to adjustment. *The World Bank Economic Review* 6 (3), 423-438.

- Thompson, J. (1967). *Organisations in Action.* New York, NY: McGraw-Hill.

- Ulrich, D. & Smallwood, N. (2007). *Leadership brand: Developing customer-focused leaders to drive performance and build lasting value.* Boston, MA: Harvard Business School Press.

- Walker, O. & Ruekert, R. (1987). Marketing's role in the implementation of business strategies: A critical review and conceptual framework. *Journal of Marketing* 51 (July), 15-33.

- Webster, C. (1995). Marketing culture and marketing effectiveness in service firms. *Journal of Services Marketing* 9 (2), 6-21.

- Wilkins, A. & Ouchi, W. (1983). Efficient cultures: Exploring the relationship between culture and organisational performance. *Administrative Science Quarterly* 28, 468-481.

- Yutchman, E. & Seashore, S. (1967). A system resource approach to organisational effectiveness. *American Sociological Review* 32, 891-903.

Chapter 8

Services Management and Corporate Performance

Kwaku Appiah-Adu

Abstract

Services, both consumer and business, are essential and intrinsic to the working of modern economies, and in many national, regional and local economies, dominate the business landscape. This chapter attempts to determine the effects of services management on corporate performance. It begins with historical developments that led to the birth of the service sector. Next, an effort is made to understand the definition and characteristics of services and what makes them unique in nature. Owing to the link between competitive advantage and corporate performance, the two concepts are investigated in an attempt to gain a deeper understanding of performance. In this context the chapter sheds further light on the relationships between performance and each of the three peculiar Ps of services; people, physical evidence, and processes. Also highlighted are the links between service encounters and competitive advantage, types of service encounters in developing economies, and the notion of strategic service vision. Furthermore, the service triangle model is highlighted, touching on internal, external and interactive marketing. Subsequently, the significance of employee satisfaction and customer satisfaction in a business is presented, leading to an overall assertion of the importance of services management to corporate performance. Finally, implications of the findings and conclusions of this chapter for business practitioners is discussed.

Keywords: *Services; Management; Performance; Value; Competitive advantage; Customer satisfaction;*

Introduction

Global trends have altered the traditional balance between customers and suppliers during value creation such that new communications, technology and the establishment of reasonably competitive business models have empowered customers with unlimited choices. The needs of these multi-faceted customers translate into increased and sophisticated perceptions of desired product or service outcome. Spurred on by competition, businesses are challenged to be more customer-centric in their attempts to identify, establish and maintain profitable customer relationships. Business competition dominates disparate tête-à-têtes within the academic and industrial landscape; mostly driven by analysts' desire to understand the dynamics of the environments in which strategies are executed. A detailed sectorial analysis by (Teece, 2010) revealed that while value embedded interactions yield sustainable competitive advantage, the challenges they present remain dynamic; thereby, creating uncertainties and the accompanying potpourri of camaraderie, fear and doubt.

Traditionally, economic activities were captured as primary, secondary, and tertiary with primary activities hugely apparent in the colonial era even though it still remains the spine of many developing nations. The late 18th century to early 19th century witnessed the industrial revolution which birthed the secondary sector (manufacturing). This was followed by the novel service sector (tertiary) in the mid-20th century, a sector which now dominates developed economies. All these economic activities transit through value adding stages. Thus, whether countries or industries, the most efficient player hammering value into its string of activities is most likely to exhibit superior performance. These series of value driven activities performed by corporations to gain competitive advantage is captured by Michael Porter (1985) in his book "Competitive Advantage: Creating and Sustaining Superior Performance". Using this viewpoint, Porter described a chain of activities common to all businesses, and divided them into primary (inbound logistics, operations, outbound logistics, marketing and sales and services) and support activities (firm infrastructure, human resource management, technology development and procurement).

Critics of Porter's value chain bluntly describe it as antiquated in the light of the world's evolving social and technology era and that it was developed at a time when economies of scale were perceived as key aspects to competitive advantage and profitability, and manufacturing was dominant. Consequently, these critics argue that the relevance of Porter's value chain in a service driven era, which is assuming new proportions in a hugely technologically driven business environment, characterised by dynamism and turbulence, is debatable. While critics of Porter's value chain may appear to have a case, the fundamentals of business operations relating to efficiency, effectiveness, economy, productivity, and cost reduction, which are fundamentals on which Porter's value chain is founded, without a doubt, are commonsensical ingredients required by any organisation that seeks to run sound business operations and achieve excellent returns on its investment.

120

Services

Generally, services are collectively defined by scholars as a set of capabilities, with each capability being a set of actions performed by an entity (acting like a server) in response to a (constrained) request issued by another entity (being the client). Zeithaml, Bitner and Gremler (2013) simply refer to services as deeds, processes, and performances provided or co-produced by one entity or person for another entity or person. Today, in many parts of the world, services are leading contributors to the gross domestic product (GDP) of their economies and it is contended that, there is a growing market for services and increasing dominance of services in economies worldwide. This growth is apparent in established economies as well as emerging economies such as China where the central government has placed priority on service sector growth, thus witnessing a growth in the contribution of services to GDP from 43% in 2010 (CIA World Factbook, 2011) to 50.5% in 2015 (CIA World Factbook, 2016). In the final decade of the 20th century, many firms jumped on the service bandwagon, investing in service initiatives and prompting service quality as ways to differentiate themselves and develop a competitive advantage. This was followed by academic and industrial inquiry into the nitty-gritties that characterise services to provide a better understanding of the service paradigm that was now dominating the business environment.

Characteristics of Services

Fitzsimmons and Fitzsimmons (2011) maintain that ignoring the differences between manufacturing and services requirements will lead to failure but more importantly, recognition of the special features of services will provide insights for enlightened and innovative management. Thus, the distinction between a product and service is difficult to make because of the tangibility spectrum (the purchase of some products are accompanied by facilitating service and the purchasing of a service often includes facilitating goods). Intangibility is the most basic distinguishing characteristic of services because services are performances or actions rather than objects; they cannot be seen, felt or tasted like tangible goods.

Heterogeneity, another characteristic of services reveals that because services are performances frequently produced by humans, no two services will be precisely alike. The employees delivering the services are the service to the customer and people may differ in their day-to-day performances. Variability also results because no two customers are precisely alike and have different perceptions and expectations. Whereas goods are produced first and then sold and consumed, many services are sold first and then produced and consumed simultaneously because the customer is part of the value delivery network and performs co-creating functions. Perishability is the last characteristic of services in no particular order and refers to the fact that services cannot be saved, stored or returned. Significant contributions of academics to the service management literature have stressed that in services, a distinction must be made between inputs (customers) and resources (labour and capital).

Services Management

Successfully positioning an enterprise, strategically assembling the product portfolio, properly deciding on the accurate allocation of resources, and deciding what an acceptable level of performance might be in such a competitive environment are key decisions of top management who must craft business models for their value propositions. Owing to the age-old feud between business rivals, competition for profits has intensified as both services and manufacturing firms have been on the receiving end and continuously attempt to craft strategies that will land them on the winning side of the feud. Service strategy, a key to achieving competitive advantage, is developed by top business executives and driven by a vision of the purpose and place of the organisation to address concerns about the target market (Fitzsimmons and Fitzsimmons, 2011).

Services Marketing Mix and Competitive Advantage

Resting on Zeithaml et al's (2013) definition of services; the deeds, processes or performances provided or co-produced must be communicated and delivered to the recipient. In view of this, scholars have developed the extended mix for services to augment the traditional marketing mix initially designed for manufactured products. The extended marketing mix is a toolkit of controllable variables that the service provider blends to communicate and deliver its offerings to consumers. Indeed, the notion of a mix implies that all the variables are interrelated and depend on each other to some extent. Thus, the extended marketing mix encapsulates "people, process and physical evidence". Theoretical evidence within the competitive advantage and competitive strategy literature has demonstrated that for firms to outperform the competition at arm's length, an optimal mix of the tools must be carefully aligned and integrated towards understanding the needs of the customer. In essence, the characteristics of services influenced the extension of the marketing mix to cater for the weaknesses of the traditional marketing mix because while advertising and sales promotion are important to both products and services, the simultaneity traits of services require service delivery personnel to be involved in real-time promotions even if their job description is operational in nature.

People and Competitive Advantage

In order to stay in the game and survive turf wars, global and indigenous companies must follow certain prerequisites and fulfil conditions that determine success in their respective sectors. A unique service, strong electronic commerce, financial stability and excellent customer service are just a few of the many qualities businesses in this current day and age should possess. All these factors constitute the fundamentals for start-ups and successful brands. However, logistics and operations can be mimicked by competitors; impressive process, modern technology, and astute business models will be scrutinised and even copied after launch often enabled by the low entry barriers of the service industry which allow new entrants to follow suit and possibly become competitors. How then can companies differentiate themselves from their competitors? From being a pleasure to work with, to being the most knowledgeable asset for customers, people constitute one critical asset that can make a firm unique and thrive.

In the context of services, "people" are all human actors who play part in service delivery, and thus, influence the buyer's perceptions: namely, the firm's personnel, the customer and other customers in the service environment. The extant literature has continually underlined the essence of people, and particularly, the importance of service employees cannot be over-emphasised. From a promotional standpoint in the context of services, employees are adjudged as walking billboards of service organisations. They are an embodiment of the service and prior to service consumption, their appearance, attitudes and behaviours help influence customer perceptions of the service. They also play an all-important role in the service delivery and subsequently, customer satisfaction conundrum. Irrespective of the type of service offered, it is a well-documented fact that employees are the service providers, hence are the service in the eyes of the consumer, also serving as a focal point that customers fixate on in real-time.

Unconsciously, research has revealed that, attempts to discuss the people variable of the extended marketing mix have adopted a one-sided approach; focusing wholly on the employee and neglecting the customer. Because services are co-produced and consumed simultaneously, customers influence the outcomes of service encounters as well as the outcomes of other customers. Leading practitioners and contributors to the services management and marketing literature have speculated that to deliver effective service quality through people, *hiring the right people* (competing for the best people, hiring for service inclination and service competencies, being the preferred employer), *developing people to deliver service quality* (training for technical and interactive skills, empowering employees, promoting teamwork), *providing the needed support system* (measuring internal service quality, providing supportive technology and equipment, developing service-oriented internal processes) and *retaining the best people* (competing for the best people, measuring and rewarding strong service performers, treating employees as customers, including employees in the company's vision) are key strategies for developing a firm's sustainable competitive advantage.

Physical Evidence and Competitive Advantage

The intangibility characteristic of services burdens consumers and customers of services to rely on environmental and tangible cues in much the same way that they rely on packaging to categorise and form their initial beliefs (perceptions) about consumer goods. The physical evidence variable of the extended services mix includes all the tangible representations of the services such as the brochures, signage, equipment as well as the web pages and in some instances, the physical facility where the service is offered. This is referred to as the servicescape; a term coined by Booms and Bitner,(1982). They continue to speculate that regardless of the type of service offered, the physical evidence of the service will influence the flow of the experience, the meaning customers attach to it, their satisfaction and emotional connections with the company delivering the experience, as well as their social and personal interactions with others experiencing the service.

The servicescape (physical facility) has been well documented across the pertinent literature as one of the most important elements used in positioning a service organisation, and thus, play many strategic roles simultaneously. Among the numerous roles is the physical facility's role as a package which presents the servicescape as a "wrapper" that conveys to customers an external image of what is "inside". Thus, the servicescape is a visual metaphor of the intangible service and helps consumers and prospects create perceptions about the expected service. This image projecting function of the physical facility possesses meaning-filled episodes of customer encounters which is synonymous with the advantages of unique brands; an intangible asset that translates to sustainable competitive advantage and consistent superior performance.

Again the servicescape assumes the role of a facilitator during moments of truth by aiding the performance levels of persons in the environment. The design of the servicescape enhances or inhibits the efficient flow of activities with the service setting; thus, a well-designed, functional facility can make the service a pleasure to experience from the customer's perspective and assist employees to accomplish their goals. This creates a mutual win-win situation between the actors within the consumption setting; indeed, satisfaction of either customer or employee has proven to be a leading contributor to organisational performance translating into firm advantages.

The servicescape design also aids in the socialisation of both employees and customers in the sense that it helps to convey expected roles, behaviours and relationships. The simultaneity trait of services creates the need for the presence of both providers and consumers during service delivery. Thus, a clear delineation of tasks and roles expedites the delivery process while cushioning customer satisfaction with a little margin for error. Like consumer goods, research has revealed that, reducing the lead time and satisfying customers' needs in a timely manner have significant positive impacts on corporate objectives (Fitzsimmons and Fitzsimmons, 2011).

Last but not least, the physical facility that aids service delivery in real-time plays the role of differentiator by separating a firm from its competitors and signalling the market segment of its offerings and value propositions. The organisational performance literature has produced favourable remarks for organisations that excel in competencies which are distinct from the competition and its effects on sustainable competitive advantage (Andrews, 1971; Prahalad & Hamel, 1990; Sleznick, 1957).

Process and Competitive Advantage

Global and local markets have become highly competitive and turbulent, and as they constantly change, conditions continuously evolve with rapid pace. Indeed, they have moved from being simple to complex, stable to dynamic, and benign to hostile (Neu and Brown, 2005). In response to changing market conditions, both manufacturing and service organisations have traditionally become more customer-centric and innovative; in a way that customers receive products and services that better fit their needs. The only way this is possible is attributed to the process variable of the extended marketing mix which describes the procedures, mechanisms and flow of activities by which the service is delivered; namely, the service delivery and operating systems. The degree of complexity in delivery steps that the customer experiences or the operational flow of the service also give customers evidence on which to judge the service. Empowering employees to meet customers' needs in a timely fashion is favoured over hierarchical structures that result in bureaucratic practices requiring the customer to follow a complicated and extensive series of actions during service delivery.

Responsive feedback mechanisms are relevant to firms in their quest to deliver superior performance but organisations are often in a managerial dilemma because of "the tip of the iceberg" principle which avers that about 50% of customers who encounter service failure do not complain to either frontline employees or top management. How would an organisation manage the servicescape and the processes it has engineered to deliver ultimate satisfaction to its clientele without continuous feedback? The key to this dilemma somewhat rests in the bellies of the concept of a service culture. Indeed, experts have suggested that a customer-oriented, service-oriented organisation will have at its heart a service culture, that is, a culture where an appreciation for good service exists, and where giving good service to both internal and external customers is considered a natural way of life and one of the most important norms exhibited by everyone (Appiah-Adu and Amoako, 2016; Webster, 1995; Zeithaml et al, 2013).

Clearly, a service culture is crucial to the creation of a customer-focused organisation and has been identified as a source of competitive advantage in companies. The genesis of a strong service culture is captured in a strong exhibition of service leadership by superiors through developing a service culture and ending with transporting the service culture to the customer. It is worth noting that, the extended marketing mix is salient for services only and

126

the three elements (people; physical evidence and processes) are controllable; meaning they are within the control of the firm and an optimal mix will influence the customer's perception of the service, their level of satisfaction and their willingness to make repeated purchases and referrals.

Service Encounters or Moments of Truth and Competitive Advantage

Service encounters are regarded as the building blocks for customer perceptions. These encounters present the avenue for the providers to meet the customers in real-time. Experts associate several accolades with the service encounters like "where the rubber meets the road", "real-time marketing" and the "moments of truth" because it is in this arena that promises made by the providers or their companies are kept or broken and it is from these encounters that customers build their perceptions. At this juncture, the episodes of interactions between the actors provide the customers with a snapshot of the firm's service quality, thus, each episode contributes to the customer's overall satisfaction and results in their willingness to fast-forward the encounter, end the episode or repeat the episode. The moments of truth also present an organisation with the opportunity to prove its potential as a quality service provider and to increase customer loyalty.

Types of Services Encounters in Developing Economies

The type of service encounter is hugely dependent on the servicescape usage (whom the servicescape will affect) and the servicescape complexities (very simple; lean; very complicated environment; or elaborate). A typology of services is captured by Zeithaml et al (2013) to include self-service or technology mediated encounters, interpersonal service encounters or face-to-face encounters and remote services. The most prevalent encounters operated from the developing countries perspective, particularly Ghana is vastly the interpersonal or face-to-face services with a growing trend towards the remote service encounters. Organisations operate these encounters due to reasons like the meagre technology adoption rate, high illiteracy rate, growing affluent proletariat, and the lack of appreciation for the prowess of services to transform nations.

Banking by ATMs has become natural to many customers to the extent that even in developing economies, bank employees are becoming the only people who regularly see bank interiors. With ATMs becoming a way of doing business for many customers, all banks have had to distribute their services (and the customer's money) through ATMs in order to remain competitive. In addition, ATMs have further developed with time, to include the use of these services to settle utility and other bills.

Current trends suggest that ATMs were just the first step, with home banking and electronic banking now playing a key role in banking operations. With their PCs, phones and other electronic devices, whether from home or their offices, consumers can now track their accounts, apply for loans and credit cards, make transfers and pay bills electronically to anyone with a bank account number. The regulatory bodies such as Central Banks as well as information and communications technology providers are providing the necessary infrastructure and platforms for these transactions to become a reality in many developing economies.

Apart from banking, other areas where processes are being used to deliver effective service and meet customer needs are education and business-to-business communication. In the corporate world, video conferencing is becoming very popular in enhancing service delivery. It is believed that this form of conducting business will be the answer to escalating corporate travel costs and increasingly stressed employees. The systems have been around for years but are now being purchased and used widely by companies.

Indeed, for organisations operating in both developing and industrialised economies, the contribution of service encounters to competitive advantage is paramount because it is at this juncture that all the variables of the extended marketing mix converge with their distinctive competencies to form a nexus or hub for delivering superior service performance to customers which, all things being equal, further translates to profitability, market share, brand equity and other consequences of sustainable competitive advantage.

Strategic Service Vision

A strategic service vision encapsulates the service delivery system, operating strategy, service concept and the target segments that management's idea or value proposition intends to satisfy. The relatively low entry and exit barriers, the minimal opportunities for scale economies, and erratic sales fluctuations that confront the services industry, have burdened strategic managers to adopt strategic planning tools for effective business outcomes

(Fitzsimmons and Fitzsimmons, 2011). The 7S Model developed by McKinsey has been widely used by academics and practitioners and remains one of the most popular strategic planning tools. It sought to lay emphasis on human resources (Soft S), rather than the traditional mass production tangibles of capital, infrastructure and equipment, as a key to higher organisational performance. The goal of the model was to show how seven elements of the company: Structure, Strategy, Systems (hard components of the 7S) and Skills, Staff, Style, and Shared values (soft components of the 7S) can be aligned together to achieve effectiveness in a company. The key point of the model is that all the seven areas are interconnected and a change in one area requires change in the rest of a firm for it to function effectively.

Corporate Performance

Regardless of the sector in which it operates, any organisation that desires to excel in its selected industry needs to seek and obtain evidence to ascertain and monitor payoff and payback of new investments in service. Gaining competitive advantage and enhancing a firm's performance relative to competitors are two of the main objectives that businesses strive to achieve. In order to attain a competitive advantage that cannot only match that of business rivals but also surpass industry performance averages, a firm must first comprehend the relationship between the internal strengths and weaknesses of the organisation, as well as the potential effects on its competitive advantage and performance (Ismail, Che Rose, Uli, & Abdullah, 2011).

Turf wars between business giants have been prevalent in terms of pricing, promotional campaigns, distribution strategies and innovative products. These turf wars have contributed to the re-engineering of business structures and systems, companies diversifying, acquisition and mergers as many organisations have engineered major overhauls in order to compete successfully. This has also triggered the quest for more efficient and effective service delivery systems; a central topic cutting a swathe through scholars and business executives. Business strategy scholars have argued that achieving a position of competitive advantage is the precursor to the significant performance of a firm (Barney, 1991; Fahy, 2000). It is also widely acknowledged that organisations that possess a sustainable competitive advantage demonstrate superior growth and their income statements reflect continuous profitability which is also a key to survival (Ma, 2000; Fahy, 2000; Gimenez and Ventura, 2002; Wang and Lo, 2003; Wiklund and Shepherd, 2003; Bowen and Ostroff, 2004).

Service and Profitability

There is a tendency for managers to view service and service quality as costs rather than as contributors to profits, partly because of the difficulty in tracing the link between service delivery and financial returns. The focus of services management and marketing is on promises; promises made and promises kept to consumers. A strategic framework referred to as the service triangle by Zeithaml et al (2013) visually reinforces the importance of people in the ability of firms to keep service promises and succeed in building customer relationships. The triangle presents the three interlinked groups (company, customers and providers) that work together to develop, promote and deliver services.

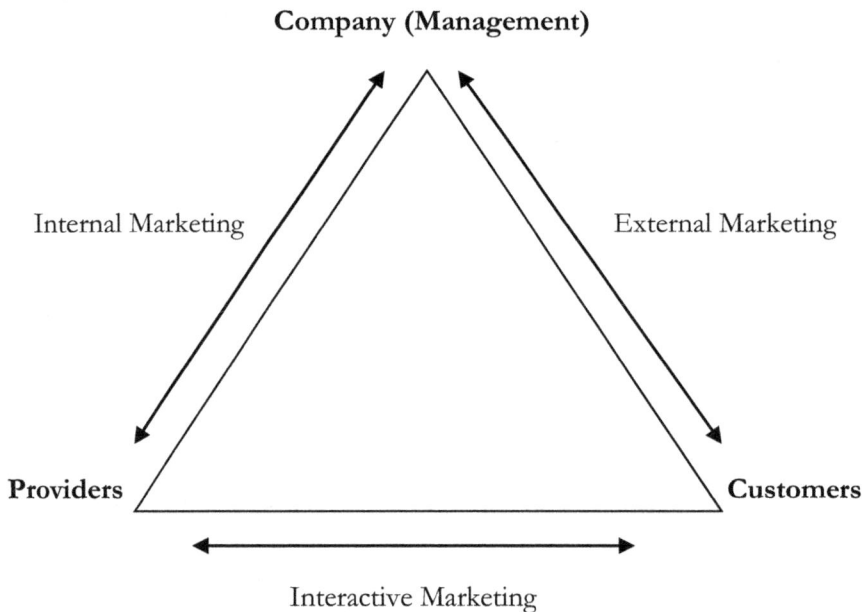

Company (Management)

Internal Marketing   External Marketing

Providers   Customers

Interactive Marketing

Figure 8.1: Services Triangle (Adapted from Zeithaml, Bitner and Gremler, 2013)

Activities on the Service Triangle

On the right hand side of the triangle are the external marketing efforts that the firm engages in to develop its customer's expectations and make promises to customers about expected service delivery. This is achieved through marketing communication tools such as advertising, public relations, exhibitions, direct marketing, sponsorship, social media marketing, sales promotion and other promotional activities.

The bottom of the triangle is captured as interactive marketing which reflects delivering promises in real-time. It occurs between the services resources and the inputs of the service. Employees' roles are critical at this stage of the service delivery process. Most visible activities are the service encounters, personal selling, servicescape and customer service centres. The left-side of the triangle suggests the critical role played by internal marketing and deals with the attempts made by management to aid providers deliver on the service promises. It involves recruiting, training, motivation and providing equipment as well as technology.

Employee Satisfaction, Customer Satisfaction and Profitability

Satisfied employees make for satisfied customers and satisfied customers can, in turn, reinforce employees' sense of satisfaction in their jobs. Schneider and Bowen's (1985) ground breaking research reported that; a climate for both *service* and *employee well-being* are highly correlated with overall customer perceptions of service quality. The relationship between service quality and competitive advantage has been extensively researched with significant positive correlations between the two variables (Dominic, Nee, Wong & Yoke, 2010; Jelčić, 2014). The underlying logic connecting employee satisfaction and loyalty to customer satisfaction and loyalty and ultimately profits is illustrated by the service profit chain (Heskett, Sasser & Schlesinger, 1997; Heskett, Sasser & Wheeler, 2008). The service profit chain suggests that there are critical linkages among internal service quality, employee satisfaction, productivity, the value of services provided to the customer and ultimately customer satisfaction, retention and profits.

Services Management and Corporate Performance

Reynoso (2010) stipulates that "top-level executives of outstanding service organisations spend little time setting profit goals or focusing on market share, the management mantra of the 1970s and 1980s". Instead, they understand that in the new economics of service, frontline workers and customers need to be the focus of management concern. Successful service managers pay attention to the factors that drive profitability in this new service paradigm: investment in people, technology that supports frontline workers, revamped recruiting and training practices, and compensation linked to performance for employees at every level.

Management practitioners and scholars believe that the new economics of service requires innovative measurement techniques. That is, because of the characteristics of services and the low entry-exit barriers characterising the service industry, business models must be flexible to adapt to the rapidly changing business environment. These business models must calibrate the impact placed on employee satisfaction, loyalty, and productivity on the value of products and services delivered so that managers can build customer satisfaction and loyalty and feed-off its corresponding impact on profitability and growth. As a matter of fact, it has been found that the lifetime value of a loyal customer is astronomical, especially when referrals are added to the economics of customer retention and repeat purchases of related products (Reynoso, 2010).

The service-profit chain establishes relationships between profitability, customer loyalty, and employee satisfaction, loyalty, and productivity. According to Heskett et al (2008), the links in the chain (which should be regarded as propositions) are as follows: profit and growth are stimulated primarily by customer loyalty; loyalty is a direct result of customer satisfaction; satisfaction is largely influenced by the value of services provided to customers; value is created by satisfied, loyal, and productive employees; employee satisfaction, in turn, results primarily from high-quality support services and policies that enable employees to deliver excellent services, value and results to customers.

The Nature of Competitive Advantage

Conventional management thinking is wedded to the notion of sustainable competitive advantage, that is, the significant and distinctive advantages that an organisation has over its competitors which can be readily translated into added value for its customers. This notion of an advantage has an intuitive appeal because of its apparent simplicity. Advantages may include technical excellence, reputation, low costs, a quality product, a powerful and instantly recognisable brand, organisational culture, leadership and innovative propensity, power over suppliers and distributors, reputation for service quality, customer service, and value for money. These advantages permit the organisation to add more value than its competitors in the same market but they may be easily imitated (Porter, 1980, 1985; Lynch, 1997). Drawing from Peteraf's (1993) theoretical conditions for competitive advantage, some business and management scholars; have argued that as markets are so powerful, seeking sustainable competitive advantage for most companies is not realistic, and indeed only the largest companies with considerable market shares will achieve and sustain any advantages. This view equates competitive advantage (and hence added value for customers) unequivocally with market power (and consequent economies of scale) – although this is not a view that can go unchallenged.

Sustainable competitive advantage must then pass three specific tests:

1. The advantages must be significant not modest, persist over time and provide real benefits to the customer and the business;

2. The advantages must be recognisable and clearly linked to customer benefits that they will value;

3. The advantages must be capable of resisting competitor imitation, erosion or attack (Barney, 1991).

Companies must possess distinctive competencies different from the competition (a capability gap) and this gap must make a difference to the customer (Reynoso, 2010). These differences must be reflected in product attributes that are key buying criteria.

Improving Business Performance

All firms either explicitly or implicitly employ a particular business model which describes the design or architecture of the value creation, delivery or capture mechanisms employed (Teece, 2010). The essence of a business model is that it crystallises customer needs and ability to pay; defines the manner by which the business enterprise responds to and delivers value to customers; entices customers to pay for value; and converts those payments to profit through the proper design and operation of the various elements of the value chain. Businesses operating in this fiercely competitive context must develop customer-centric business models that envisage the customer as paramount and core to its business activities.

Contributors to the corporate performance literature have argued with varying degrees of success, that superior corporate performance is realised by developing a strong and continuing customer orientation (Kohli and Jaworski, 1990; Reichheld, 2006) in all business functions, and ensuring that every function understands that they exist not to serve their own narrow interests but those of the customer (Martin and Bush, 2006). Ultimately the customer must be the judge of product quality. Many successful companies have wrestled with the fundamental conundrum - how to increase product quality while bringing down costs.

The key task of management is clearly to focus on only those activities that create and maintain customer satisfaction and loyalty (the creation of value for customers) by delivering high quality products at a competitive cost. The core value-adding processes are innovation (a firm needs a steady stream of new products or faces a future of sales and prices being driven down by the competition); efficient operations (being able to design, produce and deliver high value products at low cost) and customer creation; support and retention (which requires knowledge of how the market is segmented, the benefits customers want, how their buying decisions are made and how these wants and buying behaviours may change over time plus competitor analyses).

To create good business performance one must start from the strategic imperative of what services and markets to concentrate on and in so doing, strive to achieve high levels of customer satisfaction and their profitable retention. Inevitably this means keeping out of some markets - one needs to get better business not just more business; and it also means investing selectively in those distinctive capabilities of the business which generate high customer perceived values (that is, the business needs strategic intent). This means creating demonstrable value advantages either by way of dramatically superior quality or major cost savings. The business world has usually interpreted business success or excellence to be one or a combination of good profitability (return on capital, equity and sales); revenues or turnover increases significantly; or significant market share improvement vis-à-vis competitors.

Each one of these success criteria has significant problems. First, profit measures are subject to well-known problems of being easily manipulated (for example, by the treatment of depreciation, stock valuation, research and development expenditure and foreign currency transactions). A company can improve profits to a considerable extent by drastically cutting costs (particularly delivery costs), restricting new investment and raising prices but the long-term cost will be deterioration in the company's market position. However, this is not the only problem with profit measures. Average profits can be very much higher in some

134

industries than others, and have very little to do with management quality but everything to do with market structure (barriers to entry, number of competitors, relative power in the supply chain, etc.).

Second, revenues are an insufficient and rather misleading indicator of success. More business is not enough - we must get *better* business. Better business is simply business which is more profitable than business currently or previously obtained, while delivering targeted and superior customer value. A firm is usually reluctant to turn away business, even if it is low profit business, and usually hopes to secure better total profits by generating large volumes. Such actions are easy to justify particularly when trading conditions are tough, and indeed our culture generally rewards a businessperson for gross revenues generated rather than profit contribution. However, of even greater concern is the incipient insecurity of this approach - the lack of confidence in our marketing ability to attract and retain the very best (profitable-high value) business.

Third, market share depends on how the market is defined and measured (imprecise and subjective at the best of times, and indeed, market delineation and measurement is poorly considered in both the scholarly literature and in business practice). Moreover, market share depends not on management quality per se but often on inherited resources and circumstances which have enabled a company to secure a dominant market position without having to work hard for it.

Rather than rely on profit and other performance criteria, the most appropriate measures of performance are customer satisfaction and customer loyalty. Customers satisfied with the value provided will purchase again and again, thus, generating better profitability and market share. Customer satisfaction is clearly a function of how the value experienced by customers matches up to that which they expected, and most importantly, what they perceive could have been obtained from competitors. It is not an end in itself but a means of achieving and holding on to competitive advantage. Customer satisfaction generates repeat purchases (thus lowering costs), referrals, word of mouth promotion, and loyalty, but not promiscuity or switching buying behaviour.

Finally, firms must also probe internally whether customer acquisition helped to improve organisational skills and competitiveness. Skills and reputations deteriorate over time if they are not constantly topped up. Sales are either achieved by *asset-milking* (the taking advantage and exploiting of existing skills, reputations and relationships) or *asset-building*, with opportunities to develop new skills by developing innovative products, building new and far stronger relationships with customers and creating a strong reputation in new market segments (Maister, 1997). Too much asset-milking leaves a business highly exposed strategically.

We have certainly moved on from the 1980s when spurred on by the book authored by Peters & Waterman (1982) titled 'In Search of Excellence, managers worked hard to achieve 'excellence' and sustain 'excellence'. Unfortunately 'excellence' is not an unambiguous concept and many of the firms identified by Peters and Waterman's as excellent are no longer top tier organisations, and indeed, many are no longer in existence.

Levitt researching innovation in management as far back as 1962 clearly wrote concerning the success of a company - 'the thing that really mattered was the whole cluster of non-product benefits with which the company surrounded its generic product' (Levitt, 1962: 74-75). Success then is due, at least in part, to the complex bundle of value satisfaction offered to customers, of which the generic core product is only a part.

In order to capture the essence of the proposition advanced and developed in this chapter, a conceptual model of improving business performance is presented in *Figure 2* (Appiah-Adu, 2016) as a basis for further empirical research. This model is based on frameworks developed by Heskett, Jones, Loveman, Sasser & Schlesinger (1994) - the service value chain; and Bharadwaj, Varadarajan & Fahy (1993) - sustainable competitive advantage in service industries. The model brings together the various elements discussed and developed in this chapter. Below is a conceptual model of improving business performance.

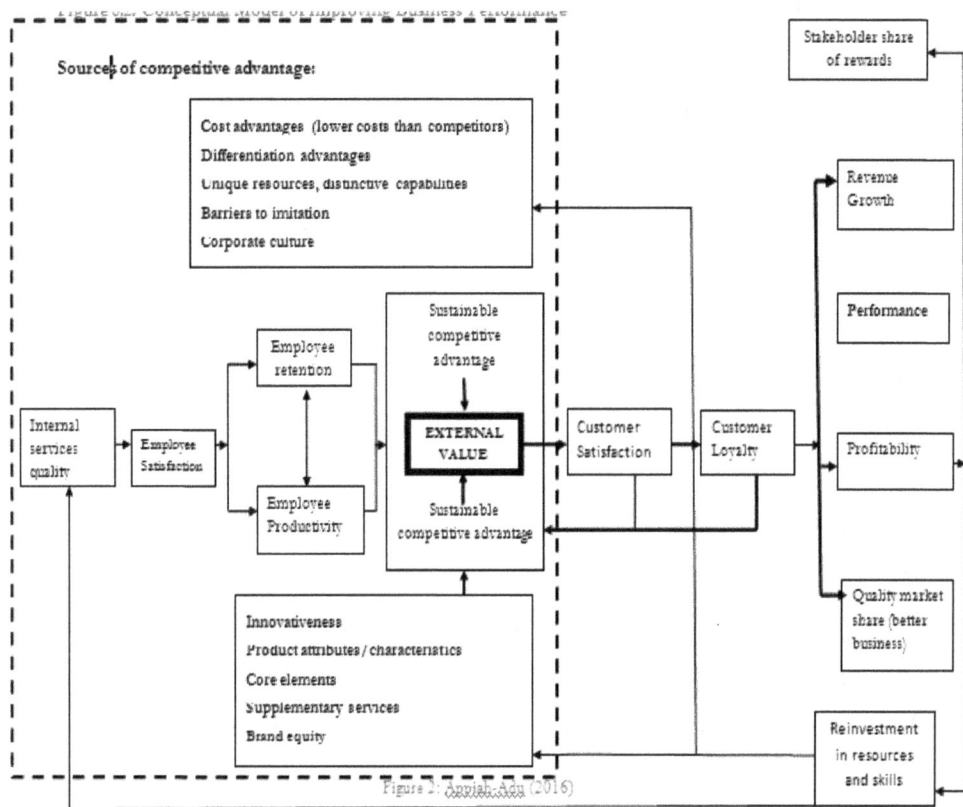

Figure 2: Asriah Ada (2016)

Implications for Scholars and Managers

Building on the basic proposition that services add to the perceived value of a product, and in turn enduring value is one of the bases for sustainable competitive advantage, this chapter challenges scholars to continuously seek a deeper understanding about the processes and issues presented in Figure 2. Herein lies one of the routes to improving business performance. For firms and their executives, we can summarise the implications of these issues as follows.

Firstly, a firm's skills and resources are potential sources of competitive advantage but only if value is generated for customers; value is created when customers receive perceived benefits, which in turn creates customer satisfaction. High levels of customer satisfaction results in customer loyalty. Secondly, attaining sustainable competitive advantage is not the end of the journey but the beginning - wealth for stakeholders is created through delivering consistent value to customers. Thirdly, achieving lasting differentiation advantages by enhancing value through the bundling of supplementary services may actually be the most enduring source of competitive advantage because they add to the reputation of the business. Finally, durability of sustainable competitive advantage and providing long-term value depend critically on reinvestments as well as new investments in new skills and resources.

References

- Appiah-Adu, K. (2016). Paper presented at the Dean's Research Club. Central University, July.

- Andrews, K. (1971). *The concept of corporate strategy*. Homewood, IL: Irwin Publishing.

- Appiah-Adu, K. & Amoako, G. (2016). The execution of marketing strategies in an emerging developing economy: A case study of selected market leaders. *African Journal of Economics and Management Studies*, 7 (1), 1-21.

- Barney, J. (1991). Firm resources and sustained competitive advantage. *Journal of Management*, 17 (1), 99-120.

- Bharadwaj, S., Varadarajan, R. & Fahy, J. (1993). Sustainable competitive advantage in service industries: A conceptual model and research propositions. *Journal of Marketing*, 57 (October), 83-99.

- Bowen, D. & Ostroff, C. (2004). Understanding HRM-Firm performance linkages: The role of the strength of the HRM system. *Academy of Management Review*, 29 (2), 203-221.

- Booms, B. & Bitner, M. (1982). Marketing services by managing the environment. *Cornell Hotel and Restaurant Administration Quarterly*, 23 (1), 35-40.

- Central Intelligence Agency. (2011). *The World Factbook*. Washington, DC: USA.

- Central Intelligence Agency. (2016). *The World Factbook*. Washington, DC: USA.

- Dominic, P., Nee. K., Wong, D. & Yoke, Y. (2010). The importance of service quality for competitive advantage – with special reference to industrial product. *International Journal of Business Information Systems*, 6 (3)

- Fahy, J. (2000). The resource-based view of the firm: Some stumbling-blocks on the road to understanding sustainable competitive advantage. *Journal of European Industrial Training*, 24 (2/3/4), 94-104.

- Fitzsimmons, J. & Fitzsimmons, M. (2011). *Service management*. New York, NY: McGraw-Hill.

- Gimenez, C. & Ventura, A. (2002). *Supply chain management as a competitive advantage in the Spanish grocery sector.* Published Working Paper. No. 2, 04/2002, Universitat Pompeu Fabra (UPF), Barcelona, Spain.

- Heskett, J., Jones, T., Loveman, G., Sasser, W. & Schlesinger, L. (1994). Putting the service-profit chain to work. *Harvard Business Review*, 72 (2) (March-April), 164-174.

- Heskett. J., Sasser. W. & Schlesinger, L. (1997). *The service profit chain: How leading companies link profit and growth to loyalty, satisfaction and value.* New York, NY: Free Press.

- Heskett, J., Sasser. W. & Wheeler, J. (2008). *The ownership quotient: Putting the service profit chain to work for unbeatable competitive advantage.* Boston, MA: Harvard Business Press.

- Horne, J. & Wachowicz, J. (2001). *Fundamentals of financial management.*Upper Saddle River, NJ: Prentice Hall.

- Ismail, A., Che R., Uli, J. & Abdullah, H. (2011). The relationship between organisational resources and systems: An empirical research. *Asian Social Science*, 7 (5). http://dx.doi.org/10.5539/ass.v7n5p72

- Jelčić, S. (2014). Managing service quality to gain competitive advantage in retail environment. *TEM Journal*, 3 (2), 181-186.

- Kohli, A. K. & Jaworski, B. J. (1990). "Market Orientation: The Construct, Research Propositions, and Managerial Implications". *Journal of Marketing* 54.2: 1.

- Levitt, T. (1962). *Innovation in marketing.* New York, NY: McGraw Hill.

- Lynch, R. (2006). *Corporate strategy.* London: Financial Times & Prentice Hall.

- Ma, H. (2000). Competitive advantage and firm performance. *Competitiveness Review,* 10 (2), 16-32

- Maister, D. (1997). *True professionalism.* New York, NY: The Free Press.

- Martin, C.A. & Bush, A. J. (2006). Psychological climate, empowerment, leadership style, and customer-oriented selling: An analysis of the sales manager-salesperson dyad. *Journal of the Academy of Marketing Science*, 34(3), 419-438.

- Neu, W. & Brown, S. (2005). Forming successful business-to-business services in goods dominant firms. *Journal of Service Research*, 8 (1), 3-17.

- Peters, T. & Waterman, R. (1982). *In Search of Excellence,* New York, NY: Harper & Row.

- Peteraf, M. A. (1993) "The Cornerstones of Competitive Advantage: A Resource-Based View". *Strategic. Management Journal.* 14.3: 179-191.

- Porter, M. (1980). *Competitive strategy.* New York, NY: Free Press.

- Porter, M. (1985). *Competitive advantage.* New York, NY: Free Press.

- Prahalad, C. & Hamel, G. (1990). The core competence of the corporation. *Harvard Business Review,* May-June, 3-15.

- Reicheld, F. (2006). *The ultimate question driving good profits and true growth.* Boston, MA: Harvard Business School Press.

- Reynoso, J. (2010). Review of the ownership quotient: Putting the service profit chain to work for unbeatable competitive advantage. *Journal of Services Management,* 21 (3), 413-417.

- Schneider, B. & Bowen, D. (1985). Employee and customer perceptions of service in banks: Replication and extension. *Journal of Applied Psychology,* 70 (3), 423-433. http://dx.doi.org/10.1037//0021-9010.70.3.423.

- Selznick, P. (1957). *Leadership in Administration: a Sociological Interpretation.* Evanston, IL: Row, Peterson.

- Teece, D. (2010). Business models, business strategy and innovation. *Long Range Planning,* 43 (2-3), 172-194.

- Wang, Y. & Lo, H. (2003). Customer-focused performance and the dynamic model for competence building and leveraging: A resource-based view. *Journal of Management Development,* 22(6), 483-526.

- Webster, C. (1995). Marketing culture and marketing effectiveness in service firms. *Journal of Services Marketing,* 9 (2), 6-21.

- Wiklund, J. & Shepherd, D. (2003). Knowledge-based resources, entrepreneurial orientation, and the performance of small and medium-sized businesses. *Strategic Management Journal,* 24, 1307–1314.

- Zeithaml, V., Bitner, M. & Gremler, D. (2013). *Services marketing.* New York, NY: McGraw-Hill Irwin.

Chapter 9

Impact of Effective Financial Management on Corporate Performance

Williams Abayaawien Atuilik

Abstract

All organisations are set up to achieve certain set targets and objectives. The ability of a firm to achieve their set objectives is referred to as corporate performance. A firm can only achieve its objectives if it applies effective financial management practices which involve the planning, operating and monitoring of the finance function of the organisation. Given the rapidly changing and competitive nature of the business environments in which modern organisations operate, if firms are to survive, corporate managers must appreciate the need to develop and make full use of financial management tools. Effective financial management has a direct and positive impact on corporate performance. That is, a good financial management system will lead to better and improved corporate performance, and similarly, a weak financial management system is likely to result in poor corporate performance.

Keywords: Corporate performance; financial management; Budgeting; Working capital management.

Introduction

How does effective financial management influence corporate performance? An answer to this question has relevance for organisations in all sectors of a nation including national governments. This is because, regardless of the sector in which an organisation operates, organisations are set up to pursue and achieve some objectives. Some firms are set up to maximise value for the owners through profitable and productive ventures whilst others are set up to undertake activities that promote the public interest by resolving specific societal challenges.

Whatever the rational may be for setting up an organisation, all corporate entities must work towards the achievement of their set targets and objectives which are varied and different. It is worthy to note that regardless of the objective of an organisation, actions need to be taken to achieve those objectives. Some of the conditions necessary to achieve good corporate

141

performance include good corporate governance; skilful, hardworking and experienced human capital along with a good compensation scheme; and existing demand for the goods and services the organisation provides just to mention a few.

An organisation needs to put structures and processes in place to be able to undertake its business in order to achieve the set objectives. These structures include having a board of governors to lead the organisation, attracting and retaining competent employees through competitive compensation schemes and good working conditions as well as putting in place efficient operational arrangements to guide the delivery of goods and services. To do all of the above, there is the unavoidable need to secure the right amount of financial resources from the right sources, in the right mix, at the right cost, and at the right time and to effectively manage these financial resources.

The process involved in doing this is what is often referred to as financial management. This chapter analyses the impact of effective financial management on corporate performance. The chapter begins with an introduction, and then discusses corporate performance followed by a discussion of the processes of good financial management. The chapter then draws the link between effective financial management and corporate performance and concludes by drawing attention to the implications of the analysis for business executives, policy makers, and scholars and for future research.

What is Corporate Performance?

A number of empirical studies have established a positive relationship between a myriad of variables and corporate performance. It has been documented that a positive relationship exists between corporate performance and good corporate governance (Klapper & Love, 2004); optimal corporate diversification (Lang & Stulz, 1993); discharge of corporate social responsibility (McGuire, Sundgren, & Schneeweis, 1988); good corporate reputation (Roberts & Dowling, 2002); good corporate social performance (Griffin & Mahon, 1997; Orlitzky, Schmidt, & Rynes, 2003; Preston & O'bannon, 1997; Waddock & Graves, 1997); equity based compensation schemes for corporate agents and employees (Mehran, 1995); good human resource management practices (Huselid, 1995); and, appropriate mix of debt to equity financing for the activities of organisations (Williamson, 1988).

142

Corporate performance relates to the ability of a firm to achieve its set qualitative and quantitative objectives. The business of organisations necessarily involves the carrying out of activities aimed ultimately at helping the firm achieve some objective. Organisational objectives are both quantitative and qualitative. Goals relating to the quantity of goods and services to produce and sell, the number of customers or clients to attract, the amount of sales value, target profits, cost ceilings etc. are quantitative objectives. Qualitative goals include: levels of efficiency in delivering services, the quality of products and services, quality of management etc. When an organisation is able to achieve its stated objectives, it is said to have performed well. If corporate objectives are not met; the organisation is said to be non-performing. Thus, the ability of a firm to attain its set targets reflects how well or badly it has performed. Corporate performance is thus a multidimensional construct which attempts to measure the ability of organisations to achieve their set goals and objectives (Zahra & Pearce, 1989).

Corporate performance may be measured by assessing movements in the market value of the organisation, profit levels attained by the firm, its ability to meet current and future obligations and remain sustainable, the ability of the organisation to fulfil its corporate social obligations and more generally, its ability to accomplish what it sets out to do. Corporate performance could be viewed from the perspective of financial performance, operational performance, or a firm's ability to meet different corporate social responsibility targets. It is obvious that corporate performance, no matter how it is conceived, is the core essence for the existence of the firm. A number of studies have suggested that an organisation's performance is linked to a number of factors. The question that begs for an answer is: what is the impact of effective financial management on corporate performance? To answer this question, one needs to understand the processes of effective financial management. The next section therefore explains the processes involved in effective financial management.

The Financial Management Framework

Figure 9.1 below presents the conceptual framework of a functional financial management system and suggests that a functional financial management system should lead to improved corporate performance.

FINANCIAL MANAGEMENT FRAMEWORK

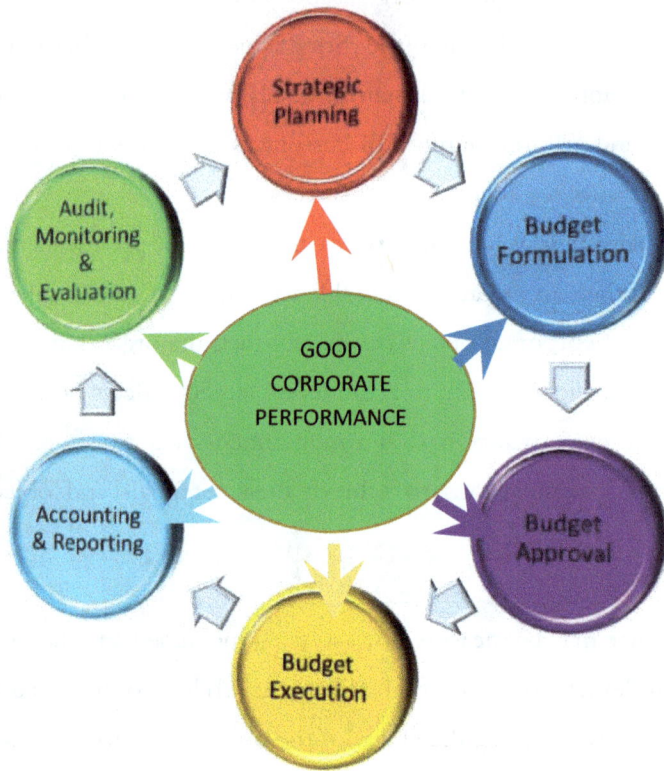

Figure 9.1: Financial Management Framework

What is Financial Management?

According to Horne and Wachowicz (2001) "financial management is concerned with the acquisition, financing and management of some assets with some overall goal in mind" (p.2). It can be deduced from this definition that financial management is the planning, operating and monitoring of the finance function of an organisation in order to achieve its objectives. Financial management encompasses all the processes involved in managing the finances of corporate organisations. These processes include the identification of corporate objectives through medium to long term planning; formulation of short term corporate budgets to implement the medium to long term plans; identifying funding sources and raising the funds to finance operations and projects identified in the budget; managing budget execution processes through effective working capital management; making investment decisions regarding the kind of assets to hold as an organisation that will ensure the achievement of objectives; and making decisions regarding how to distribute returns to stakeholders in the

144

form of dividends and other forms of compensations.

In effect, financial management is about taking deliberate and intentional actions to look after the health of an organisation, and not leaving things to chance. Financial management to a corporate organisation is like maintenance is to a vehicle. Just like a vehicle, the corporate organisation requires good quality fuel and oil and regular servicing and maintenance in order to function well. If neglected, just like a vehicle, the organisation will eventually break down and fail to reach its intended destination.

An effective financial management system ensures that the organisation has resources to achieve its objectives. An effective financial management model will necessarily involve the following phases; the planning phase, the budgeting phase, the budget execution phase which includes revenue mobilisation or fund raising, financial reporting phase, as well as the auditing, monitoring and evaluation phase. The roles of each phase in financial management are depicted in figure 9.2 and discussed in turns.

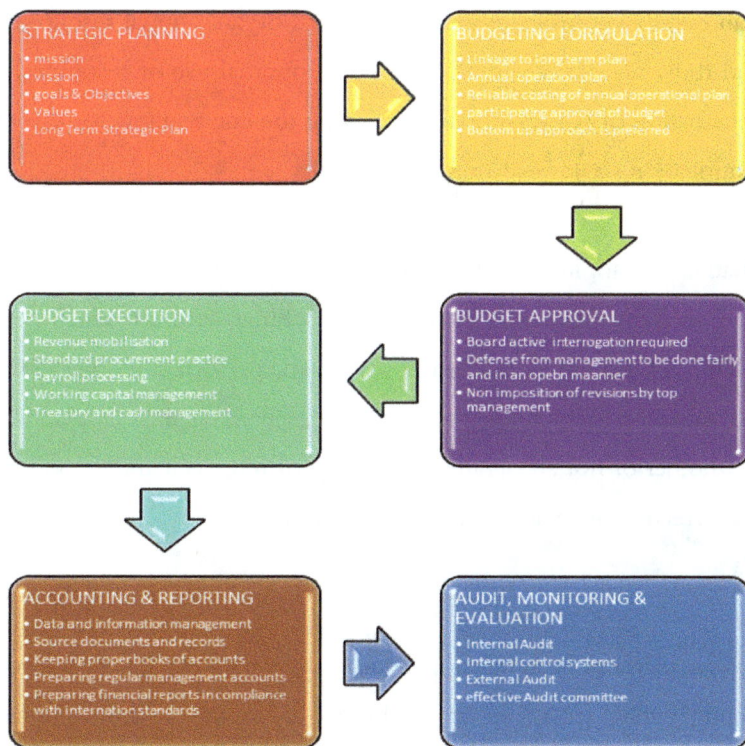

Figure 9.2: Detailed description of financial management framework

145

Planning

A number of studies have shown that good planning within organisations has a positive association with corporate performance (Miller & Cardinal, 1994; Pearce, Robbins, & Robinson, 1987; Robinson & Pearce, 1983). Planning involves making deliberate and intentional choices regarding the future direction of an organisation. To be effective, an organisation should first identify its strategic focus by defining its vision, which represents the organisation's long term goals, and its mission which clarifies the purpose and values of the organisation. Specific objectives that will enable the organisation to achieve its mission and vision statements are then developed out of which clear strategies for the implementation of the objectives are crafted.

These strategies can be framed in the form of strategic plans for the medium to long term. Activity plans are then crafted out of the strategic plan for relatively shorter time horizons to facilitate implementation. When developing strategic plans for organisations, there is the need to consider the resources available to the firm, organisational needs which are based on the strategic choices made by the organisation in terms of its areas of operation. The strategic plan helps to coordinate the allocation of organisational resources over a long term horizon, and thus, contributes to a rational and optimal use of resources. It also allows for the early anticipation of risks that may arise along the line to allow for careful and considered analysis of mitigation strategies to resolve the risks.

Planning is an essential pillar of financial management. Without it, the organisation will only be wandering in the wilderness without any benchmark against which performance can be measured. The implication is that without a plan, performance measurement will be less meaningful. Actual performance has to be measured against a plan to come to some conclusion whether or not an organisation is performing well and a good plan is an essential feature of an effective financial management system.

Budgeting

Once a strategic plan has been developed, an activity plan can be crafted, and developed into an annual budget which could be further broken down into bi-annual, quarterly, monthly or weekly budgets. Merchant (1981) and Nouri and Parker (1998) found that a participatory budgeting system increases staff morale and job satisfaction, and ultimately makes a positive impact on productivity. This implies that good budgeting and budgetary control practices in corporate organisations should lead to improved corporate performance. A budget may be defined as a predetermined detailed plan of action, developed and distributed as a tool to guide operations for the ensuing period and to serve as a partial basis for subsequent evaluation of performance.

A budget is a detailed plan which sets out, in money terms, the estimated revenue and expenditure of an organisation for a future period of time, prepared based on some agreed underlying assumptions and objectives. Operational budgets cover the recurring and routine operating activities of an organisation, whilst a capital budget covers the investment activities of an organisation such as the acquisition of long term assets used for the production of goods and services of the organisation. Ryan and Ryan (2002) show how the fortune 1000 companies are increasingly relying on the net present value method of capital budgeting to analyse the appropriateness or otherwise of critical and important capital asset investments decisions.

Among other objectives, the budget and the process of budgeting greatly facilitate planning, help in revenue mobilisation or fund raising, and serve as tools for control through comparison of budgets with actuals throughout the year so that variances are spotted and remedial actions taken to align actuals closely to the budget. Merchant (1981) explained that the budget process positively influences managerial behaviour and helps to secure positive corporate performance and budgeting as a key feature of effective financial management.

Budget Execution

Once the budget is developed, there is need to raise the funds required to execute the budget. No organisation can carry on its business without having sufficient funds. Ensuring that sufficient funds are available in the right amount, at the right time from the right source and at the right cost is critical to organisational success. Funds may be raised from different sources: from the owners of the organisation, from the operations of the organisation, or from lenders. Again the funds that could be made available to an organisation could be long term, medium term or short term. Each of these different maturity terms of funding sources would have different cost implications and therefore have a bearing on corporate performance.

A major financial management function is to carefully evaluate how much funding an organisation requires, and to determine the appropriate mix of sources from which the funding should be raised to ensure that cost is minimised. Among the several factors that are often considered in deciding on the mix of funding sources for organisations are: the cost and risk associated with the particular source of funding, the tax implication of the source of funding, the timing and reliability of cash flows expected from the projects to be funded. Indeed, the point that an organisation needs to have sufficient funds at minimal cost in order to be able to carry out its activities is obvious.

Budget execution involves disbursements of allocated funds in the budget for their assigned purposes using processes that have been agreed upon. The budget execution process involves procurement of goods and services, payroll processing and payments, contracting processes etc. The payment of wages and salaries and the procurement of goods and services can only be done well when cash is available at the right time to meet committed needs. A number of empirical studies have established that effective working capital management practices have a positive relationship with corporate performance in a number of organisations in a number of countries (Padachi, 2006; Raheman, Afza, Qayyum, & Bodla, 2010; and Vishnani & Shah, 2007).

Working capital management which is a key financial management function ensures that funds are available in the right amount, at the right time, from the right source and at the right cost to meet the commitments of the organisation. Working capital management also ensures that the organisation does not run into deficits where there are no funds at particular points in time to finance the planned activities of the organisation; and also that organisations do not lock up surplus funds in cash balances that do not yield returns by ensuring that surplus funds are invested in appropriate investment instruments with the right maturity terms.

Good working capital management requires that organisations keep optimal levels of inventories and manage their financial relations with both debtors and creditors to avoid situations where clients keep substantial amounts of the organisation's funds for unduly long periods of time and at the same time ensure that the organisation takes advantage of optimal credit terms from its suppliers and lenders. It also requires that the organisation applies competitive procurement processes so that the organisation obtains value for money in the procurement of goods and services. Kaynak (2003) established that there is a positive relationship between total quality management which involves efficient procurement processes and firm performance. The importance of efficient procurement in ensuring good procurement cannot be overemphasised.

Financial Reporting

Financial management does not end with the disbursements of allocated funds. There is the need to ensure that a set of financial statements are prepared to report the financial transactions of the organisation. Financial reports generated from the financial management system are critical tools for enhancing corporate performance. Cunningham and Harris (2005) and Kluvers and Tippetts (2010) pointed out that relevant and understandable financial reports have the ability to clearly communicate organisational performance to stakeholders. Barton (2005) suggested that for financial reporting systems to be useful, they must possess the characteristics of: relevance, reliability, comparability, and understandability. Chan (2003) explained that financial reports are used to: evaluate an organisation's ability to meet obligations, induce others to offer resources to the organisation, and monitor the performance of the organisation. Having good financial reports helps to provide information about the organisation to allow for stakeholders to make informed decisions.

Effective financial management systems support organisations to generate financial statements that are prepared in accordance with established accounting standards to capture the material financial transactions of the organisation accurately and reliably to show the financial performance of the organisation during the reporting period, the financial position of the organisation as at the end of the reporting period and the cash flows of the organisation during the reporting period. Such information generated from the financial reporting system should allow the different stakeholders to be in a position to properly evaluate performance and make informed decisions based on this evaluation.

Auditing, Monitoring and Evaluation

Organisations are often run by trained management teams who are often different from the owners and tend to have interests which differ from that of the owners. The divergence in interest between owners and managers create what has come to be known as the agency problem. The agency problem makes it necessary for the owners to engage independent auditors to review the financial statements prepared by management and to provide assurance to the owners through their independent professional opinion as to whether or not the financial statements prepared by management reflect a true and fair view of the operations of the organisation during the reporting period and whether the assets and liabilities as at the end of the reporting period reasonably reflects the true state of financial position of the organisation.

Before the independent external auditors examine the records to provide their independent opinion, it is good financial management practice to have internal auditors, who work as part of the management team, to continuously monitor and evaluate the policies and procedures put in place by management, to assess the adequacy or otherwise of those policies in helping management achieve its set objectives. Both internal and external audit processes help to provide recommendations on the operational and financial policies and practices of the organisation which when acted upon will help to improve corporate performance (Klein, 2002).

From the above analysis on what represents a good financial management system, the question is what is the relationship between good financial management and corporate performance? The next section seeks to establish this link.

Linking Effective Financial Management and Corporate Performance

It has already been said in an earlier section that corporate performance is about the ability of organisations to achieve their set objectives whether operational or financial. For an organisation to be able to achieve its objectives, in the first place, those objectives must be properly developed through a careful and deliberate planning process which is an integral part of an effective financial management system. Without a good planning process, there will be no good objectives to meet. Once plans have been developed, they will remain plans on the shelves unless and until they are reduced to actionable activities and resources allocated to ensure that these activities are actually carried out through the budgeting and budget execution process. The fund raising function of financial management ensures that financial resources are raised at the right cost to finance the activities of the organisation.

Working capital management processes ensure that adequate cash is available at all times to ensure that the wheel of the organisation does not grind to a halt. If working capital is not properly managed, the organisation may run out of cash at critical times when it will need to carry out some activities. The consequence is that some activities may not be carried out, and this may lead to poor corporate performance.

The availability of financial information through effective financial reporting processes makes it possible for evidenced based decisions to be made by management of organisations. The absence of good information will result in a situation where decisions will simply be based on guess work and not informed by data. The point that financial decisions guided by cost benefit analysis based on financial information generated by the financial management system will more likely lead to better corporate performance as compared decisions not informed by cost benefit analysis cannot be over emphasised. The opportunity presented by the auditing, monitoring and evaluation process of the financial management system to ensure value for money, and identification of risks and weaknesses in organisational processes for redress, should have a direct and positive impact on corporate performance.

The Impact of Sound Financial Management on the Economy

Financial management at the national level also has an impact on the performance of government. Financial management of public funds has come to be known as Public Financial Management. According to Andrews *et al* (2014) Public Financial Management (PFM) refers to the way governments manage public resources (both revenue and expenditure) and the immediate, medium, as well as long term effects of such resources on the economy or society. This implies that PFM involves the processes of managing financial resources and the outcome or results achieved from those processes. PFM processes involve: planning, controlling, implementation and monitoring of fiscal policies and activities, including the reporting, audit and the exercise of oversight responsibilities on the management of public funds.

The PFM cycle encompasses the phases of budget formulation, budget approval, budget execution, accounting and reporting, monitoring and oversight activities (Kan-Dapaah, 2015; Andrews et al., 2014). The impact of a good PFM system on effective resource management at the national level cannot be overemphasised. Cangiano, Curristine and Lazare (2013) and Allen (2013) suggest that an effective PFM system promotes efficient allocation of scarce resources to activities, projects and programmes in an economy thus ensuring that scarce resources are deployed to their optimal use; leads to effective delivery of public goods and services to the citizenry at optimal prices; and helps to achieve a sustainable fiscal position for the entire economy, thus enabling economic development.

Effective PFM systems also deliver stewardship and accountability over public funds in a transparent manner. This brings about good economic governance. Good governance is a virtue that all civilised societies are trying to embrace to help improve the wellbeing of members of the society. Good governance calls for national economies to be governed and led in a manner as to ensure that resources are well utilised in meeting the needs of all stakeholders in the national economy. According to Cheema and Maguire (2001) good governance involves governance practices infused with the principles of equity, participation, rule of law, transparency and accountability. Cheema and Maguire assert further that there are three dimensions of governance: political governance, economic governance and social governance, and that all three are linked to each other and provide the platform for the effective delivery of public service. An effective PFM system ensures good economic governance.

Grindle (2004) states that "indeed, it is all too clear that when governments perform poorly, resources are wasted, services go undelivered, and citizens – especially the poor – are denied social, legal, and economic protection. For many in the development community, good governance has become as imperative to poverty reduction as it has become to development more generally" (p. 525). Cheema and Maguire (2001) find that there is a positive correlation between the practice of good economic governance and human development. Patra (2012) finds that failure of government to exhibit good PFM governance principles leads to massive scams and corruption which deprive societies of much needed resources for development and consequently lead to low levels of human development.

Conclusions and Recommendations

Today's organisations operate within rapidly changing and competitive environments. For a firm operating in the current marketplace to survive in their challenging business environments, corporate managers must appreciate the need to develop and make full use of financial management tools. In all organisations, financial management should be given a high priority. Financial management plays a pivotal role in the performance of corporate organisations. Effective financial management helps business executives to make effective and efficient use of resources to achieve corporate objectives and fulfill commitments to stakeholders, and assists corporate organisations to be more accountable to donors and other stakeholders. Sound financial management helps corporate organisations to gain the respect and confidence of funding agencies, partners and beneficiaries and therefore is able to attract more funding; it gives corporate organisations competitive advantage over their peers in the mobilisation and use of scarce resources; and assists corporate organisations to prepare themselves for long-term financial sustainability.

These reasons make it imperative and persuasive for organisations to put in place effective financial management systems. An effective financial management system should ensure consistency in the operations of the organisation, accountability over the resources of the organisation, transparency in the management of resources of the organisation, integrity of the system to preserve resources of the organisation, stewardship by managers to owners of the organisation, and use of best standards in carrying out all the different activities of the organisation, and viability of the business of the organisation.

It can therefore be concluded that effective financial management has a direct and positive impact on corporate performance. That is to say a good financial management system will lead to better and improved corporate performance and similarly a weak financial management system should lead to poor corporate performance. This has implications for business executives, policy makers, and a scholar as far as future research is concerned.

The implication for business executives is that they should ensure that their organisations do maintain effective financial management systems to guide their operations as this will ensure better corporate performance for their business organisations. Business executives should therefore endeavour to make appropriate investments towards putting in place effective financial management systems within their businesses and should also allow the financial management systems once developed to function without impediments.

Policy makers at the national level should realise the critical role of effective financial management in the realisation of all policies that they develop. They should therefore ensure that there is an effective financial management system at the national level to facilitate the smooth implementation of all policies. If this is not done, polices will only remain pieces of documents on the shelves of the policy makers. For purposes of future research, scholars should address their attention to empirically testing the conclusions made in this chapter by using data to examine the relationship between effective financial management and corporate performance for different types of organisations in order to reinforce the assertions.

References

- Allen, S. (2013). Reflections on two decades of Public Financial Management reforms. In *Public Financial Management and Its Emerging Architecture,* eds. Marco Cangiano, Teresa Curristine, Michael Lazare. Washington, DC: International Monetary Fund. 21 – 76.

- Andrews, M., Cangiano, M., Cole, N., De Renzio, P., Krause, P. & Seligmann, R. (2014). *This is PFM* (No. rwp14-034).

- Barton, A. (2005). Professional accounting standards and the public sector - a mismatch. *Abacus, 41*(2), 138-158.

- Cangiano, M. Curristine, T. & Lazare, M. (2013). Introduction: The Emerging Architecture of Public Financial Management." In *Public Financial Management and Its Emerging Architecture,* eds. Marco Cangiano, Teresa Curristine, Michael Lazare. Washington, D.C.: International Monetary Fund. 1 – 17

- Chan, J. (2003). Government accounting: An assessment of theory, purposes and standards. *Public Money & Management, 23*(1), 13-20.

- Cheema, G. & Maguire, L. (2001). Governance for human development: The role of external partners. *Public Administration & Development, 21*(3), 201-209.

- Cunningham, G. & Harris, J. (2005). Toward a theory of performance reporting to achieve public sector accountability: A field study. *Public Budgeting & Finance, 25*(2).

- Griffin, J. & Mahon, J. 1997). The corporate social performance and corporate financial performance debate twenty-five years of incomparable research. *Business & Society, 36*(1).

- Grindle, M. (2004). Good enough governance: Poverty reduction and reform in developing countries. *Governance, 17*(4), 525-548.

- Huselid, M. (1995). The impact of human resource management practices on turnover, productivity, and corporate financial performance. *Academy of Management Journal, 38*(3), 635-672.

- Kan-Dapaah, D. (2015). Parliament's role in the fight against corruption. *Institute of Economic Affairs, Ghana.*

- Kaynak, H. (2003). The relationship between total quality management practices and their effects on firm performance. *Journal of Operations Management, 21*(4), 405-435.

- Klapper, L. & Love, I. (2004). Corporate governance, investor protection, and performance in emerging markets. *Journal of Corporate Finance, 10*(5), 703-728.

- Klein, A. (2002). Audit committee, board of director characteristics, and earnings management. *Journal of Accounting and Economics, 33*(3), 375-400.

- Kluvers, R. & Tippett, J. (2010). Mechanisms of accountability in local government: An exploratory study. *International Journal of Business & Management, 5*(7), 46-53.

- Lang, L. & Stulz, R. (1993). *Tobin's q, corporate diversification and firm performance* (No. w4376). National Bureau of Economic Research.

- Mehran, H. (1995). Executive compensation structure, ownership, and firm performance. *Journal of Financial Economics, 38*(2), 163-184.

- Merchant, K. (1981). The design of the corporate budgeting system: influences on managerial behaviour and performance. *Accounting Review, 56*(4), 813-829.

- Miller, C. & Cardinal, L. (1994). Strategic planning and firm performance: A synthesis of more than two decades of research. *Academy of Management Journal, 37*(6), 1649-1665.

- McGuire, J., Sundgren, A. & Schneeweis, T. (1988). Corporate social responsibility and firm financial performance. *Academy of Management Journal, 31*(4), 854-872.

- Nouri, H. & Parker, R. J. (1998). The relationship between budget participation and job performance: the roles of budget adequacy and organisational commitment. *Accounting, Organisations and Society, 23*(5), 467-483.

- Orlitzky, M., Schmidt, F. & Rynes, S. (2003). Corporate social and financial performance: A meta-analysis. *Organisation Studies, 24*(3), 403-441.

- Padachi, K. (2006). Trends in working capital management and its impact on firms' performance: an analysis of Mauritian small manufacturing firms. *International Review of Business Research Papers, 2*(2), 45-58.

- Patra, B. (2012). Government, governance and corruption: The case of 2G spectrum scam. *Vilakshan: The XIMB Journal of Management, 9*(2), 91-108.

- Pearce, J., Robbins, D. & Robinson, R. (1987). The impact of grand strategy and planning formality on financial performance. *Strategic Management Journal, 8*(2), 125-134.

- Preston, L. & O'bannon, D. (1997). The corporate social-financial performance relationship. *Business and Society, 36*(4), 419-429.

- Raheman, A., Afza, T., Qayyum, A. & Bodla, M. (2010). Working capital management and corporate performance of manufacturing sector in Pakistan. *International Research Journal of Finance and Economics, 47*(1), 156-169.

- Roberts, P. & Dowling, G. (2002). Corporate reputation and sustained superior financial performance. *Strategic Management Journal, 23*(12), 1077-1093.

- Robinson, R. & Pearce, J. (1983). The impact of formalised strategic planning on financial performance in small organisations. *Strategic Management Journal, 4*(3), 197-207.

- Ryan, P. & Ryan, G. (2002). Capital budgeting practices of the Fortune 1000: How have things changed? *Journal of Business and Management, 8*(4), 355-371.

- Van Horne, J. & Wachowicz, J. (2001). *Fundamentals of financial management.* Upper Saddle River, NJ: Pearson Education.

- Vishnani, S., & Shah, B. (2007). Impact of working capital management policies on corporate performance - An empirical study. *Global Business Review, 8*(2), 267-281.

- Waddock, S. & Graves, S. (1997). The corporate social performance-financial performance link. *Strategic Management Journal, 18*(4), 303-319.

- Williamson, O. (1988). Corporate finance and corporate governance. *The Journal of Finance, 43*(3), 567-591.

- Zahra, S. & Pearce, J. (1989). Boards of directors and corporate financial performance: A review and integrative model. *Journal of Management, 15*(2), 291-334.

Chapter 10

Human Resource Management and Organisational Performance

Hazel Berrard Amuah

Abstract

This chapter discusses the relevance of human resource management (HRM) with due consideration for the fact that people are the most important resource of any organisation. HRM provides a planned approach to managing people effectively for performance through various HR practices. Equally important is the consistent, focused growth and skills development of the workforce as well as using performance management to ensure the alignment of individual and team objectives to the overall achievement of these targets. HRM also ensures that the total employment value proposition of an organisation meets both expectations of the employees based on their skills and competencies, is competitive in the market and affordable based on organisational performance. Very importantly, HRM is responsible for employee relations which is essentially about how the HR function of an organisation implements various philosophies of engagement, commitment, high involvement and empowerment to motivate employees and ensure that there are more objective and alternative vehicles and fora for communications.

***Keywords**: Human resource management; Workforce; Talent; Organisation; Performance.*

Introduction

Michael Porter in 1985, proposed a model he called "the value chain model" through his best seller book, Competitive Advantage: Creating and Sustaining Superior Performance. In this book, he gives a presentation of a value chain analysis using his model as a framework for the identification and measurement of the key activities that comprise an organisation's value chain. To start on the premise with a common understanding of "organisations", the definition used in this book to describe organisations is as follows: organisations are (1) social entities that (2) are goal-directed, (3) are designed as deliberately structured and coordinated activity systems, and (4) are linked to the external environment. According to Daft and Lane (2013), an organisation is not a building or a set of policies and procedures;

157

organisations are made up of people and their relationships with one another. An organisation exists when people interact with one another to perform essential functions that help attain goals. An organisation is a means to an end.

The value chain described by Porter falls within the context of organisational design. Organisation theory and design provides the necessary tools to evaluate and understand how a huge, powerful firm like Lehman Brothers can die and a company like Bank of America can emerge almost overnight as a giant in the industry. It helps to provide insight into how a band like the Rolling Stones, which is comparable in its set up and operations to a highly sophisticated global business organisation, can enjoy phenomenal success for nearly half a century, while some musical groups with equal or superior talent are not able to survive past a couple of hit songs. Organisation theory helps provide meaning and insight into what happened in the past, as well as what may happen in the future, so that organisations can be managed more effectively.

Human Resources Management (HRM)

The human resource management of any organisation is extremely critical as this function is responsible for the most important resource of any organisation. HRM is essentially about having a planned approach to managing people effectively for performance. As a function, HRM brings out the important values of trust, care, teamwork, encouragement and development which help the organisation meet the principle of being a good employer and thereby motivating staff to give their best and aims to establish a more open, flexible and caring management style so that the employees of the organisation will be motivated, developed and managed in a way that they can and will give of their best to support departments' vision, mission and objectives. To successfully execute these responsibilities, HRM is divided into various sub functions which are usually managed by specialists to provide in-depth support to the organisation.

Workforce planning

Usually in support of ensuring that the organisation has the appropriate human resource capability, every year, the organisation undergoes a business planning phase which does forecasting of the organisation's growth targets for the upcoming year, next three years, five years and ten years. This process is called Workforce Planning and it entails a systematic identification and analysis of what an organisation is going to need in terms of the size, type, experience, knowledge, skills and quality of workforce to achieve its objectives. Workforce planning can be described also as the process used to generate business intelligence in a bid to inform the organisation of the current, transition and future impact of the external and internal environment on the organisation in a way that enables it to be resilient to current structural and cultural changes to better position itself for the future.

There are two key types of workforce planning. Strategic Workforce Planning usually covers a forecast period of three to five years and is aligned to business needs and outcomes. It focuses on identifying the workforce implications, current, transition and future of business strategic objects and includes scenario planning. The other type of workforce planning is known as Operational Workforce Planning and it usually covers the next 12–18 months of the life of an organisation. It should align with the timeframe of the business planning cycle and it comprises processes and systems applied to gathering, analysing and reporting on workforce planning strategy.

Workforce planning supports the vision and mission of the organisation as well as provides insights and details as to how the organisation intends to achieve its business objectives. Through workforce planning and management, the HR function collaborates with the various business and functional heads to forecast the human resources required, related implications including costs, integration of new staff, impact on current team, team dynamics, cultural impacts etc. Different organisations use different approaches to workforce planning and management. Figure 10.1 below shows a typical ten (10) step approach to SWP.

During this ten step process, it is important to undergo certain activities which will provide the necessary information and context to complete the workforce planning process.

Step One : Review of the organisational strategy. The organisational strategy comprises the goals and objectives of the business operating unit for which the planning activity is needed. To that extent, it is necessary to: understand the rationale and scope for the workforce planning, have a summary of people-related measures (if any or define them), review the vision and mission of the organisation, as well as review the organisational performance plans, financials and budgets, organisation charts, staffing plans etc. to ensure relevance and practicality.

Strategic Workforce Planning

1. Review organisation strategy
2. Research internal labour market
3. Assess existing and planned resource pool
4. Identify future skills demands/needs and gaps/excesses
5. Model the workforce against the hypotheses
6. Define workforce requirements
7. Develop resourcing strategy with the business
8. Develop Resourcing Plan and engage with business
9. Implement and measure
10. Integrate with other planning processes

Figure 10.1: Designed by Amuah (2016)

Once this process is complete, it is necessary to nominate and set up a multidisciplinary team to conduct planning (HR, Finance, Budget, Unions and Business Leaders, etc.) and develop strategic plans, current and projected budget information, external market data/trends. There is a set of assumptions made in order to set the scope of the planning effort. These assumptions include but are not limited to: a focus of the plan (key roles, unit, function or organisation; high turnover or declining performance areas), the number of years to project for during the particular workforce planning (1-5years), a list of workforce characteristics such as permanent, temporary, FTE, non-FTE, contractors, etc., diversity and cultural issues ensuring barriers are not being created, and baseline financials (annual and projected budgets, headcount). This completes step one of the workforce planning process.

Step 2 is to research internal labour market. This is also known as workforce segmentation and it is about summarising key workforce or resource pool 'characteristics' of the group in scope. The key activities involved are: the collection of the 'people' data for the group in scope (headcount, titles, grades, performance ratings, qualifications, tenure, age, race, compensation, benefits etc.), the creation of a current workforce profile; number, turnover, location, demographics (age, gender, race), competencies, job levels , education, certifications, status (full time? part time?), the validation of findings with managers and business leaders. Care must be taken to look out for missing or bad data which should not be made up or fabricated, rather it is recommended to make reasonable, conservative assumptions around gaps and be consistent. It is useful to validate the findings as the work progresses as a surprise in the baseline will undermine credibility in the long run. It is also recommended that there is a thorough understanding of the employee lifecycle – how and where they enter, develop (move around) and leave the organisation.

Step 3 is about assessing the existing (supply) and planned (demand) resource pool. This pool can be defined as the supply side of the equation; the available human capital which is the current and future workforce that will deliver on organisational objectives. The key activities include: using the current workforce profile, identifying trends; time in position, turnover, increased/decreased compensation, growth or contradiction of value of role; validating findings with managers and business leaders. It is also necessary to create a projected workforce 'profile' based on trends and assumptions. Some relevant questions to be asked to gain information are the following: What changes (technology innovations, organisational structure, outsourcing etc.) are expected over the planning period? How will that affect volume, type and locations of work? Skill mix? What will the planned organisation look like (what competencies, how many people, what certifications)? Prioritise the top 5-8 competencies that are essential; rank these to differentiate one job level from another and summarise the projected (demand) staffing levels and competencies that can/will meet the need. While conducting this exercise, care must be taken not to validate the 'most likely' scenario with internal (experienced business leaders) external sources (peer networks, benchmarks etc.) or use the same data elements in the current and future workforce profile so gaps can be readily identified and validated. It helps to use the same data elements in the current and future workforce profile so gaps can be readily identified and validated.

Step 4 is about identifying future skills demands/needs and gaps/excesses. A gap analysis will identify how well the workforce is positioned for the future; *shortfalls require action; excesses require realignment.* The key activities include alignment of the current and projected workforce profile and identify: gaps in headcount, grades, knowledge, skills, abilities, experience, excesses in headcount, grader, knowledge, skills, abilities, and experience. Draft a solution analysis to address gaps and excesses which cover: vital skills needed for success, skills, imbalance created by turnover; retention strategies and associated costs, training versus recruiting to fill competency gaps, contractors versus staff; re-assignment of resources with excess skills to other key roles to create development opportunities and creating mentoring for staff needing nominal development. Areas to watch out for are avoiding over analysis which becomes paralysis and a focus on priority as well as critical skills. It is recommended that during this phase, there is the use of the gap/excess findings to create career development programmes that can fill projected needs organically.

Step 5 comprises the process of modelling the workforce against the hypotheses. Several scenarios are developed with the business to build understanding of the supply and demand issues. The key activities involved here are the review of findings with business leaders to validate projections and secure support; confirm gaps and excesses and define associated actions; model alternate projection scenarios, finalising agreements on overall skill needs, ranking of criticality of skills, determining broad timing and staff requirements, etc. and determining compensation structure. It is critical not to get too attached to the accuracy of the projections and outcome of the analysis as it may change and thus flexibility is imperative. It helps to collect cost data throughout the process as they will be useful in the discussions with business leaders, especially the 'order of magnitude'.

Step 6 is about defining the workforce requirements of the organisation. This can be described to be the demand side of the equation and should include the requirements of key (critical) roles. The key activities in this process are refining the needs in terms of total numbers and competency requirements, outlining how the skills can be developed; recruiting, developing through training, re-training, relocation, on-the-job etc. and the lead times involved to be fully competent. These elements must be used to define the 'workforce system' (recruiting, training, retention, realignment functions) that reflects what is required to fill the critical roles. It is necessary to also develop alternative scenarios (best case/worst case) and their consequences, e.g. lack of skills/expense of resources in market shifts focus to training; develop a communication strategy to communicate workforce plan and expectations to impacted employees, stakeholders and inventory. HR programmes which will require modification as a result of the projected requirements e.g., tuition reimbursement, certification awards, completion of training. Care must be taken when defining critical roles as these should not merely be senior roles but those that bring significant value or are 'mission critical' to the overall value chain of the business. It is helpful to ensure that HR Business Partners/Managers are connected to the business strategies of their respective operating units and capable of translating such strategies into a people agenda and set of requirements. They need to be on the look-out for new skills required in new places (geographies).

Step 7 entails developing resourcing strategy with the business. Sourcing strategy determines where an organisation will look for the talent it needs – internally, externally, build versus buy talent approach. The key activities include agreeing upon guiding principles and philosophical approach to talent acquisition; assessing labour pool in key geographies for critical skills and competencies needed and determining whether internal candidates can meet need and how internal sourcing will be handled; assessing the need for external recruiting support; establishing preferred provider contracts with reputable recruiting firms; leveraging the organisational brand to solicit better hires and identifying alternative sourcing strategies – campus/trade schools, flexible arrangements, relocation, secondments, etc. The information sources include published labour market analysis; internal skills and competency databases. Attention needs to be given to regulatory/work council complexities, cultural nuances and ways of working, internal staff distraction and disruption if internal postings are not well coordinated with internal equity issues. Looking broadly at the organisation's internal talent pool globally, knowing where the skills reside in their own organisation, leveraging technology as much as possible and being prepared to rigorously manage this as a strategic project are very critical aspects of this phase.

Step 8 is about developing a Resourcing Plan and engaging with business. A resource plan is a tactical plan to implement the resourcing strategy that integrates the defined workforce requirements. The key activities include establishing project lead and project management team(s); developing a high level action plan that includes activities and costs required to implement the sourcing strategy; reviewing with key stakeholders to gain buy-in; confirming their role and establishing critical success factors and ways of working together (collaboration on interviewing, tools in place, hiring process, who has final say on compensation, etc.); reviewing plan with legal department to determine whether any 'red flags' exist; developing mitigating actions and monitoring progress and track costs. The roles of hiring managers are critical in this process as they will need support in matching their needs to specific candidates; scheduling of interviews and time management as well as following up with candidates and assessing 'fit'. It is recommended to evaluate the need to conduct training for hiring managers on behavioural interviewing techniques, etc.; include any actions that result in plan, and pay significant attention to on-boarding to ensure that new recruits become engaged and productive quickly – assign mentors, transition coaches, tool, checklists, etc. to ease transition.

Step 9 comprises the implementation and measurement of what needs to be done. This requires an action plan that details steps required to implement the programmes and measure outcomes. This phase involves key activities such as: appointing a project team to oversee implementation and monitor progress against goals, developing a detailed action plan that includes all the tactical activities required to implement the workforce plan (Project Management Office, communication strategy, employees and leadership, training, recruiting, technology systems, policy and programme revisions and measures of success during implementation and on-going). HR managers need to beware of competing priorities and 'fire fighting' that push the implementation to the bottom of the priority list. Some useful hints in this phase include the fact that implementation requires time and resources; therefore it is necessary to make sure the team works hard on analysis not when there is no resource for execution.

Finally, Step 10 which is the last phase is about integrating with other planning processes. The SWP process will inform both talent management, succession and career paths as well as be an input to corporate/strategic plans. Critical activities and key action points to note are that SWP can be an integral part of the corporate planning cycle and scenarios from the corporate cycle can be used in scenario modeling at workforce level. In some organisations the SWP tools are part of the wider corporate toolset. It is advisable to take note of the tools and processes which get in the way of challenging and searching conversations that need to be had with BU leaders about likely futures for the business and their consequences. It helps to keep the whole process simple but searching: with a focus on the key roles first, not all of them; identifying the likely new roles and skill-sets, scenario plan; and remaining predictive and insightful.

Talent Acquisition
Recruitment versus talent acquisition

Organisations are increasingly looking to acquire external talent, although nearly half are making efforts to develop existing employees. The business case for acquiring external talent strategically is far more compelling than simply recruiting to fill positions today. Recruitment can be simply described as the process of filling open positions in organisations. It can be described as an entirely tactical event. Strategic talent acquisition is however more complex and adds more value to an organisation's talent management strategy. During this process, the candidate has an opportunity to explain his/her future career aspirations, and the recruiter gathers enough information to determine if there is a potential fit in the client organisation.

Strategic talent acquisition takes a long-term view of not just filling positions today, but using the candidates that come out of a recruiting campaign as a means of filling other positions in the future through a rigorous succession planning process. Clearly once this is properly done, the organisations benefit ultimately as they build a robust talent pipeline for the organisation. These future positions may be identifiable today by looking at the workforce plan, succession management plan, or by analysing the history of attrition for certain positions. This facilitates the process of predicting that specific openings will occur at a pre-determined period in time. In the most enlightened cases of strategic talent acquisition, organisations will recruit today for positions that do not even exist today but are expected to become available in the future.

Taking the long term strategic approach to talent acquisition has a huge impact on how an approach is made to a candidate. If the approach is purely tactical in nature, all we ask of the prospective candidate is "are you qualified and interested?" However, if the approach is more strategic in nature, the intent of the call is to go much further, and the conversation becomes more relationship building. The candidate has an opportunity to explain his/her future career aspirations, and the recruiter gathers enough information to determine if there is a potential fit in the client organisation.

Learning and development (L&D)

Learning and development is a unit of HR also referred to in some organisations as the Training unit of HR or the Training and Development unit of HR. Even though this role cuts across the different businesses and functions of an organisation, it is usually incorporated within the HR department due to its responsibility of ensuring employee growth and skills development. In large organisations, it is usually a stand-alone unit while in smaller organisations, it forms at least one fifth of the HR manager's job. It is rare to find this role separated from the HR function.

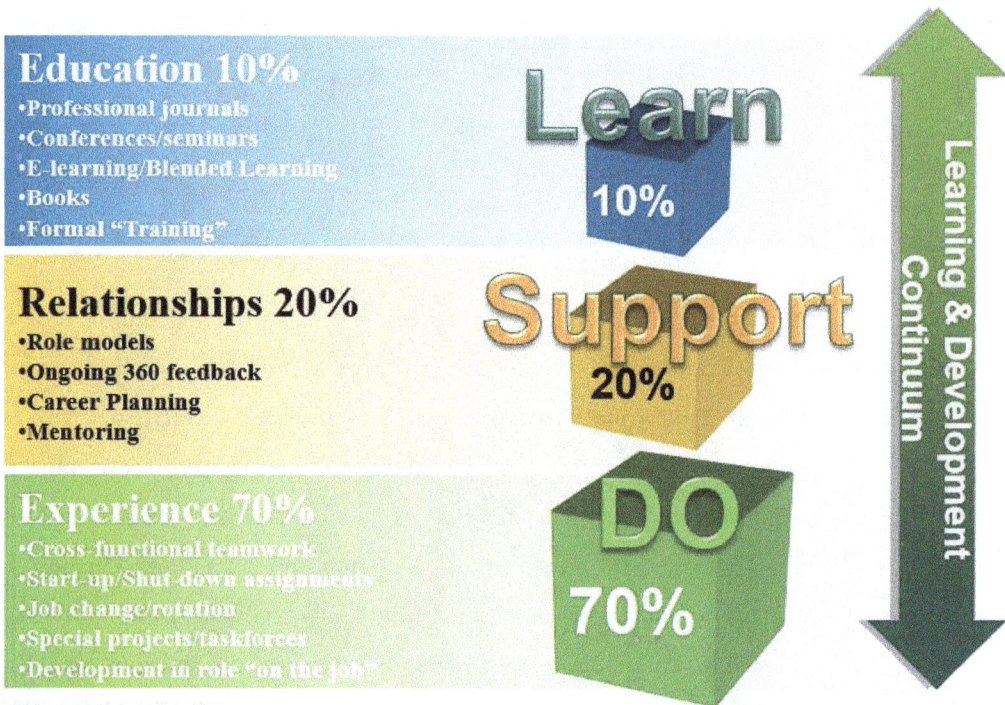

Education 10%
•Professional journals
•Conferences/seminars
•E-learning/Blended Learning
•Books
•Formal "Training"

Learn 10%

Relationships 20%
•Role models
•Ongoing 360 feedback
•Career Planning
•Mentoring

Support 20%

Experience 70%
•Cross-functional teamwork
•Start-up/Shut-down assignments
•Job change/rotation
•Special projects/taskforces
•Development in role "on the job"

DO 70%

Learning & Development Continuum

SOURCE: Princeton University USA

Figure 10.2 showing the 70-20-10 Learning strategy for organisations. Morgan McCall, Robert Eichinger & Michael Lombardo, *Center for Creative Leadership,* Princeton.

L&D is largely aligned to the overall business strategy. It must thus, be totally aligned with the needs and expectations of the organisation; and most organisations which thrive and grow, record a positive correlation between strategic learning and development aligned with business strategy and the achievement of business objectives. Lack of   clarity on the business strategy, lack of resources, and lack of interest or understanding of purpose risk being a huge barrier to alignment between L&D and the business. Modern L&D usually follows research conducted by Princeton University, USA in 2015, per Figure 2 above.

The L&D function uses the above strategy to derive and implement development interventions in consultation and partnership with both employees and line managers for the most appropriate programmes to be put in place in support of business strategy. Usually the 10% training content comprises e-learning, videos, books, journals, seminars, workshops, conferences, in-house and external training (locally or internationlly). Learning technologies are more common in larger organisations; they are more likely than smaller organisations to include e-learning courses and blended learning among their most common L&D practices and to anticipate growth in the use of various learning technologies.

The 20% focuses on development interventions which thrive on relationships. There are several ways of developing people using relationships. They include implementing 360 instruments on individuals for them to receive feedback from their direct reports, peers and superiors. The reports generated are then used to develop action plans for the individuals. The action plans focus on enhancing the strengths of the individuals as well as turning their development areas into strengths. Role models are an impactful way of developing individuals as they emulate them, their way of behaving, communicating, and going about interacting with others. Career planning helps to focus efforts of individuals to be geared towards their aspirations through exposing them to the details of the careers they aspire to have in the short to medium term. Assigning mentors also provides excellent opportunities for individuals to be developed as mentors use their experience and profound technical competencies to help develop individuals.

Seventy percent of development options is experience based and includes but is not limited to cross functional teamwork where individuals are made to be part of cross functional projects and teams or task forces set up to deliver on certain objectives. Individuals are also given practical opportunities for start up and shut down assignments for them to undergo an experience that will enable them apply themselves and learn or enhance skills and competencies that they need to develop. On the job training is also an experience based development intervention where an individual is developed in his role by enhancing his capabilities through more immersion into the role, setting of stretch targets and enabling the individual to apply creativity and innovation in challenging the status quo in his current job.

L&D managers require certain core competencies to fully implement the capability agenda of the organisation. This includes but is not limited to, having a strong business and commercial acumen, emotional intelligence, innovation and creativity, programme design and delivery, presentation skills, insight into different learning styles of individuals, interpersonal skills and monitoring and evaluation skills. While face-to-face remains the most dominant approach in learning and development interventions, due to the virtual set up of most firms, organisations leverage on learning technologies to effect development interventions. The most common barrier to learning and development include fund availability, cutting of budgets allocated to learning and development, other functional managers not duly supporting the learning and development agenda to build the capability of their teams.

Performance Management

Performance management is the function of HR which can be described as the process through which line managers and supervisors share their expectations, goals, performance objectives for their teams to have an understanding of the organisational targets and functional targets and how their individual and team work contribute to the overall achievement of these targets. In the same vein, the performance management process is the vehicle for sharing feedback, identifying learning and development areas and opportunities, as well as allowing for the evaluation of performance results against the set targets. Performance management is the organisational process which sits in HR but is implemented throughout the organisation with all levels of employees; that is used to create and sustain an environment; that places value on continuous improvement; strives to achieve stretch targets; fosters innovation and creativity; assesses and responds to change; promotes learning and professional development in ways that engage and reward superior performance.

Performance management is that organisational tool that is used to differentiate performance through processes such as compensation and benefits and recognition in the organisation. The foundation and success of performance management is using a tool that captures the essence of performance i.e., the targets that an individual should work to achieve during the year and the specific organisational behaviours that the individual must demonstrate in working to achieve their objectives. Some performance management tools include a section to capture the development needs of the individual and the designated interventions agreed to improve performance. Usually there are five steps and four formal meetings throughout the year to formally manage performance discussions with individuals. These steps are pictorially represented and described in Figure 3 below.

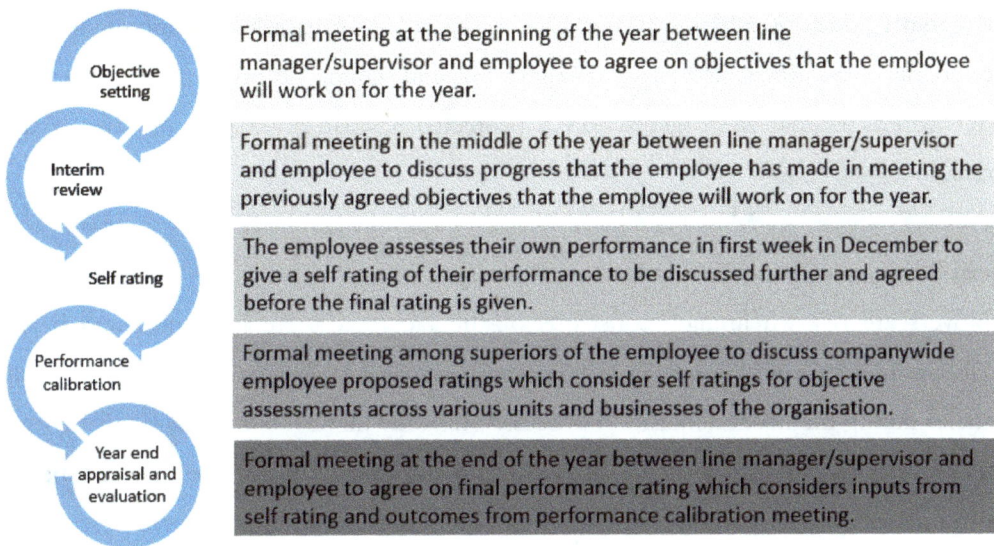

Figure 10.3 describing the performance management cycle (Amuah, 2016)

Individuals who consistently do not meet minimum performance expectations over a two year period are put on Performance Improvement Plans (PIP) or initiatives which essentially are plans which focus on monitoring the individual through a micromanagement approach to set targets and review daily or weekly to track performance and highlight challenges the employee may be facing. Before PIPs are implemented, there is a formal discussion with the employee by the line manager/ supervisor and the HR manager responsible for the purpose of alignment and clarity on the purpose of PIP, which is usually over a six month period, and extended up to an extra three months but not more. Usually organisations use different templates and forms for this activity. Every work target is thus recorded on this template and performance tracked and recorded and signed off by both employee and line manager/supervisor. At the end of the stipulated six month period, both parties sign off together with HR validating the outcome of the PIP process.

There are usually two possible outcomes from this process. The first one, which is the expected outcome is that the PIP will correct any performance challenges and have the employee's performance improved. The second outcome which is not what the organisation prefers is when the employee is not able to meet expected standards and must be managed out of the organisation. Occasionally some organisations put the employee in a different position where there is a perception that there is a wrong person-position fit to give them an opportunity to demonstrate that they can still contribute to organisational success in another function, business or unit. The involvement of HR and signing off on all the documents duly for record ensure that the organisation is protected against any claims or suits of unfair termination.

Talent Strategy and the Talent Review Process

Employers are overwhelmingly conscious of the fact that there is a mismatch between available candidates and the needed technical and employable skills as a key obstacle in filling vacancies during the talent acquisition process. This only highlights the reality of the war on talent as there is a global shortage of talent and the magnitude of the disparity between supply and demand will increase over time. The skills demanded by regions may vary but on the global landscape, the need for skilled trade workers, engineers and sales representatives remains quite high. It is critical for business leaders to always have a thorough understanding of their business vision and strategy and the specific human resource capital needed to drive this goal. To remain competitive and grow requires a solid talent benchmark as this is the lifeline to the future success of any organisation.

The urgent need for developing high potentials in every organisation is a crucial component of a company's business strategy because it feeds or depletes the pool of talent capable of filling impending senior leadership vacancies. It is for this purpose that the talent strategy of an organisation is critical for its viability and growth. The talent strategy of an organisation is typically about how an organisational strategy develops and implements the plan which ensures that the right people are in the right positions to drive the organisational agenda to success. The starting point is assessing the capabilities of the current workforce especially those in key and critical positions to ascertain their potential and sustained performance.

Most organisations use the nine-box grid as a commonly used tool to aid in a discussion of employee strengths and development needs.

It is believed that the nine-box grid or matrix was originated by McKinsey with the aim of assessing different business units and to prioritise the investment in individuals in an organisation. Apparently, McKinsey developed it for General Electric in the late 1960s and 1970s to make it possible then to assess the potential of individuals in its business and prioritise its investment and overall strategy. Apparently the concept of the nine-box grid was inspired by the Boston Consulting Group and their "Boston Box" of business or product potential. In the Boston Consulting Group grid, products are placed in the various boxes based on their performance and potential and this concept is applied to how individuals are placed in the nine-box grid.

Typically it is used in a group setting where managers collectively review current and sustained performance and future potential of a specific segment of their workforce, usually those who are in lower levels of the hierarchy. The segmentation of the employees is based on their job levels and reporting lines so typically superiors will review one or two levels below them. The essence of these multiple perspectives is to ensure they eliminate subjectivity and enforce an objective and balanced view of an employee's skills and growth areas which are ultimately used to prepare individuals for future roles with due consideration for business needs and the career aspirations of the individual. In that regard line managers also use the talent grid information to position employees in alignment with organisational needs and the critical job roles and capabilities in the organisation. Insights and outcomes of this process also serve as inputs into the development plans of employees.

The Talent Review Process

Figure 4 below is a pictorial representation of the process flow the end to end process of the talent review process. There is the initial step of planning with the key stakeholders to discuss the purpose, benefits, expected outcomes and governance regarding commitment, time and ground rules as this is a confidential conversation about people. The next step is about the alignment of the context within which this process is being managed. It is about the strategy, challenges, opportunities, work goals and priorities. It is also important to clearly define the boundaries and scope of the roles and tasks for the discussion and engage the team to brainstorm the knowledge and required attributes for the productive and fruitful discussions for the specific population to be reviewed and discussed for plotting in the various boxes. Once this has been clearly established, there is the group discussion of the key talents while reviewing their sustained performance over a period as well as their potential to identify their readiness for future roles and assignments. In this context also, their strengths and development needs are discussed to feed into the development planning process of these individuals at the end of which recommended training and development interventions, other developmental considerations like mentoring etc., are discussed for proper planning and the identification of the right programmatic interventions in support of expected growth. The feedback of the developmental discussions, assignments and initiatives are then communicated to the relevant stakeholders for implementation.

Figure 10.4 showing the process flow of the Talent Review Process (Amuah, 2016)

Below is the 9-box Talent Grid in which individuals are plotted based on sustained performance and potential per the discussion above.

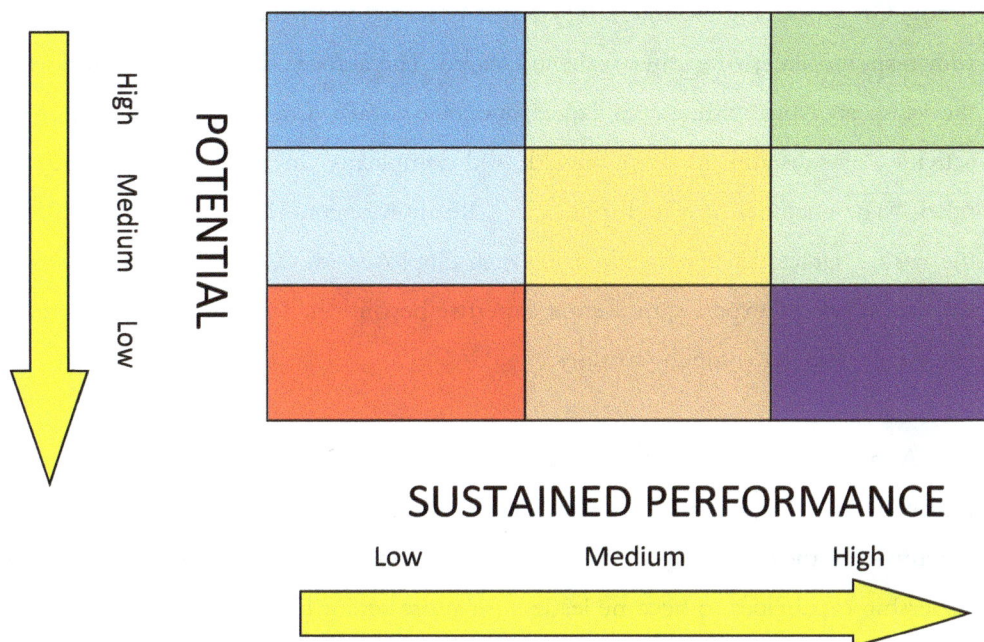

Figure 10.5 Demonstrating the Nine-box talent grid for talent review

Defining High Potential

Having discussed the talent grid and placing individuals in the various talent boxes with due consideration for their sustained performance, the following discussion will be to discuss what high potential is and is not. The term "high performer" is often used interchangeably with "high potential," however, the two are not synonymous. Research has shown that high potentials are almost always high performers, but the reverse is not always true. An assessment of most companies studied for this chapter confirms that the best firms understand that an individual's current performance and his or her future potential for advancement are two fundamentally different measures. Performance is typically defined during the talent management process and is often a combination of delivering business results (the "what") with the exhibition of certain behaviours expected of leaders (the "how"). While performance is evaluated in a historical context, typically over the past six months to a year, potential is a future-directed assessment. Specifically, a person's potential refers to their ability to take on a position of greater responsibility within a specific time period.

In a *Harvard Business Review* article, "How to hang on to your high potentials", Fernández-Aráoz, Groysberg and Nohria (2011) define potential as a person's ability to succeed in roles with responsibilities of greater scale and scope. The authors define 'greater scale' as a job in the same area but with, say, a larger budget or staff. 'Greater scope' is a job involving activities of substantially more breadth and complexity. In a *Business Strategy Review* article titled, "The anatomy of a high potential", Ready, Conger, Hill, and Stecker (2010) identify the basic characteristics of a high potential employee as: delivering strong results credibly and not at others' expense; mastering expertise beyond the technical; and, behaving in ways, consistent with the company's values.

The Aon Hewitt approach to defining high potential builds on a multi-faceted approach pictorially represented below and which states that organisations typically identify high potentials as those employees, or leaders, who possess the business acumen, vision, and leadership capabilities to become leaders (or more senior leaders) within the company. They look for the skills and attributes that allow top talent to propel into more challenging roles within a relatively short time frame. However, this definition of high potential fits only one piece of the puzzle.

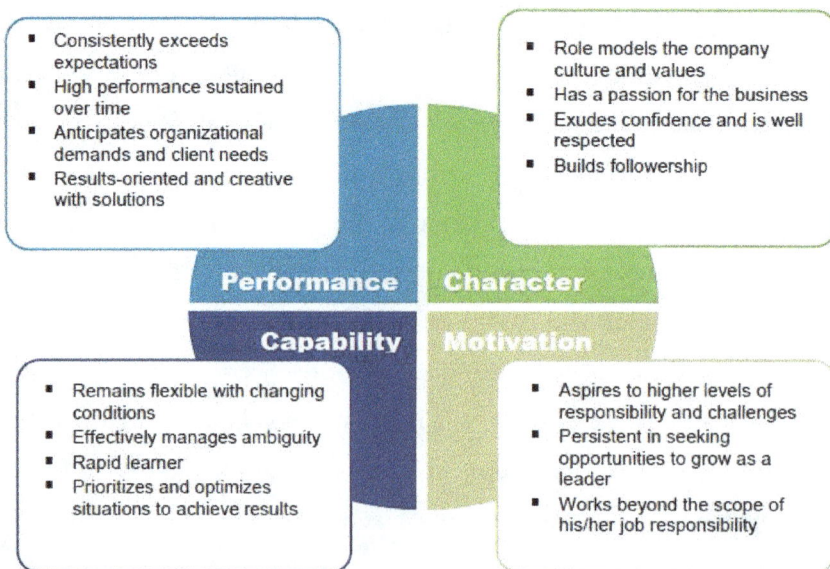

Performance
- Consistently exceeds expectations
- High performance sustained over time
- Anticipates organizational demands and client needs
- Results-oriented and creative with solutions

Character
- Role models the company culture and values
- Has a passion for the business
- Exudes confidence and is well respected
- Builds followership

Capability
- Remains flexible with changing conditions
- Effectively manages ambiguity
- Rapid learner
- Prioritizes and optimizes situations to achieve results

Motivation
- Aspires to higher levels of responsibility and challenges
- Persistent in seeking opportunities to grow as a leader
- Works beyond the scope of his/her job responsibility

Figure 10.6 the Aon Hewitt Potential definition chart

Organisations must focus their efforts on employees who demonstrate potential combined with readiness. Aon Hewitt defines potential as the assessment of an employee's ability to rise to and succeed in a more senior or expanded role. Potential considers individuals' performance, character, capability and motivation.

These definitions are very critical in how they contribute to the succession planning and leadership drive of any organisation.

Succession Planning

"A person who does not worry about the future will shortly have worries about the present" (Ancient Chinese Proverb). Succession planning is a talent management programme that is vital to an organisation's long-term health, growth and stability. Where the leadership of an institution plans strategically, there is clear recognition that they are strategically managing the human capital to drive transformation and to support the accomplishment of the institution's goals; that is, succession planning is a necessary part of the process. Conducting an appropriate gap analysis and developing professional competencies is understood as key to future organisational success. Succession planning is the deliberate and systematic effort made by leadership of organisations to recruit, develop and retain individuals with a range of leadership competencies capable of implementing current and future organisational goals (Leibman et al., 1996, Seniwoliba, 2015). Succession planning can also be described as the application of a consistent set of specific procedures to ensure the identification, development, and long-term retention of talented individuals. While this general definition works well, firms view succession planning in many different ways (Schoonover, 2011).

For some firms, it simply means making sure there are replacement candidates for key positions; for others with a more comprehensive perspective, succession planning represents a deliberate and systematic effort to ensure leadership continuity in key positions; retain and develop intellectual and knowledge capital within key employees for the future; encourage individual advancement; ensure the stability or 'bench strength' of key personnel; provide an overarching approach to continue effective performance of the firm; and organise concerted programmes for the development, replacement, and leveraging of key people to ensure a deep talent pipeline. The importance of succession planning and management cannot be overemphasised as the above discussion has highlighted that it is necessary for several reasons: the continued survival of the organisation depends on having the right people in the right positions at the right time. Seniwoliba (2015) opines that, succession planning is essential to encourage diversity and multiculturalism and avoid 'homo-social reproduction' by managers and succession forms the basis for communicating career paths, establishing development and training plans, establishing career paths and individual job moves.

To have a successful succession planning model in an organisation, every effort must be made to develop employees to ensure that they become highly qualified employees who are capable of filling critical positions in the organisation today and in the future. Succession planning is therefore a vital element to both workforce planning and strategic planning in any organisation. In today's dynamic world where competition is high, work is fluid, environment unpredictable, organisations flatter, and where the organisational configuration repeatedly changes, the old view of succession planning by defining specific individuals for specific tasks does not work. Modern organisations perceive the necessity for creating a pool of high-potential future candidates, at all organisation levels, to fill any needs, at any time. In the past, organisations were busy searching for a substitute for top executives and CEOs when their current top leaders were due to move out. At present, organisations are more aware of the importance that succession planning possesses new perspective; and that, selecting at all levels of the organisation, preparing, developing, and retaining high-potential future leaders is their bridge to maintaining sustainable competitive advantage in today's highly revolutionary environment. Developing and retaining future leaders is important to make sure that those human assets are there and ignore any outside temptation to leave their organisations.

During this process of succession planning, there are several steps which are followed to ensure that talents are ready to succeed in the roles they are being prepared for. Figure 10.7 below highlights these stages. First of all, there is a clear time line defined for the preparation, training and development of the talent for the role in question. Secondly, there is a defined 'content' comprising the skills, knowledge (WHAT) and the leadership style, values (HOW) which are used to develop the individual through an 'outside-in' training and development intervention using the 70-20-10 model earlier discussed under Learning and Development. These are done over a four step strategy cutting across the three dimensions of normative, strategic and operational aspect of work.

Step one is to clearly define the skills, knowledge, abilities, aptitudes, values, leadership skills and styles expected of the role in question for the individual. Step two involves the assessment of the individuals identified to have the potential to fit in the role against the earlier defined criteria in step one. The next step, step three, is the selection of the best fit candidate who will then undergo a development intervention and capability taking into consideration their current knowhow, skills and abilities in comparison with the expectation from the position they are being prepared for. Finally, step 4 involves the practical aspects of gradually initiating the individual into the role by making them take on some responsibilities in the new role for which they will be assessed. Throughout this process, there is always the ongoing SWOT to ensure that the individual is in touch with internal and external trends and the capability plans are adjusted accordingly.

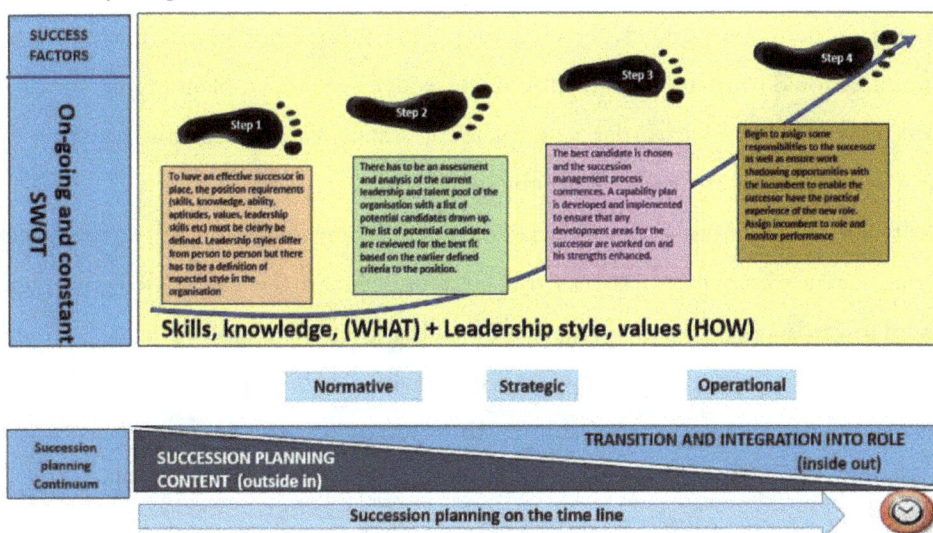

Figure 10.7 showing the steps and process flow for succession planning (Amuah, 2016)

Importance of Succession Planning

Today, organisations find themselves in a fast moving, high pressured, competitive society, where the slightest advantage may give one firm a valuable edge especially with globalisation where national boundaries have become porous and almost non-existent. For any organisation to grow and expand it is imperative that it is built and maintained on strong foundation. Undoubtedly, the best and strongest foundation for any firm is a pool of capable, talented individuals, who have grown with the firm, have imbibed its culture, gained a thorough understanding of the procedures, policies, processes and systems as well as absorbing its knowledge. Such individuals are ready to move up to higher and more senior and pivotal leadership roles in the organisation.

When an organisation loses talents to other firms and have to replace the workforce, the workforce might be replaced in a short time, but what the firm actually loses is a large quantity of organisational memory and essential skills. There are many factors which influence succession planning to be successful and effective, even though each organisation will be quite unique in its specific features. Meharabani and Mohamed (2011) came up with the following factors as part of their research findings:

i.) Training: Training plans help the employees to learn new skills and knowledge and therefore give them new abilities. Trained people are more empowered. Therefore, training programmes should be made available for any effective succession planning.

ii.) Management Support: In order to implement a successful succession planning system, there is a need for a lot of support from the managers.

iii.) Clarifying the career path is another factor where an organisation clarifies the career path that would eventually help employees to better understand the career objectives and also help them towards a better implementation of succession planning.

iv.) Another factor is creating a positive vision which will help create a positive insight towards succession planning programmes thus removing fear in employees who think succession planning is a threat to their positions in the organisation. Having a strong organisational culture which provides values, beliefs, standards and paradigms for all employees also affects effective succession planning.

Employees can consider these values, beliefs, standards and paradigms as a guideline for their everyday performance. Therefore, these values and standards should support the succession:

- Reduced time to fill critically-important positions
- Reduced turnover of high-potentials
- Improved customer service
- A more systematic and cost-effective approach to developing high potentials
- Improved alignment between staffing and organisational strategic goals

- Improved alignment between employee development efforts and organisational strategic goals

- A better match between the people you need and the people you have

- A deeper talent pool available for you to draw on as needs arise

- Better decision-making about who to promote

- Enhanced competitiveness by focusing promotion decisions on issues more effectively linked to the organisation's competitive advantage

The assessment evaluated organisational performance in four succession planning programme dimensions.

- Identification: How well the firm has identified its succession planning needs, linked needs to goals, and goals to strategic vision. The *identification score* is a weighted factor in the overall 'potential' rating of the firm's programme.

- Assessment: How well the organisation has used the identification pieces to assess their needs, and assess individual/department promotion potential. The *assessment score* is a weighted factor in the overall 'potential' rating of the organisation's programme.

- Development: How well the firm has worked with individuals to shrink the development gaps, and moved forward in helping each area develop talent pools. The *development score* is a weighted factor in the overall 'performance' rating of the firm's programme.

- Management: How well the organisation has actively kept senior management, department level management, and individuals appraised of progress, encouraged active participation on succession planning programming, and evaluated the programme and then responded to needed changes. The *management score* is a weighted factor in the overall 'performance' rating of the organisation's programme.

Job descriptions must be used as a foundation for all talent management programmes including succession planning as they help identify and communicate expectations of the role, requirements, accountabilities and the attributes that underpin success in the organisation. Job descriptions facilitate talent matching through the assessment of an individual's readiness and capability for the roles they have been identified to succeed in. The process also needs to take into consideration the individual career aspiration as career progression and changes in roles of individuals which do not excite the successor could ultimately lead to their downfall.

Employee Relations

Employee relations is essentially about how the HR function of an organisation implements various philosophies of engagement, commitment, high involvement and empowerment to motivate employees and ensure that ultimately there are more objective and alternative vehicles and fora for communications. Employee relations skills and competencies remain important and pivotal to an organisation achieving performance benefits. Employee relations has evolved over the period to focus on gaining and retaining employee commitment and engagement in the organisation and mitigating demotivation and employee turnover resulting from resignation.

Employee relations include several aspects of the contract of employment between an employee and the organisation. Some of these activities are:

- Managing the employment contracts of employees which include core aspects like compensation, working conditions, code of conduct, discipline, absence, health and safety, legal basis, etc.

- Ensuring that that the organisation is compliant with all legislature pertaining to employment, redundancies, termination of contracts, minimum wage, working hours, unfair dismissal, discrimination, etc.

- Ensuring and driving direct communication with employees through engagement sessions, direct communication, individual/team briefing, management of employee surveys for data collection and information, etc.

- Promoting retention, involvement and engagement through policies which enhance work-life balance, working in teams, collective bargaining negotiations and discussions with or without unions and key opinion leaders, and establishing a partnership mentality with the workforce.

More often than not, line managers are able to identify employee voice as contributing to performance and productivity when they are able to express their concerns, opinions about work. When employees feel engaged with the organisation, there is higher employee commitment and satisfaction than what is derived from the machinery for negotiation and consultation. Employee relations also entail mechanisms which are used to drive two-way communication through joint consultation, project teams, etc. Firms can drive engagement further by leveraging on technology which is used to drive higher performance in recent times.

Avenues such as electronic media, attitude surveys, etc., are options available to the firm. Attitude surveys usually provide organisations feedback about the state of the psychological contract between the firm and employees. HR practices have a strong impact on the way people feel about their work. The attitude of employees towards job satisfaction, commitment to work, work-life balance and the state of employee relations of an organisation are profoundly impacted by the sense of belonging that employees feel towards and trust the firm, their perception of how fairly they are being treated, and the extent to which they perceive that the organisation has fulfilled the terms of their agreement.

Employee relations is a very critical role in HR because the HR function is assessed based on the effectiveness of their employee relations and how visible HR is perceived in organisational activities which seek both employee satisfaction and productivity. Employee relations is perceived as synonymous with the entire field of HR. Employee relations is very strategic and the HR function should be able to manage and deal with employees from both an individual and representative perspective. Employees usually join an organisation with enthusiasm, motivation and desire to grow and contribute to its viability and growth. How this mindset is maintained is indicative of how well employee relations are implemented in an organisation.

Employee relations specialists need to have the following critical skills to have an impact on employees: mastery of the legislature governing collective bargaining, employee representatives, general employment, facilitation, negotiation and communication skills, business acumen; understanding of how to develop trust and respect as well as exhibiting personal qualities of objectivity, robustness, confidence and courage to express themselves to employees across the hierarchy of the organisation including senior management, emotional intelligence and diversity management. These competencies are critical because in most organisations, it is not senior management who engage employees or trade unions or opinion leaders or employee representatives in negotiations and discussions, it is the employee relations specialist who does that. This highlights how important it is for a firm to acquire the right talent to manage this function successfully.

Compensation and Benefits

Compensation and benefits is that sensitive part of the employment contract that usually is perceived to be the element that employees are most interested in when considering the total employment value proposition of an organisation and it usually scores low in employee surveys. Other organisations also refer to it as remuneration and benefits. Regardless of how this unit of HR is called, it is usually linked to the organisational structure, talent acquisition and recruitment, employee retention, motivation, performance management, feedback, and satisfaction and these elements in total are the attraction and attrition forces of most organisations. For most employees, compensation is the equivalent to not only how they are paid, but ultimately, to how they are valued by the organisations they work for. The compensation or remuneration package is usually considered from a total rewards perspective as they include non-monetary, direct and indirect elements.

Non-monetary compensation or rewards are any form of benefit that an organisation gives to an employee but does not hold any tangible value. Usually some organisations have a structured and well defined recognition programme which also falls under non-monetary compensation. Monetary compensation, also known as direct compensation is the employee's basic wage which can be in terms of annual salary, monthly salary, weekly salary or an hourly wage that the employee receives in return for their services to the organisation. Direct compensation options include the cash wage paid to the employee as earlier mentioned, or/and an incentive pay which is a variable pay or bonus paid to employees when specific performance objectives are met. Some organisations also offer stocks or shares to reward excellent performance. There are also other types of bonuses which comprise a gift occasionally to applaud exceptional performance or for specific occasions.

Indirect compensation varies from firm to firm. However, there are statutory requirements such as social security and disability payments that every organisation must ensure is paid on behalf of the employees to state designated institutions. Other indirect compensation are retirement or pensions, paid leave, health insurance, relocation expenses etc., which are covered by the organisation for the employee. Flexible working hours especially for mothers and those working on lower jobs for work-life balance are other ways that organisations can make their compensation more appealing to employees. Competitive compensation packages are developed when there is a good combination of monetary, non-monetary, direct and indirect compensation to employees based on their position they are going to occupy, level of complexity, scope, impact as well as their skills and experience etc. Regardless of the various aspects of a compensation package, the non-negotiable aspects from an employee perspective is that the package should cover basic living expenses, be reviewed in response to economic indicators in a country such as inflation and currency depreciation against major world currencies.

A very important element in the compensation strategy for any organisation is internal and external equity. It is absolutely critical for the sanity of any organisation that they ensure that this is duly in place. Internal equity is the fairness and objectivity that is applied to the salaries of employees with the same or similar scope of work, impact, job descriptions, level, business, etc., while external equity refers to the relative wage/salary fairness compared to similar jobholders in different organisations within or without industry. A fair wage/salary is arrived at through intra and inter industry surveys usually conducted by a third party for all the participating organisations to do comparator analysis of jobs, levels, scope, impact and wages for individuals and map them to determine what a fair wage looks like on the labour market. Periodically organisations must conduct review of job descriptions for all positions as well as job evaluations across the organisation to enhance equity in compensation. Job evaluations allow for a more systematic and rational approach where jobs are evaluated according to compensable factors like experience, education, knowledge, skills, responsibilities, etc.

Some organisations also apply the broad-banding approach to compensation as used in a

183

Cornell University study (Milikovich & Bloom, 1995). With this approach, employees are placed on a five level scale which is developed based on parameters such us authority to make decisions, skills level and supervisory capacity. Other organisations also apply a skill-based approach where similar skills and qualifications are used as a basis of compensating employees rather than the job they do itself. This is typically done through grouping the individuals into skills classes to determine their pay levels for jobs. Eventually therefore, employees of similar skills are grouped together regardless of job titles or positions.

Conclusions and Implications

From the foregoing discussions, it is plausible to conclude that there is a positive relationship between effective human resource management, employee attitudes, commitments and business performance. The Human Resources function is a support function that governs the most important resources of an organisation. The above presentation clearly shows that though this function is very critical to the success of any business, it is imperative that organisations put in place procedures, processes, policies and structures across the various HR practices to make them useful and significant in the value chain of the firm. Until this is done, there is little or no chance for any organisation to experience business viability, growth and profitability.

This chapter serves as a manual for HR practitioners to play the role of effective business partners using HR as a key driver for business success. Other areas that need further research in human resource practice is how when these functions are outsourced to third party organisations, the firm would stand a better chance of growing further in the context of a lean organisational structure where core business is the focus.

References

- Daft, R. & Lane, P. (2013). *Management.* Mason, OH: Cengage Learning..
- Fernández-Aráoz, C., Groysberg, B. & Nohria, N (2011). How to hang on to your high potentials. *Harvard Business Review* 89 (10), 76-83.
- Leibman, M., Bruer R. & Maki, B. (1996). Succession management: The next generation of succession planning. *Human Resource Planning* 19 (3), 16-29.

- Mehrabani, S. & Mohamad, N. (2011). Brief review of succession planning and management approach, 3rd International Conference on Advanced Management Science, IACSIT Press, 19.
- Milikovich, G. & Bloom, M. (1995). Issues in managerial compensation research. *CAHRS Working Paper Series.*
- Ready, D., Conger, J., Hill, L & Stecker, E. (2010). The anatomy of a high potential. *Business Strategy Review* 21 (3), 52-55.
- Schoonover, C. (2011). Best practices in implementing succession planning. Schoonover Associates, LLC.
- Seniwoliba, J. (2015). Succession planning: Preparing the next generation workforce for the University for Development Studies, *Pearl Research Journals* 1 (1).

Chapter 11

Systems Development, Technology and Business Performance

Albert Antwi-Boasiako

Abstract

The relationship between Information Technology (IT) and business performance has been explored extensively within the industry and in academic research. The benefit of adopting IT innovation supported by a standardised systems development framework for business performance in a developing economy is generally understood within the business sector and well crystallised in strategic business documents. Even though some research findings suggest IT innovations may not primarily translate into business profitability (Koellinger, 2008), evidence suggests adopting an IT innovation generates IT business value which directly impacts on organisational performance (Melville et al, 2004; Koellinger, 2008). Further industry analysis suggests generating IT value from adopting IT innovation does not necessarily guarantee competitive performance for businesses. Thus, for businesses to achieve competitive performance from IT innovations, a strategic IT innovation model for competitive performance is required. The chapter explores the application of this model for sustainable competitive performance as well as its implications for business executives.

Keywords: *Systems development; IT innovations; IT business value; Competitive performance*

Introduction

Businesses and organisations have adopted Information Technology (IT) innovation by aligning technology initiatives with business goals in order to improve organisational performance. Adoption of IT innovation has seen significant increase in developing economies including Ghana. IT innovations have been implemented across all sectors of the economy and areas such as banking, insurance, e-commerce, education, health and e-government have seen significant investments. According to the World Bank Group, IT innovations are principal requirements for sustainable economic development[1] (2012).

---

[1] The World Bank Group – ICT for Greater Development Impact: *World Bank Group Strategy for 2012-2015.*

Considering the importance of Information and Communications Technologies, the United Nations Development Programme (UNDP) has developed the Information and Communications Technologies for Development (ICT4D) initiative to support growth and economic development with IT innovations in developing economies[2].

In the business environment, research has established a correlation between adoption of IT innovations and business performance. The term IT business value is usually used to refer to the impact of IT innovations on businesses. The IT business value is measured with different metrics including a firm's productivity, increased profitability, cost reduction, inventory reduction, overall competitiveness of the business and other business performance metrics (Hitt & Brynjolfsson, 1996; Kohli & Devaraj, 2003; Mukhopadhyay et al, 1995). Recent studies have identified IT business value as the organisational performance impacts of IT innovations that measure both efficiency impacts and competitive impacts (Melville et al, 2004). The above findings apply to both process and product IT innovations.

However, research has also established that adoption of IT innovation does not necessarily translate into competitive performance. Evidence exists that process improvements through IT initiatives may not necessarily translate into business profitability (Barua et al, 1995; Hitt & Brynjolfsson, 1996; Koellinger, 2008). For example, adopting electronic banking (e-banking system) by a financial institution enhances banking operational procedures and processes but this does not automatically translate into business profitability. Available evidence suggests businesses may also achieve immediate profitability through the adoption of appropriate IT innovations but such performance may not be competitive and sustainable. Thus, businesses may not be able to generate the full IT business value from such innovations due to both internal and external factors.

In addressing the issue of IT innovations and competitive performance, this chapter presents a practitioner's perspective on systems development, technology and business performance by asking critical questions. How and to what extent does the adoption of IT innovation translate into sustainable competitive performance? What are the key system development requirements for competitive performance through IT innovations? How can IT innovations

---

[2] The United Nations Development Programme (UNDP) - Information and Communications Technologies for Development (ICT4D)

guarantee competitive performance? What internal and external factors could impact on IT innovations for competitive performance in a developing economy? The chapter examines organisational practices which underpin IT innovations for competitive performance through analysis and application of a proposed Strategic IT Innovation Model for Sustainable Competitive Performance. The practical implication of the proposed model on businesses is further explored.

Technology & Business Performance

The relationship between technology and business performance continues to impact on organisational processes and practices. Most organisations rely heavily on information technology for their business functions which impacts on the firm's reliability, efficiency and responsiveness to the growing needs of customers and stakeholders in the current technology-enabled business environment. In today's IT marketplace, different technology options are available to choose from. There are available technologies for each kind of business environment. A multinational mining firm may decide to deploy an expensive Enterprise Resource Planning (ERP) system while a retail shop may focus on acquiring a Customer Relationship Management (CRM) system to enhance its business activities. Currently, one important characteristic being experienced in the industry is the customisation of IT-based innovations to meet firms' specific business needs.

Economic theory suggests business performance is mediated by certain innovative organisational initiatives and activities. IT innovation in particular has been identified as an enabler of a firm's performance. IT innovation in the business sector has focused on two primary areas – product innovations and process innovations. Product innovation represents the generation of a new production function, distinctive from an existing product while process innovation corresponds to the implementation of a new or significantly improved business process or a shift of a business process or delivery method with lower variable costs in the development of an existing product or service (Dasgupta & Stiglitz, 1980; Kamien & Schwartz, 1982; Shaked & Sutton, 1982; Vickers, 1986).

The application of technology-enabled product innovation and process innovation in the banking sector with specific examples will be helpful in explaining what constitutes both product innovation and process innovation. The introduction of a pre-paid payment card such as Visa in the banking sector represents product innovation. Thus, a new payment system has been introduced to facilitate payments for goods and services. This is a typical example of an IT engineered product innovation. The impact of this product innovation is significant – payment for goods and services can be made instantly. In addition, customers can pay for goods and services beyond the borders of the card-issuing country. An example of process innovation in the banking sector is the introduction of the internet banking system. With this IT-based innovation, customers are able to transfer funds both within the country and abroad through the internet without having to physically visit the branch.

The introduction of Visa pre-paid cards and adoption of the internet banking system by a financial institution may not directly translate into profit for the firm. This is because the relationship between technology innovation and business profitability is highly complex to be measured with such a simplistic economic analysis. Other macro-economic and micro-economic elements would have to be considered in such an analysis. However, the above account of product innovation and process innovation engineered by IT innovations highlights specific changes in organisational practices and activities which result in product and process-based benefits to the firm. Thus, there is a correlation between the adoption of either a product-based innovation or a process-based innovation by a firm and business performance. This is because in economic terms, business performance is measured not just in terms of the firm's direct profitability but with other business performance benchmarks.

In relation to this subject, the IT business value generated from the adoption of a particular IT-based innovation is another important business performance variable. Even though the adoption of IT innovations may produce some direct and immediate benefits such as enhancing specific business processes and activities, IT-based innovations may be implemented for strategic reasons that will provide sustained competitive advantage and superior performance for the firm (Melville et al, 2004).

The relationship between IT-related innovations and business performance can be examined further from a different perspective. IT-enabled innovations can be implemented not only to improve individual processes or to generate a new product or service but also to enable process and service synthesis and integration leading to improved efficiency and organisational performance (Basu & Blanning, 2003). For example, a banking software application may be deployed to integrate a customer's existing account with his or her pre-paid Visa card or a mobile money account. Firms adopt IT-based innovations to create the technology platform that enables integration of organisational processes as well as new products and services.

This section of the paper has established that IT-enabled innovations impact on business performance through the generation of new products or services, enhancement of intermediate business processes to improve organisational practices, and an integration of the firm's processes and services. There is compelling empirical evidence that IT-enabled innovations are clearly valuable for business performance (Koellinger, 2008; Kohli & Devaraj, 2003; Melville et al, 2004). However, the above business performance impacts do not necessarily translate into competitive performance for firms.

There are several internal and external factors that play a role in IT business value generation leading to competitive performance. The next section of this chapter investigates why IT-enabled innovations may not necessarily lead to a firm's competitive performance.

Why IT Innovations may not necessarily translate into Competitive Performance?
Adoption of IT innovation for competitive performance is influenced by both external and internal factors. A business may not be able to realise competitive performance from a cutting-edge IT innovation because of organisational-specific attributes and other external factors. Industry analysis suggests that the effect of external factors on IT innovation for competitive performance is quite significant in developing countries. This section analyses these micro and macro attributes that affect a firm's realisation of competitive performance.

Bharadwaj (2000) has identified three key factors that impact on IT-based innovations for competitive performance, namely IT infrastructure, human IT resources and IT-enabled intangibles. For a firm to achieve competitive performance, IT innovation should address these competitive performance factors. The example below illustrates how the combination of these factors impacts on competitive performance for a banking firm. An appropriate IT infrastructure such as a software application and other supporting IT infrastructure are required to adopt internet banking. It is equally important to have a team of IT professionals with skills and knowledge to manage an internet banking system across the bank. Other factors such as top management's involvement to align the project to the firm's goals, customers' orientation and their ability to use the internet banking platform are considered essential for the firm to realise the full goal of the innovative project. Firms which are unable to leverage these performance impact factors may fail to achieve competitive performance.

Industry analysis suggests some firms have failed to realise the full IT value from the adoption of IT innovations because of their failure to effectively integrate the nature of their businesses and the required IT innovations. A failure in business profiling in order to adopt corresponding system development information has been identified as a major constraint for competitive performance. Even though the business in question may realise some financial gains from IT innovations, the question of competitive performance over a period of time in an emerging competitive IT environment remains. A detailed analysis covering the nature of the business, the firm's operational and strategic goals and the macro environment in which the firm operates is required to generate the firm's profile. This will impact on the outcome of the system development analysis for the firm to adopt a particular IT innovation.

Firms operating in developing economies face further external challenges in realising competitive performance from IT innovations. There are specific factors that impact on the macro environment in which the firm operates. For example, government policy and regulation on IT, availability of specific IT based skills, national IT infrastructure, the general prevailing IT culture and availability of critical national infrastructure that supports IT growth and development could impact on how businesses benefit from IT innovations on a sustainable basis (Dewan & Kraemer, 2000; Jarvenpaa & Leidner, 1998).

While this chapter is not meant to analyse the entire macro environment for the adoption of IT innovations, it is imperative that these external factors are highlighted. This is because businesses are directly interlinked with specific in-country structures and systems which directly or indirectly impacts on business performance. For example, poor telecommunications infrastructure could affect a firm's adoption of internet banking. Lack of reliable and constant supply of power is a major constraint to firms providing data storage and hosting services – which directly supports IT-based services.

Government policy that promotes and provides incentives for IT adoption, state protection for online transactions, IT infrastructure such as national data centres and tax incentives to promote the development and adoption of IT are examples of initiatives that could impact positively on a firm's adoption of IT innovations in a developing economy.

A case in point which highlights experiences from developed economy is presented below. In the United Kingdom, it costs less to purchase a mobile phone using a credit or a debit card than to make the purchase with cash. This incentive has led all major retailers to integrate Point of Sale (POS) devices and online payment platforms into their operations. The incentive has also led to substantial patronage of such services by customers. The competitive performance impacts arising from such innovation is evident.

Evidence suggests some firms have failed to realise the full value from IT innovations because of their inability to re-align their IT innovations to the evolving competitive IT environment (Chesbrough, 2007; Melville et al, 2004; Powel & Dent-Micallef, 1997). A firm may achieve initial competitive performance from IT innovations but imitation over a period of time and the availability of the IT innovation in the market weakens such competitive performance. Technology is not static and therefore continuous innovation of IT-driven projects is required for a firm to achieve sustainable competitive performance. The next section of the chapter proposes a model for firms to adopt IT innovations to achieve sustainable competitive performance.

A Strategic IT Innovation Model for Competitive Performance

For a firm to achieve competitive performance from IT innovations, the adoption of the IT project itself should be guided by a competitive performance framework. This section reviews a proposed *Strategic IT Innovation Model for Competitive Performance*. The proposed model is designed to integrate key strategic and operational activities which underpin the adoption of IT innovations for competitive performance:

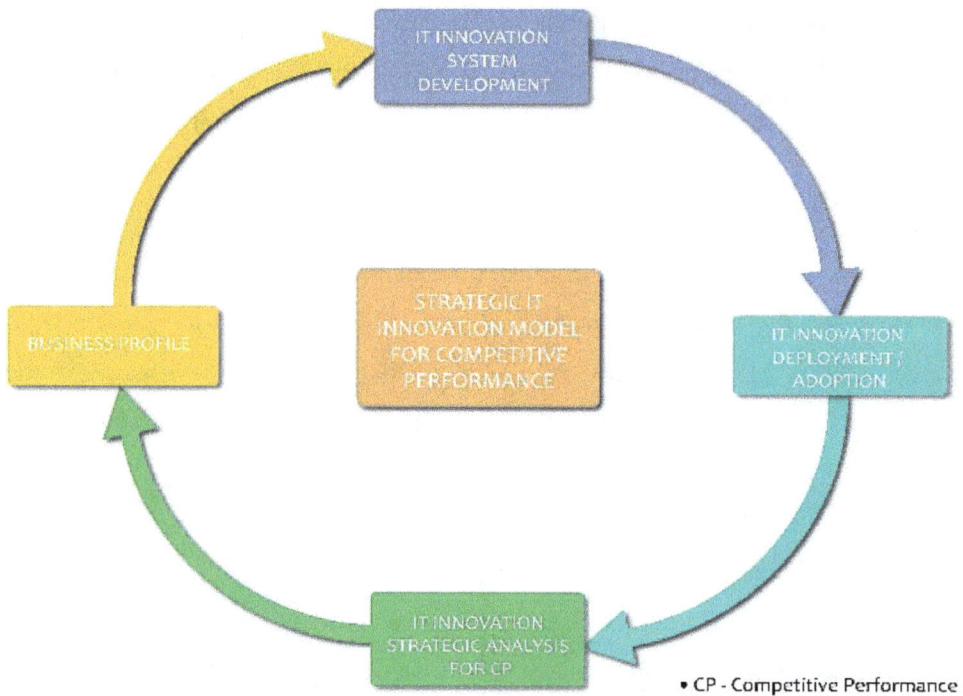

Figure 11: Strategic IT Innovation Model for Competitive Performance

The above model identifies four strategic and operational activities required to adopt any IT innovation, namely *Business Profile, IT Innovation System Development, IT Innovation Adoption/Deployment* and *IT Innovation Strategic Analysis for Competitive Performance*. The four strategic and operational activities are interconnected and hence impact on each other in order to realise the core objectives and performance expectations from IT innovations.

Business Profile – Business profile constitutes the profile of the firm and it is a product of a business analysis conducted before the adoption of IT innovations. For a firm to adopt any IT innovation, a detailed analysis covering the nature of the business, existing business operations practices and systems, the firm's strategic goals, competitive IT environment, market trends, the IT culture of the target market as well as other macro environment factors is required. For a firm to derive competitive performance, IT innovations should be responsive to the fundamental requirements of the business in a short, medium and long term. The business profile analysis is required to capture this essence before the systems development stage.

IT Innovation System Development – This stage covers gathering of requirements, analysis of the requirements and the design of IT-based innovations among other system development level considerations. System development requirements are based on the *Business Profile* for the adoption of IT-based innovation. The firm in question is required to analyse information from the *Business Profile* and ensure the IT innovation is strategically aligned with organisational goals. The firm is required to analyse the proposed IT innovation to ensure the system is compliant with the prevailing standards and best practices before the system is designed. Flexibility of the system and ability to integrate other technologies into the system are factors which are considered at the IT Innovation system development stage. This is because, the proposed *Strategic IT Innovation Model for Competitive Performance* requires re-alignment and re-engineering of existing IT innovations to achieve sustainable competitive performance. IT innovation system development specification is produced at this stage to serve as a blueprint for the design of the system.

IT Innovation Deployment/Adoption – Testing of the IT innovation system or platform, evaluation of the system's testing (pre-deployment test) and re-engineering (if required) to conform to system development requirements constitute this phase. IT innovations are deployed after the testing and evaluation. Firms are required to ensure that system development requirements – both for immediate deployment of the system and future re-engineering and possible IT-based integrations in the future are met.

IT Innovation Strategic Analysis for Competitive Performance (CP) – This is the most important component of the proposed IT model for competitive analysis. Firms which fail to realise the full value of IT innovations usually fail to consider this activity as an essential component for competitive performance. This stage requires firms to analyse results for competitive performance from IT innovations. Since IT innovations are dynamic, strategic analysis for CP requires businesses to examine the IT innovation from two perspectives – micro and macro analysis.

The first is a strategic analysis in relation to performance results, competitive IT value being generated from the adoption of the particular technology or innovation. Secondly, the IT innovation should be analysed in relation to other emerging technologies and innovations in the market for the competitive value. A practical demonstration is the adoption of online banking by a commercial bank. Current developments in mobile and SMS banking have rendered the traditional online banking system less attractive to customers and therefore less competitive. For example, analysis suggests other innovative products such as third party platforms – 'Aggregators'[3] are being introduced into the Ghanaian financial services industry to take advantage of the emerging mobile money market. Therefore, for a commercial bank which has already adopted internet banking, it becomes imperative to re-engineer the existing IT-based innovation (traditional internet banking) and integrate the new online business model to achieve competitive performance.

The nature of the business is also an important factor in strategic analysis for CP. For example, a profile of a firm may change in 3 or 5 years after the adoption of an IT-based innovation. In order to achieve competitive performance, the IT innovation should reflect on the new business profile of the firm.

Managing Technology Risks for Competitive Performance

Adoption of IT innovations creates specific risks for a firm. It is essential that business operators identify potential risks associated with the adoption of IT-based innovations in order to implement appropriate risk management tools and strategies to address them. Risk management is an essential component of a successful IT innovation for competitive performance. The risks associated with IT innovations are both technical and non-technical in nature. While each technology comes with its peculiar vulnerabilities and risks, managerial and human factors have been identified as major contributors to risks associated with IT-based innovations.

Business operators in developing economies face peculiar challenges pertaining to risks associated with IT innovations. Industry analysis suggests attack against Confidentiality, Integrity and Availability (CIA) of information systems has been identified as the topmost risks confronting firms operating in developing economies. The resulting data breaches and

---

[3] Aggregators are third party technology applications providers and platforms that assemble different Mobile Money operators such as MTN Mobile Money, VodaCash, Airtel Money and TigoCash onto a single platform. They provide services to the financial sector by integrating their centralised mobile money platform (application) into the core banking system. This enables customers to directly transfer funds from their accounts to any of the Mobile Money services.

fraud have wider regulatory impacts on firms as well as financial losses. It is essential to highlight one critical deficiency along the chain of IT based projects which precipitates attacks targeting IT-based infrastructures. Firms of all sizes have largely ignored security aspects of IT based innovations and this corporate culture has contributed to serious financial losses and reputational damages to firms. For example, a financial institution operating in Ghana lost more than 2 million euros to fraud through fraudulent transfer engineered by external hackers who compromised the core banking application. Analysis of the incident suggests security measures including intrusion detection systems, anti-malware programmes and other cyber security tools and controls to protect the application were not implemented when the core banking application was deployed. Further analysis suggests security considerations were marginally considered during the *IT Innovation System Development* stage.

Businesses in Ghana and other developing countries continue to suffer from fraud and other losses due to lack of user awareness arising from poor cyber security culture, inadequate cyber security control measures and business reliance on sub-standard IT applications and systems. Analysis conducted by e-Crime Bureau suggests businesses in Ghana lose an average of at least USD 150,000 per week to cyber facilitated fraud.[4] In an environment where IT regulation is almost non-existent, businesses are unable to distinguish between trusted IT applications and systems from sub-standard products which in many instances facilitate cyber-attacks. Firms' patronage of counterfeit IT products including pirated software programmes have also been identified as a major contributing factor to the high rate of cyber-attacks and fraud targeting firms.

While businesses face several IT related risks, cyber-attack remains the topmost risks faced by firms adopting emerging IT innovations. Industry analysts suggest businesses especially in financial services sector, IT-based businesses such as e-commerce and e-payment service providers and SMEs will continue to suffer cyber-related attacks until a substantial investment in cyber security is made to secure and protect IT-based innovations. Lack of

---

[4] The USD 150,000 figure quoted relative to cyber fraud is based on figures correlated from financial losses suffered by businesses who reported cyber fraud incidents for investigations and recovery in the year 2015. The Bureau received reports directly from affected businesses and also law enforcement including the Criminal Investigation Department (CID) of the Ghana Police Service and the Financial Intelligence Centre (FIC).

regulations, standardisation and enforcement of cyber security best practices have contributed to the problem. Government is therefore required to develop a comprehensive national cyber security policy and strategy with the aim of ensuring business security relative to IT innovations.

Implications for Policy Makers & Business Executives

We need to draw specific lessons from the above narrative pertaining to IT innovations and competitive performance. It has been established that, in the current technology-based economy, a mere adoption of IT innovation may not guarantee a firm's competitive performance. This is because an investment in IT has become a common business practice and adoption of IT innovation is evident across all sectors of the economy. The following pointers will guide both policy makers and business operators in adopting IT-based innovations to achieve a sustainable competitive advantage and superior performance:

- For a firm to realise the full IT value for competitive performance, the macro environment in which the firm's operates must be conducive. A policy that promotes adoption of IT innovation is required. Specific incentives such as tax waiver on IT-based services will encourage greater adoption and patronage of IT based products and services.

- Critical infrastructure such as electricity and telecommunications networks are major drivers of IT innovations for competitive performance. Policy makers should ensure the availability of such critical infrastructures in order to support adoption of IT innovations.

- Adoption of the right IT innovation to meet specific business requirement is key in achieving competitive performance. Business analysis is required to generate a *Business Profile* which forms the basis of system development requirement for a particular IT innovation.

- Technology is dynamic. Similarly, business profile changes from time to time. To achieve competitive performance, firms are recommended to re-engineer their IT innovations to re-align with the new business profile. Flexibility in IT innovation system development is therefore required.

- Adoption of IT innovation does not necessarily lead to competitive performance. It is recommended that organisational resources such as required skills, business operational practices, change initiatives and culture of orientation are harnessed to interface with the IT innovation in order to derive the maximum IT value on sustainable basis.

- For a firm to achieve competitive performance, it is not enough for business executives to protect their technological innovations from imitation. In our globalised economy, it is becoming almost impossible to protect technological innovations from competitors. As a result, business executives should rather focus on investing in the next technological innovation to sustain competitive performance.

- Risks are inherent in all IT based innovations. To achieve competitive performance from IT based innovations on a sustainable basis, firms are advised to treat IT risk management as a business investment.

Conclusions

This chapter has demonstrated that business innovations are mediated by information technology. Evidence suggests the adoption of IT innovation improves operational efficiency and leads to either process or product innovations. However, industry analysis strongly suggests that the adoption of IT innovation may not necessarily lead to the intended competitive performance. Both micro and macro factors have been identified as major constraints confronting firms from deriving full IT business value from such innovations. Other risk factors such as cyber-attacks targeting confidentiality, integrity and availability of information have been identified as the topmost IT risks facing firms which adopt IT innovations.

While appreciating that both internal and external factors affect a firm's drive to achieve sustainable competitive performance, the chapter has outlined specific policy recommendations and management best practices aimed at ensuring that IT-based innovations generate expected returns on sustainable basis. The proposed *Strategic IT Innovation Model for Competitive Performance* is recommended as a strategic management tool for business executives to adopt IT innovations, to analyse expected competitive performance measures and also to study the impacts of other IT innovations in the business operating environment in order to re-engineer and re-align existing IT innovations for sustainable competitive performance.

References

- Barua, A., Kriebel, C. & Mukhopadhyay, T. (1995). Information technologies and business value: An analytic and empirical investigation. *Information Systems Research* 6(1), 3-23.

- Basu A. & Blanning, R. (2003). Synthesis and decomposition of processes in organisations. *Information Systems Research* 14(4), 337-355.

- Bharadwaj, A. (2000). A resource-based perspective on information technology capability and firm performance: An empirical examination. *MIS Quarterly* 24(1), 169-196.

- Chesbrough, H. (2007). Business model innovation: it's not just about technology anymore. *Strategy & Leadership* 35(6), 12-17.

- Dasgupta, P. & Stiglitz, J. (1980). Industrial structure and the nature of innovative activity. *Economic Journal* 90, 266-293.

- Dewan, S. & Kraemer, K. (2000). Information technology & productivity: Evidence from country-level data. *Management Science* 46(4), 548-562.

- Jarvenpaa, S. & Leidner, D. (1998). An information company in Mexico: Extending the resource-based view of the firm to a developing country context. *Information Systems Research* 9(4), 342-361.

- Kamien, M. & Schwartz, N. (1982). *Market Structure and Innovation.* Cambridge: Cambridge University Press.

- Koellinger, P. (2008). The relationship between technology, innovation, and firm performance: Empirical evidence on e-business in Europe. *Research Policy* 37(8), 1317-1328.

- Kohli, R. & Devaraj, S. (2003). Measuring information technology payoff: A meta-analysis of structural variables in firm-level empirical research. *Information Systems Research* 14(2),127-145.

- Melville, N., Kraemer, K. & Gurbaxani, V. (2004). Information technology and organisational performance: An integrative model of IT business value. *MIS Quarterly* 28(2), 283-32

- Mukhopadhyay, T., Kekre, S. & Kalathur, S. (1995). Business value of information technology: A study of electronic data interchange. *MIS Quarterly* 19(2), 137-156.

- Powel, T. & Dent-Micallef, A. (1997). Information Technology as Competitive Advantage: The Role of Human, Business, and Technology Resources. *Strategic Management Journal* 18(5), 375-405.

- Shaked, A. & Sutton, J. (1982). Relaxing product competition through product differentiation. *Review of Economic Studies* 49, 3-13.

- The World Bank (2012). *ICT for Greater Development Impact: World Bank Group Strategy for 2012-2015.* Washington, DC: World Bank. Retrieved from: http://documents.worldbank.org/curated/en/2012/06/16557117/ict-greater-development-impact-world-bank-group-strategy-2012-2015

- Vickers, J. (1986). The evolution of industry structure when there is a sequence of innovations. *Journal of Industrial Economics* 33, 515-529.

Chapter 12

Strategic Thinking and Business Performance

Kwaku Appiah-Adu

Sam Aning

Nana Kegya Appiah-Adu

Abstract

This chapter explores the effect of strategic management on business performance and offers a range of methods to help executives to adjust their firms to the business environment in an effort to attain their primary goals. Properly utilised, strategic management can engender harmonious decision making and camaraderie. Nonetheless, to a large extent realisation of corporate strategy is dependent on the right conceptual viewpoint as opposed to particular devices, since devices by themselves can actually become an impediment to creative thinking, particularly in markets that are extremely turbulent, demanding steady adjustment and matching of strategy to varying conditions. Strategic management functions optimally when understood as a way of learning rather than a holy grail to follow. Consequently, the purpose of this chapter is to delineate strategic thinking using a developing country as an illustration for business executives operating in such settings to be ingenious and think creatively in respect of the typical challenges within their business environments. This chapter seeks to shed additional insight into the appreciation of the conceptualisation and realisation of strategic thinking processes in different contexts.

Keywords: *Strategy; Strategic thinking; Strategic management; Strategic planning; business performance; developing economies.*

Introduction

The 21st century's dynamic and highly competitive market environments call for managers who are well positioned to adapt expeditiously to change. Numerous paradigms have been advanced to help business practitioners in adapting to market evolutions and revolutions. Strategic management consists of techniques for developing a firm's long-term focus, articulating plans derived from internal and external environments and taking the appropriate action to realise the organisation's goals. It is suggested that strategic management models generate information, to facilitate a comprehensive deliberation of options, to forestall surprises, to cultivate ideas, to encourage motivation and to enhance internal discourse and other laudable organisational attributes.

Nevertheless, becoming an expert of strategy transcends the application of these techniques; it is a thoughtful process (Crosby, 1991; Jacobides, 2010; Martin, 2007; Mintzberg, 2008; Simons, 2010). A creative, strategic utilisation of the mind is not easy to prescribe. The techniques of strategic management are anticipated to promote problem solving, but the techniques can also become ends in themselves to the disadvantage of what they are projected to attain. By itself, accepting strategic management through the completion of forms and fulfilling the requirements of planning is not the only vita issue, but indeed it must also be supported by the capacity to think strategically.

This chapter seeks to present the distinct components of strategic thinking and expressly ascertain what it is. Using the experience of businesses and managers operating in Ghana, we also seek to share how managers in other emerging developing economies can become creative and think innovatively in respect of the specific challenges within their business environments. Through this approach, it is hoped that we can offer managers a dynamic approach in adapting to the unpredictable character and turbulence in the business environments of developing countries, particularly those in Africa.

As a concept, strategic thinking thus comprises ideas, processes and tools, of discovering fresh and creative methods to resolving problems, applying policy proposals and methodologies that facilitate for sound execution, monitoring, evaluation and feedback to improve the status quo. Though strategic management may not provide a universal cure or magic wand for changing the fortunes of organisations and other bureaucracies, it does not imply that its tools should be disregarded in organisational performance. This chapter hypothesizes that for firms operating in developing economies, if employed suitably as a basis to innovative and harmonious thinking, where unity in diversity can be arrived at, strategic management techniques may shed additional light on future prospects for businesses.

Strategic Thinking: The Conceptual Model

With respect to developing economies and the examples provided, it can be suggested that the starting point of strategic thinking is usually the recognition that there is a challenge that needs to be addressed or a matter that requires a solution. Nevertheless, the strategy to be formulated should take into consideration the internal capabilities and limitations of the firm in respect of the opportunities and threats in the marketplace. Using this process, strategies to be executed would be developed on a stronger footing and be better directed at addressing issues that need to be tackled. Consequently, strategic thinking is a reiterative cycle and as and when required the process can continuously be innovatively replicated to realise the appropriate strategy.

Figure 12.1: Strategic Thinking Chart

Strategy

While several definitions of strategic management have been proffered, the shared thesis that runs through most definitions is that it consists of the following elements:

- explicit objectives;
- environmental assessment;
- strategy crafting;

- evaluation of different sets of strategies;

- expressly stated assumptions;

- review and decision by executives;

- amalgamated plan;

- action programmes;

- monitoring and evaluating performance;

- review and feedback.

Clearly, strategy is management's ploy for strengthening the firm's locus, fulfilling customer needs and meeting performance objectives (Ackerman, Eden & Brown, 2004; Johnson, Paladino, 2010; Porter, 2008; Johnson, Scholes & Whittington, 2008). A soundly devised and executive strategy is one that amply enhances a market position and is buttressed by a relatively resilient organisation to deliver exceptional performance, despite the issues of unexpected occurrences, including fierce competition and internal challenges. This is particularly the case for private businesses.

Strategic decisions are cohesive and all-encompassing. They influence the whole firm and encapsulate either the vast majority or all of its elements. Strategic decisions are of high importance to a firm's progress and must be given the prominence they deserve. Examples in the market environment include: new business development; new market entry; mergers and acquisitions; exits or divestments. For strategy to be successful, executives need to appreciate the firm in question, its strengths, current markets and possible future markets. Moreover, they need to assess factors in the external environment that impact the capacity of the firm to achieve it selected targets. Furthermore, they need to determine and sustain a fit between the external and internal factors. This fit can be realized by including main constituencies in and outside the firm who can shape or affect its activities substantially.

Superior business performance is believed to result from being astute or judicious and from apportioning resources aptly among contending prospects to optimise the effect of the firm's capabilities. Failure is ascribed to lacklustre reactions to changes in environmental settings. It is difficult for a firm to maintain superior performance if it does not possess a sound approach to tailor its internal capabilities to driving factors in the external environment.

The Concepts of Strategic Planning and Strategic Management

As a notion, strategy has become sophisticated over the decades. At its inception, the foundation of a sound strategy was long-range planning. In the 1960s, many big firms established strategic planning departments for this task. This new approach encompassed a quest into new market and business arenas that the organisation should endeavour to move into, in contrast to the earlier method of forecasting the future based on the present, a method that was regarded as rather crude and optimistic (Drucker, 1974).

Owing to the complex market environments that made it almost impossible to forecast distant results too far into the future, strategic planning was not considered as a thorough approach to offer a springboard for a firm's development (Courtney, Kirkland & Viguerie, 1997; Neilson, Martin & Powers, 2008; Parker & Stacey, 1994). Therefore, by the 1970s, the focus had begun changing from strategic planning to strategic management. Rather than emphasising internal and external analysis and the formulation of splendid plans, implementation and evaluation became the focus as major components of a firm's success (Ansoff, Declerk & Hayes, 1976). These are the action and evaluation elements of strategy, without which mere planning is destined to be ritualistic, with insignificant practical impact.

By promoting implementation as a major component, strategic management underscores the political factor of managing institutions. Because strategic decisions originate from both organisational politics and objective evaluations, successful executives should negotiate, bargain and develop alliances in order to realise effective strategy implementation (Balogun & Hailey, 2008; Benveniste, 1989; Piercy, 2002;). Consequently, the strategic management process may be considered as consisting of five main elements which are *iterative* and not exactly successive in approach as outlined below:

- *Mission and Goals:* appreciating the firm's raison d'etre and developing a vision of where the firm should be seeking to be.

- *Analysis:* assess the external environment and internal capabilities.

- *Formulation:* devise a strategy to place the firm solidly, exploiting the competencies and prospects in the business environment.

- *Implementation:* assess performance and effect best-fit changes founded on intelligence and experience acquired and moreover in accordance with the evolving business environment.

Strategic Thinking

Owing to the evolution of pristine changes in the world of business, some advocates seem to be inclined toward the expression *strategic thinking* in firms (Martin, 2007; Wilson, 1994). This inclination may be attributed to the idea that, in reality, strategy cannot be managed. Actually, when faced with changing and turbulent business conditions, firms tend to depend on well-versed instincts and what has been learned from experience. Managers have to make decisions within the context of contradictory or imperfect information. They have to be creative and employ their experiential skills to make decisions and resolve challenges.

Noteworthy is the fact that informal strategies have constantly formed a part of managers' psyche. Also worthy of note is the fact that in today's business environment, good fate and inventiveness can have more far-reaching consequences than holding on rigidly to a strict strategic management archetype. Interestingly, without explicit adherence to strategic management techniques, many firms still perform creditably. While prescribed approaches may *enhance* informal procedures, the problem is that structured processes can *constrain* strategic thinking. What is needed is a deft combination of analytical and intuitive expertise. A strategic thinker should be innovative, open-minded, inspired and capable of managing successfully. Being at least one step ahead of change also involves collaboration and dedication to being vigilant and ready to embrace innovative ideas. Some of these intuition propensities are incompatible with methodical strategy theory and are not easily taught and imitated.

The approaches used by strategic management can boost strategic thinking – if these approaches do not become formalities that hamper the creativity of mind instead of motivating them. Unfortunately, the subject tends to have a methodological inclination (Cherulinam, 2008; Daft & Buenger, 1990). Equally, books for practitioners do not highlight the issues associated with strategy development and execution, with techniques that are relatively silent on the human aspect and tend to focus more on the figures (Bower and Gilbert, 2007; Freeman and Gilbert, 1988; Jacobides, 2010; Piercy, 2002; Simons, 2010). Although no authority can profess to possess total knowledge about sound strategic management so as to proffer a perfect template, strategic management cannot be viewed as a sheer routine procedure.

Strategy and Management in Developing Economies

Gleaning from prospects that creative thinking can be taught and replicated, strategic management paradigms have become widely accepted in several firms. This notion of management which originates from progressive change and benevolent environments seems gradually obsolete. Hence, the new view in developing countries is for managers to conduct themselves like entrepreneurs with strategic management providing direction.

Strategic management is regarded as a means of fortifying firms in developing countries (Appiah-Adu, 2000; Blunt & Jones, 1992; Brinkerhoff, 1991). Some private sector firms in developing countries are let down by the laidback mindset of their managers. Strategic management is an apt process of helping business practitioners in developing economies to be more responsive to their customers or clients.

In this context, local consultants and international donors have instituted interventions to build capacity in the development and implementation of strategic management. Under the auspices of these interventions, host nation firms usually worked with consultants to re-assess their visions, missions, goals, objectives and remits, to identify their internal strengths and weaknesses in respect of the marketplace and to undertake a stakeholder evaluation and other assessments pertinent to the business under consideration.

An important rationale for all of these interventions is the view that strategic management is culturally pertinent, globally valid, has worldwide appeal and unanimous value. This does not mean that the tools will be applicable equally in all corners of the globe. It is widely held that strategic management tends to be better suited to firms operating in industrialised or developed countries as opposed those in emerging, transition or developing countries. This cannot be ascribed to the cultural tendencies of strategic management techniques; instead, the turbulent socio-economic conditions of developing countries inhibit a firm's attempts to stick to its strategic plan (Appiah-Adu, 2000; Austin, 1990; Courtney, Kirkland & Viguerie, 1997; Jacobides, 2010). Undoubtedly, until the financial and economic difficulties faced by many of the world's economic superpowers in the first decade of the 21st century, major factors for ascertaining growth such as interest rates were usually steady. In several developing countries, the experience has been the opposite.

Compared to their colleagues in advanced nations, managers in developing countries have a tougher task in their efforts to detect and adjust to changes in the business environment. Nonetheless, this is an area where they appear to be deficient. Managers in developing countries seem to emphasise tactical concerns instead of strategic concerns. Actually, this tendency could be a response to the instabiity in their marketplaces. Strategising in the unstable conditions tends to involves reorganisation of resources earmarked for strategic management to crucial functional sections. A short sighted view and failure to reflect and act with the long term in mind may signify the start of a downhill swirl for the firm. In times of shortage and re-allocation, inflexible management systems typically do not permit the application of resources to generate fresh ideas or engender creativity that may have the ability to change developments.

Strategy therapy or Strategy axiom?
A firm that excels must have an effective strategy in one shape or form, because one distinctive characteristic of businesses that excel is to follow a plan that produces significant results. Alternatively, a waning organisation by description has a mediocre strategy or else it would not be on a downward spiral. Unfortunately, what represents an effective strategy is not easy to define. Although there are several maxims and techniques in strategic management, there are no strict tenets to mould the sequence of action.

Let us consider the concept of strategic innovation. It is widely contended that firms achieve superior performance by pushing out beyond existing frontiers into new ones (Balogun, Hailey, Johnson & Scholes, 2008; Hamel, 1994; 1996; Paladino, 2010). Managers who challenge their firms to aspire towards greater achievements instead of being content with the status quo tend to make major advances in their sectors. Some years ago, hardly did entrepreneurs consider the field of waste management as a potentially huge business opportunity in Ghana. Yet in the country's current business environment, it is common knowledge that the creative concept of providing services to the waste sector has made a company such as Zoomlion a household name. Not only has the company made appreciable efforts to tackle the issue of waste; it has indeed forged ahead to determine how waste can be converted to energy and other forms of use in the economy. A less radical approach inhibited by conservative confines would not have unearthed this novel area of business.

Nevertheless, it should be appreciated that breaking *the frame* is not a universal concept. One cannot overstate the importance of a time and tested principle in business, one that has been effective over the years, also known as *sticking to the knitting* (Peters & Waterman, 1982). Time is needed to master and reap maximum benefits from a ground-breaking strategy and firms would do well to exercise patience. As a decision-making guide, the presence of a strategy offers executives direction. Since strategy provides a framework for determining alternatives and selecting among them, it assists managers to appreciate and manage volatility and complexity.

Emphasising options could end up being beneficial for firms operating in developing countries that typically have turbulent socio-economic business environments and where resource constraints may compel managers to react to every change in the business environment. Three admirable cases of organisations in Ghana which have demonstrated superior performance in their respective sectors by being extremely successful at employing the 'sticking to the knitting' plan are Interplast Ghana Limited, Ecobank Ghana Limited and Rancard Solutions Limited.

Interplast Ghana Limited is West Africa's leading producer of plastic pipe systems. The company is a fully Ghanaian owned company with active export business in more than 20 African countries. It currently employs over 600 people. As one of the largest manufacturing companies in Ghana, Interplast is continuously expanding its production facilities and its product portfolio. Interplast invests considerably in its state-of-the-art manufacturing facility and quality raw materials. The company believes in creating quality products in order to bring a lasting difference in the infrastructural development of Sub-Sahara Africa. Interplast therefore produces not only according to the highest quality and current European standards but has also adopted the ISO standards for company management and operational procedures according to ISO 9001 and has been certified for many years. For over 40 years

Interplast's choices have provided its customers with reliable and quality materials. As a result, the company has earned the trust of many West African Governments, European construction companies and numerous other respected clients in many different fields of operation.

Ecobank Ghana Limited is engaged in merchant banking, investment banking and retail banking. It also operates through two wholly owned subsidiaries Ecobank Investment Managers Limited, engaged in the management of investments, and Ecobank Leasing Company Limited, which is engaged in providing finance lease facilities. The Bank is a subsidiary of Ecobank Transnational Inc. It has emerged as the Best Bank of the Year in Ghana's Annual Banking awards over the last few years. Ecobank's focus is on providing high quality products and services to its customers who comprise individuals, small and medium scale companies, large local corporates, parastatals, non-governmental organisations and multi-national companies. A state of the art technology, excellent customer service and a reliable telecommunication system constitute the backbone of the bank's product delivery strategy. In addition to the traditional products and services, the bank offers products and services including internet banking, telephone banking, and Ecobank regional cards. Because its aim is to consistently offer its customers efficient, reliable and excellent service, the bank forms an integral part of the Group's One Bank concept, which aims at standardising the Group's processes and procedures irrespective of geographical location or language differences.

Rancard Solutions Limited is a privately held, profitable software company focused on delivering software programmes and services to businesses and organisations who intend to deliver services and content to mobile users. Its name, Rancard means two things; information and rendezvous. The combination of these two words is very important to the company because this is what Rancard does. Its mission is to connect the world's leading brands to relevant mobile audiences at the minimum cost per subscriber acquisition. Rancard sets out to create a truly world class technology company out of Africa which would solve relevant problems of scale for businesses across the continent and beyond. Rancard is focused on helping leading companies everywhere connect better with relevant mobile audiences.

These firms have steadily sharpened and enriched their skill in the offering of 'products' and 'services' in their respective business sectors and are at the present moment a step ahead of their competitors, not only in Ghana but indeed in the whole of West Africa. 'Sticking to the knitting' may not be the best option in all conditions because a traditional or conventional strategy can disintegrate into unfruitful, knee-jerk rejection of a positive transformation. Nonetheless, what distinguishes champions (such as Interplast Ghana Limited, Ecobank Ghana Limited and Rancard Solutions Limited) from the also-rans in the midst of those who employ such a strategy is the capacity to re-package themselves based on deep-rooted tenets of success in an inimitable manner that leaves their rivals constantly battling to catch up. The issue with strategic management is that the subject offers incomplete guidance as to what kind of strategy is most suitable in a given set of existing circumstances. Retroactively, identifying a sound strategy is simple – it can be done basically by assessing the best-performing firms. The exercise is more arduous when predicting the future. Sound knowledge and judgment are needed as opposed to quantitative techniques to resolve this matter.

Strategic Management Tools

Regardless of the challenges associated with strategic management, strategic thinking continues to be a valuable element of management's responsibilities and organisational development. Though it may be needless to assert that a firm's superior performance is attributed to possessing the *appropriate* strategy, it is reasonable to submit that executives are likely to fare better if they analyse their business and the prospects available to it. Making an attempt to foresee events is superior to leaving matters to fate.

Executives who apply strategic management tools consider that it sharpens their focus, improves their understanding of the marketplace, fuels their readiness to change, and offers a range of tangible and intangible benefits (Appiah-Adu, Morgan & Katsikeas, 1996; Appiah-Adu, 2000; Kaplan & Norton, 2008; Kim & Mauborgne, 2009). Nonetheless, few executives know how to create better outcomes employing these tools. The inclination is to be obsessed with the frills of strategic management, hardly ever tackling the tough, creative duties needed to implement the task successfully. When the techniques turn into a routine ceremony, they cause a problem of suffocating the firm rather than offering a thrust for its development.

Firms in developing economies have a greater propensity to face serious challenges in undertaking the day-to-day tasks of management, let alone tackling strategy. In this respect, strategic management tools can become the foci of strategy on their own, and the crux of strategy is misplaced, a fact which may be well appreciated by giving greater thought to the tools of strategy.

Mission and Goals

Strategic management is established on the notion that successful firms have a continuity of goals and accord on fundamental principles and what is to be achieved. In turbulent environments, an assured uniqueness can promote change management by providing a pivotal focus for all in the firm. A major function of strategic management is to engender this sentiment of team spirit.

For firms operating in developing countries the principle of having a mission is highly important due to the propensity for executives to be overwhelmed by day-to-day operational issues. It is essential for managers to be mindful of this and for them to expressly address the broader longer-term mission of their firms continually.

Over the last decade, many development partner programmes have encapsulated attempts that have been made to work with managers of local firms to improve their mission statements. Examples of some of these interventions are those that have been made by the Danish International Development Agency (DANIDA), Business Sector Advocacy Research Fund (BUSAC), African Project Development Facility (APDF) and the erstwhile Enterprise Support Services for Africa (ESSA) to assist small and medium-sized firms to formulate sound strategies to provide them with the opportunity to compete successfully in their respective business environments.

A point that cannot be disregarded is how to develop mission statements, which tend to involve a summation of the firm's strategic aspiration and business orientation. These assertions are currently trendy as a way of maintaining the firm on track. Contemporary mission statements tend to focus on collaboration, creativity, quality, quest for excellence and customer value, among other ideals (Davenport, 2006; Neilson, Martin & Powers, 2008; Paladino, 2010). Nevertheless, mission statement tools are quite challenging to apply in real life. Mission documents are usually orthodox, bland and inconsistent with the true competencies of the firm, with the result that the grand expressions they encompass are hardly taken seriously.

This is not to say that the idea of mission statements is deficient; on the contrary, it suggests that gaining commitment from the workforce for a unified purpose is not easy to attain. Firms with stunning mission statements devote significant resources to forums in an effort to get their workforce to achieve a better understanding and gain their support for each distinct element of the mission. A slightly more challenging facet may be to establish commitment to the mission through actions or conduct. A pretentious mission is inferior to having none since the former triggers staff scepticism, which, in turn, has an adverse effect on the firm.

Analysis

Under the auspices of strategic management, managers are encouraged to assess their firms internally as well as the external marketplace for business opportunities. One popular technique undertaking this scan is the Strength, Weaknesses, Opportunities and Threats (SWOT) analysis. The idea is to look for fits between the firm's competencies and opportunities but against this backdrop, the firm should be seeking to minimise the potential effects of its weaknesses and the threats posed by conditions in its business environment. This technique has been applied widely in the private sector. Various development partner projects have endeavoured to foster the ability of managers to apply the SWOT technique to many developing countries, with positive results. Participants in workshops to develop linkages amongst businessmen and women in West Africa attest that the SWOT tool is one of the useful analytical techniques they employed (Davenport, 2006; Hitt, Ireland & Hoskisson, 2006; Orsini, Courcelle & Brinkerhoff, 1996).

Nonetheless, this tool must be applied with an understanding of its limitations. While there is no conceptual basis for determining the key internal and external factors, there is neither a non-subjective technique for measuring their significance. One staff member's view of the firm's internal strengths may be another staff member's internal drawback.

Perspectives of market prospects and threats may also be affected by analogous misperceptions. To large extent, managers are likely to perceive threats more readily compared with market prospects and, therefore, in assessing the marketplace, managers erroneously overstate the undesirable and underplay the positive. A successful firm may tend to be content with the business environment, leading managers to think that the marketplace is benevolent, while in actual fact it may not (Courtney, Kirkland & Viguerie, 1997; Hitt, Ireland & Hoskisson, 2006; Milliken & Lant, 1991; Simons, 2010).

Strengths, weaknesses, opportunities and threats which are usually derived from the analysis of the internal environment of a firm as well as the external environment comprising the political, economic, social, technological, legal, ecological and demographic conditions in which the firm operates, are all susceptible to personal perceptions and action. The attributes and specific circumstances of an organisation may change vary in reaction to what the pertinent actors assume they are. The point is that the consequences of SWOT assessment can be diverse and subjective or highly reliant on who is undertaking the assessment. Consequently, attempts must be made to tackle this issue by involving diverse stakeholders in strategy development.

Formulation

Currently strategy is perceived as a process to be navigated, not imposed. This shift of emphasis sets the focus on stakeholder assessment, involvement, collaboration and support. Stakeholder assessment seeks to address issues such as: on whom is the firm reliant for its existence? Who are the winners and losers amongst the stakeholders from a selected strategy? Who has been excluded? Who can be left out without creating damage? What should be done to gain the support of all important groups? The commitment of stakeholders for a chosen strategic posture leads to effective strategy development and implementation. In developing countries, it is widely recognised that important stakeholders need to be included for most projects to succeed and have an impact (Appiah-Adu, 2000; Appiah-Adu & Aning, 2012; Cullen, 2008; Kinsey, 1988). In today's business environment, stakeholder assessment assumes greater importance as a more egalitarian means of decision making.

It is important to note that in developing strategy, managers in developing countries must endeavour to determine stakeholders and involve them in the process. Amongst several managers in developing nations, additional insight is engendered when they understand the importance of collaborating with major stakeholders (Appiah-Adu & Singh, 2011; Ink, Klaus & Boynton, 1994; White, 2004). The task here is to be able to recognise major stakeholders instead of prospective groups. It is also vital for managers to respond positively to what they deem to be concerns of their stakeholders or else they are likely to fall short of expectations. Where executives get fixated with the trapping rather than the substance of stakeholder participation, it may exclude groups and cause further problems. Stakeholders must be granted the needed consideration for this technique to be successful.

Implementation

An essential feature of effective strategy implementation is the culture of the firm, also referred to as the patterns of shared values. A match between culture and strategy is a powerful lever for transforming behaviour and job performance in a refreshing strategy-supportive manner (Piercy, 2002; Mankins & Steele, 2005; Balogun & Hailey, 2008; Paladino, 2010). Managers would do well to employ both tangible and intangible approaches of developing cohesion. Managing organisation culture involves working on shifting any aspects of cherished principles that are impeding the execution of strategy. The task here is to recognise which forms of culture lead to which magnitude of performance in what types of firms within what business conditions.

Effectiveness in assessing and changing values in a firm is critical because they impact on the firm's policies (Eisenhardt & Sull, 2001; Mintzberg, Lampel & Quinn, 2007; Piercy, 2002; Simons, 2010). It is important to recognise that a formidable group culture does not necessarily provide the assurance that strategy execution will be successful. This is a challenge in several developing country firms that are restrained by severely embedded regressive cultures. The ultimate collapse of many consultancy assignments undertaken for private firms operating in developing economies is, partly, due to the failure of the organisations' employees to adapt to fresh thinking and approaches to getting things done. Unquestionably, positive advancement is achievable. Though new culture attitudes and conduct can be instituted through the endeavours of a firm's executives, they are difficult to maintain over the long haul and not necessarily easy to reproduce in different settings.

Implication for Managers

When the concept of strategic thinking is promulgated, one is referring to a successful strategy which guarantees that firms continuously demonstrate superior performance regardless of the difficulties and the turbulence in the business performance. Therefore, though a suite of techniques, processes and systems may be useful, it is neither the techniques nor the systems per se which deliver the strategic advantage.

Executives need to recall that inability to be creative and envision continuously with regard to the complexities of business environments in developing countries would make it rather hard for them to achieve growth. The subtleties of the business environment are constantly fluctuating and certainty grounded in established factors may not constantly be present or conceivable. Therefore, a propensity for analysing the marketplace developments and possessing an adaptable mind-set that facilitates coherent thinking and creativity is what is needed. This approach would permit the alignment of internal organisational requirements to the external opportunities and dynamics so that appropriate strategies are formulated to guarantee superior performance (Appiah-Adu & Singh, 2011).

This kind of coherent reasoning, together with configuration, sequencing and successful communication, is also needed to realise organisational goals (Appiah-Adu & Aning, 2012). When this has been successfully achieved, it is essential to execute the fresh initiative. Though concerns about competing resources would constantly be an issue, for several executives operating in the developing world, this can be surmounted by successful prioritisation in the strategy development phase.

Conclusions

Evidently, strategic thinking, which is perceived as the capacity to learn from the environs as the firm embraces a broader viewpoint, is a peculiar characteristic of effective management. Drawing conclusions from a universal perspective is crucial because of the shifts in the marketplace which most firms will experience as we advance into the twenty-first century.

Additionally, it is quite clear several executives in developing countries usually tackle their issues in parts instead of being strategic. Rather than focussing on events in the marketplace, they dwell unduly on internal issues. Owing to budget reductions, growing competition, swift changes in technology, and changing demand for their products, this short sighted posture is totally what is needed in emerging developing countries.

Any methodology that allows executives to focus on the big picture and limits opportunities to place needless emphasis on routine procedures is worthwhile. Strategic management can be a valuable tool, but, equally, it can be an encumbrance if applied in a monotonous manner. A problem which executives must be aware of is that strategic management techniques are usually reductionist, separating strategy into discrete tasks. Completing these tasks can supersede the actual goal of formulating the complex, total design of a firm's strategy. Inflexible or arbitrary judgment, even regarding strategic direction, is at variance with the all-inclusive, amalgamated approach which is needed. Instead of providing solutions to the problems faced by a firm, strategic management might even aggravate the difficulties by moving a firm's attention away from operational functions which themselves are areas that are characterised by serious management deficiencies.

It is not easy to explain how one can avert the trappings of strategic management and focus more on the substance of strategic thinking. Nevertheless, our different consultancy and project experiences among private firms in developing countries offer some fascinating suggestions. In developing economies, symptoms of where insights have been gained indicate that strategic management has produced the most productive results when conceptualised, developed and implemented using a consensual approach. An inflexible process usually turns out to be retrogressive (Eisenhardt & Sull, 2001; Ink, Klaus & Boynton, 1994; Jacobides, 2010; Neilson, Martin & Powers, 2008). If the strategic approach and techniques are custom-made to suit the environmental settings of a firm, nation or relevant region, it tends to be useful as a way of aiding executives to embrace a broad, long-range perspective or think strategically. Although there is no mystic recipe for effective strategies, oftentimes the judicious utilisation of strategic management techniques can be a stride on the right track.

References

- Ackerman, F., Eden, C. & Brown, I. (2004). *The practice of making strategy*. London: Sage Publications.

- Ansoff, H., Declerk, R. & Hayes, R. (eds) (1976). *From strategic planning to strategic management.* London: John Wiley.

- Appiah-Adu, K. (2000). Managerial perceptions of strategic planning benefits: A study of Ghana. *Journal of African Business*, 1(3), 7–28.

- Appiah-Adu, K. & Aning, S. (2012). Enhancing government's policy management and decision making system: Ghana's central governance reforms project, *Canadian Public Administration Journal*, 55(1), 125–47.

- Appiah-Adu, K., Morgan, R. & Katsikeas, C. (1996). Diagnosing organisational planning benefits: The efficacy of formalisation. *Journal of Strategic Marketing*, 4(4), 231–8.

- Appiah-Adu, K. & Singh, S. (2011). The role of strategy in national development: A marketing perspective. Paper presented at the 1st World Marketing Forum, Accra, June.

- Austin, J.E. (1990). *Managing in developing countries: Strategic analysis and operating techniques.* New York, NY: Free Press.

- Balogun, J. & Hailey, V. (2008). *Exploring strategic change.* London: Prentice Hall.

- Benveniste, G. (1989). *Mastering the politics of planning.* San Francisco, CA: Jossey-Bass.

- Blunt, P. & Jones, M. (1992). *Managing organisations in Africa.* Berlin: Walter de Gruyter.

- Bower, J. & Gilbert, C. (2007). How managers' everyday decisions create or destroy your company's strategy, *Harvard Business Review*, 85 (February), 72–9.

- Brinkerhoff, D. (1991). *Improving development program performance.* Boulder, CO: Lynne Reinner.

- Cherunilam, F. (2008). *Strategic Management.* Upper Saddle River, NJ: Prentice Hall.

- Courtney, H., Kirkland, J. & Viguerie, P. (1997). Strategy under uncertainty. *Harvard Business Review*, 75 (November), 67–79.

- Crosby, B. (1991). Strategic management and strategic planning: What they are and how they are different? Technical Note No.1 (Washington DC: US Agency for International Development. Implementing Policy Change Project).

- Cullen, J. (2008). *International management: A strategic perspective.* Upper Saddle River, NJ: Prentice Hall.

- Daft, R. & Buenger, V. (1990). Hitching a ride on a fast train to nowhere: The past and future of strategic management research. In J.W. Frederickson (ed.), *Perspectives on Strategic Management*. New York: Harper Business, 81–103.

- Davenport, T.H. (2006). Competing on analytics. *Harvard Business Review*, 84 (January), 98–107.

- Drucker, P. (1974). *Management: Tasks, responsibilities, practices*. New York, NY: Harper & Row.

- Eisenhardt, K. & Sull, D. (2001). Strategy as simple rules. *Harvard Business Review*, 79 (January), 102–16.

- Freeman, R. & Gilbert, Jr., D. (1988). *Corporate strategy and the search for ethics*. Upper Saddle River, NJ: Prentice Hall.

- Hamel, G. (1994). Breaking the frame: Strategy as stretch and leverage. In H. Thomas et al. (eds), *Building the Strategically-Responsive Organisation*. Chichester: John Wiley & Sons, 45–97.

- Hamel, G. (1996). Strategy as revolution. *Harvard Business Review*, 74 (July), 62–77.

- Hitt, M., Ireland, D. & Hoskisson, R. (2006). *Strategic management*. Upper Saddle River, NJ: Prentice Hall.

- Ink, D., Klaus, R. & Boynton, P. (1994). *Implementing policy change project: Mid-term evaluation*. Washington DC: Academy for Educational Development.

- Jacobides, M. (2010). Strategy tools for a shifting landscape. *Harvard Business Review*, 88 (January–February), 76–84.

- Johnson, G., Scholes, K. & Whittington, R. (2008). *Exploring corporate strategy, Text with cases*. Upper Saddle River, NJ: Prentice Hall.

- Kaplan, R. & Norton, D. (2008). Mastering the management system. *Harvard Business Review*, 86 (January), 62–77.

- Kim, W. & Mauborgne, R. (2009). How strategy shapes structure (a structuralist approach vs. a reconstructionist approach). *Harvard Business Review*, 87 (September), 72–80.

- Kinsey, J. (1988). *Marketing in developing countries*. London: Macmillan.

- Mankins, M. & Steele, R. (2005). Turning strategy into great performance. *Harvard Business Review*, 83 (July), 65–72.

- Martin, R. (2007). How successful leaders think. *Harvard Business Review*, 85 (June), 60–67.

- Milliken, F. & Lant, T. (1991). The effect of an organisation's recent performance history on strategic persistence and change: The role of managerial interpretation, *Advances in Strategic Management*, 7, 129–155.

- Mintzberg, H. (2008). *Tracking strategies: Towards a general theory of strategy formation.* Oxford: Oxford University Press.

- Mintzberg, H., Lampel, J. & Quinn, J. (2007). *The strategy process: Concepts, contexts and cases.* Upper Saddle River, NJ: Prentice Hall.

- Neilson, G., Martin, K & Powers, E. (2008). The secrets to successful strategy execution. *Harvard Business Review*, 86 (June), 60–70.

- Orsini, D., Courcelle, M. & Brinkerhoff, D. (1996). Increasing private sector capacity for policy dialogue: The West African Enterprise Network. *World Development*, 24(9), 1453–66.

- Paladino, B. (2010). *Innovative Corporate Performance Management: Five Key Principles to Accelerate Results.* New York: John Wiley & Sons.

- Parker, D. & Stacey, R. (1994). *Chaos, Management and Economics: The Implications of Non-linear Thinking.* London: Institute of Economic Affairs.

- Peters, T. & Waterman, R. (1982). *In Search of Excellence: Lessons from America's Best Run Companies.* New York, NY: Harper & Row

- Piercy, N. (2002). *Market-led strategic change.* Oxford: Butterworth-Heinemann.

- Porter, M. (2008). Five competitive strategies that shape strategy, *Harvard Business Review*, 86 (January), pp. 23–41.

- Simons, R. (2010). Stress-test your strategy. *Harvard Business Review*, 88 (November), 92–100.

- White, C. (2004). *Strategic Management, Competitiveness and Globalisation: Concepts and Cases.* Upper Saddle River, NJ: Prentice Hall.

- Wilson, I. (1994). Strategic planning isn't dead – it changes. *Long-Range Planning*, 27(4), 12–24.

Chapter 13

Organisational Culture and Corporate Performance

Francis Mensah Sasraku

Abstract

Organisational culture tends to have a complex relationship with corporate performance. Such a complex interrelationship can either have a positive or negative causal or reverse causal effect on each other, depending on the envisioning stage the organisation is in, and the dynamic nature of the organisation's culture. This complex relationship is discussed from two broad perspectives. The first concerns the traditional approach to looking at how norms and practices in organisations affect corporate performance through creativity and innovation. The second part discusses the planks of cultures that influence developing countries in their business activities and how these practices impact both the business environment and the growth of businesses. This partly explains why few conglomerates are flourishing in developing countries like Ghana. The work challenges managers to develop cultures that are stretching and also project positive attitudes that support real creativity, innovation and more critically generational continuity.

Keywords: Organisation; culture; performance; innovation; creativity; developing countries.

Introduction

There are many definitions of culture. Schein (2004) defines organisational culture as the basic assumptions and beliefs that are shared by members of an organisation that operate unconsciously, and define in a basic taken-for-granted fashion, an organisation's view of itself and its environment. Schein provides four layers of organisational culture to include values (explicit), beliefs (specific), behaviours and taken-for-granted assumptions. Organisational culture is important because it varies in context and tends to affect individuals, contributes to how groups of people respond and behave in relation to issues they face. Again, it has important influences on the development and change of organisational strategy.

The extensive works by Hofstede (1980; 2001; 2003; 2011) on national and organisational cultures, and other writers including Soares et al. (2007) have shown that attitudes to work, authority, equality, and other important factors differ from one country to another. He suggests that such differences have been shaped by powerful cultural forces concerned with history, religion, and even climate over many centuries. The implication is that organisations that operate internationally need to understand and cope with such differences, which can manifest themselves in terms of different standards, values and expectations in the various countries in which they operate. Indeed, the issue of sub-national or regional cultures cannot be underestimated by businesses when it comes to issues relating to colour, period of advertising and product launches which may conflict with regional, festive or cultural activities.

The cultural frame of reference is defined to include the organisational field which is a community of organisations that interact more frequently with one another than with those outside the field and that have developed a shared meaning system. Such organisations, they suggest may share a common technology, set of regulations or education and training. More importantly, they tend to cohere around a recipe: a set of assumptions, norms, and routines held in common with an organisational field about the appropriate purposes and strategies of field members. For example, in the financial services sector of developing economies such as Ghana, banks tend to hold to a common recipe determined through regulation due to the nature of the industry.

Underlying the organisation field is legitimacy. Legitimacy is concerned with meeting the expectations within an organisational field in terms of assumptions, strategies and behaviours. Strategies can be shaped by the need for legitimacy in several ways including regulation and normative expectations such as treating one's customers fairly. These influences affect the cultural web of an organisation which is defined to have at its centre, the set of assumptions held in common and taken for granted in an organisation generally termed the paradigm. The paradigm then interrelates with the stories, symbols, power structures, organisational structures, control systems, rituals and routines.

Corporate Culture

Corporate culture has long been linked to company performance, but how exactly are the two related? A recent study by Boyce et al. (2015) suggests the relationship is strong, but nuanced. For instance, a positive corporate culture - one that engages and motivates employees - helps a company's bottom line, according to the study of car dealerships by a group of university and corporate researchers. However, the reverse apparently is not true: a company's success is not enough to ensure a positive culture, the researchers found - and companies that succeed without a positive culture are likely to see their performance decline. According to Boyce et al. (2015) prior research supports a link between organisational culture and performance but generally falls short of establishing causality or determining the direction of a culture–performance (C-P) relationship.

Using data collected from 95 franchise automobile dealerships over six years, Boyce et al (2015) studied longitudinal culture-performance relationships to determine whether culture or performance has causal priority, or alternatively, whether a reciprocal relationship exists. Results from cross-lagged panel analyses indicate that culture "comes first," consistently predicting subsequent ratings of customer satisfaction and vehicle sales. Furthermore, the positive effect of culture on vehicle sales is fully mediated by customer satisfaction ratings. The challenge is to ascertain if there is a link between national culture and corporate culture.

This work had earlier been considered by Hofstede (1980; 2001; 2011) who classified cultures into six cultural dimensions: Power Distance; Uncertainty Avoidance; Individualism vs. Collectivism; Masculinity vs. Femininity; Long-term vs. Short-term Orientation; and Indulgence vs. Restraint. Hofstede developed his original model as a result of using factor analysis to examine the results of a world-wide survey of employee values by IBM between 1967 and 1973 and refined the model after subsequent studies. The original theory proposed four dimensions along which cultural values could be analysed: individualism-collectivism; uncertainty avoidance; power distance (strength of social hierarchy) and masculinity-femininity (task orientation versus person-orientation). Independent research in Hong Kong led Hofstede (2003) to add a fifth dimension, Long-term vs. Short-term Orientation, to cover aspects of values not discussed in the original paradigm. Relatively recently Hofstede (2011) added a sixth dimension, Indulgence vs. Self-restraint.

Power distance index (PDI): The power distance index is defined as "the extent to which the less powerful members of organisations and institutions (like the family) accept and expect that power is distributed unequally." In this dimension, inequality and power is perceived from the followers, or the lower level. A higher degree of the index indicates that hierarchy is clearly established and executed in society, without doubt or reason. A lower degree of the index signifies that people question authority and attempt to distribute power.

Individualism vs. collectivism (IDV): This index explores the "degree to which people in a society are integrated into groups." Individualistic societies have loose ties that often only relate an individual to his/her immediate family. They emphasise the "I" over the "we." Its counterpart, collectivism, describes a society in which tightly-integrated relationships tie extended families and others into in-groups. These in-groups are laced with undoubted loyalty and support for each other when a conflict arises with another in-group.

Uncertainty avoidance index (UAI): The uncertainty avoidance index is defined as "a society's tolerance for ambiguity," in which people embrace or avert an event relating to something unexpected, unknown, or contrary to the status quo. Societies that score a high degree in this index opt for stiff codes of behaviour, guidelines, laws, and generally rely on absolute truth, or the belief that one lone truth dictates everything and people know what it is. A lower degree in this index indicates more acceptance of differing thoughts/ideas. Society tends to impose fewer regulations, ambiguity is more accustomed to, and the environment is more free-flowing.

Masculinity vs. femininity (MAS): In this dimension, masculinity is defined as "a preference in society for achievement, heroism, assertiveness and material rewards for success." Its counterpart represents "a preference for cooperation, modesty, caring for the weak and quality of life." Women in the respective societies tend to display different values. In feminine societies, they share modest and caring views equally with men. In more masculine societies, women are more emphatic and competitive, but notably less emphatic than the men. In other words, they still recognise a gap between male and female values. This dimension is frequently viewed as a taboo in highly masculine societies.

Long-term orientation vs. short-term orientation (LTO): This dimension associates the connection of the past with the current and future actions/challenges. A lower degree of this index (short-term) indicates that traditions are honoured and kept, while steadfastness is valued. Societies with a high degree in this index (long-term) view adaptation and circumstantial, pragmatic problem-solving as a necessity. A poor country that is short-term oriented usually has little to no economic development, while long-term oriented countries continue to develop to a point.

Indulgence vs. restraint (IND): This dimension is essentially a measure of happiness; whether or not simple joys are fulfilled. Indulgence is defined as "a society that allows relatively free gratification of basic and natural human desires related to enjoying life and having fun." Its counterpart is defined as "a society that controls gratification of needs and regulates it by means of strict social norms." Indulgent societies believe themselves to be in control of their own life and emotions; restrained societies believe other factors dictate their life and emotions.

Cognitive styles are recognised as core characteristics of employee creativity. A cognitive style is a person's preferred way of gathering, processing and evaluating information. It influences how people scan their environment for information, how they organise and interpret this information, and how they integrate their interpretations into the mental model and subjective theories that guide their actions (Hayes & Allinson, 1998). This study reviewed aspects of two largely disparate literatures from the adjacent fields of individual and organisational learning and identified some implications for theory and practice. The focus of attention was the extent to which the individual level construct of cognitive style could be meaningfully applied to aid the understanding of learning at the level of the organisation as well as at the level of the individual. Attention was given to the ways in which consideration of cognitive style could improve the effectiveness of interventions designed to improve individual and organisational performance.

Using the Kirton (1976) Adaptation-Innovation (A-I) theory which proposes that individuals can be located on a continuum ranging from adaptation style to innovation style, adaptors are characterised as precautious, reliable, efficient, methodological, disciplined, and conforming. They reduce problems by introducing improvements that increase efficiency and maintain maximal continuity and stability. In addition these individuals are able to maintain a high level of accuracy in detailed work over a prolonged period of time. Another important concept associated with A-I theory is that of bridging in teams. Kirton (2003) defines bridging as "reaching out to people in the team and helping them be part of it so that they may contribute even if their contribution is outside the mainstream". Bridging is thus a task and a role, which has to be learnt. Bridging is neither a cognitive style nor leading, although the skilled leader may make use of persons they recognise as good bridges to maintain group cohesion. Group cohesion means to keep the group aware of the importance of its members working well together. Kirton (2003) suggests that it is easier for a person to learn and assume a bridging role if their cognitive style is an intermediate one.

On the other hand, innovators do things 'differently', and they prefer breakthroughs to improvements. Innovators are highly original but seem to be undisciplined, impractical, unsteady, and incapable of adhering to detailed work. The differences between innovators and adaptors have often been assessed by three personal characteristics: originality and idea creation; conformity to rules and group norms; and efficiency, which is about paying attention to detail and thoroughness. The efficiency construct is measured using five items that reflect attention to detail including thorough, masters all painstaking details; enjoyers of detailed work. Creativity is a necessary precursor for innovation which pertains to the generation of new and valued ideas that often reflect a broad shift in perspective and re-orientation of existing practices. The implementation of these ideas requires major changes in organisational structures or processes (Miron et al., 2004). They found that the three cultural values of creativity (idea generation), attention to detail, and conformity, complement each other and do not compete with each other but rather can co-exist. Therefore, organisations may use different combinations of these cultural values to support their business strategies.

Creativity is not synonymous with innovation; rather innovation is the successful implementation of creative ideas by an organisation (Amabile & Fisher, 2009). They found that people do their most creative work when they are passionate about what they are doing. Such high levels of intrinsic motivation are influenced both by a person's basic interest in a particular kind of work and by the work environment surrounding the person. Managers can support creative productivity by matching people to projects on the basis of interest as well as skill, by using rewards that recognise competence and support further involvement in the work, and by establishing a work environment across the organisation - from top management level to the level of workgroups - that removes the barriers and enhances the support to active, collaborative, intrinsic involvement in the work.

In establishing that work environment, managers should strive first to remove micromanagement of creative work and limit excessive time pressure, particularly time pressure when workdays are marked by fragmented demands unrelated to the organisation's most important creative work. They should also take steps to calm political problems that play out on the battlefield of creativity, resulting in excessive criticism of new ideas and an emphasis on maintaining the status quo. Managers can enhance support for intrinsic involvement in the work by giving people tasks that are meaningful to them and that positively challenge their skills. Middle level managers should form workgroups that combine diverse perspectives and talents, and then facilitate the members of those groups to work collaboratively as they both support and constructively challenge each other's ideas. Low level managers and immediate supervisors should set clear overall goals for projects, but give people as much operational autonomy as possible; they should also serve as champions for creative projects in the organisation. Top organisational leaders can provide encouragement and support for creative work in a number of ways, including the establishment of well-coordinated mechanisms for developing new ideas and systems for recognising and rewarding creative efforts. Perhaps most importantly, the passion for creativity can be stimulated by an open flow of ideas across an organisation in which people feel safe to give honest, constructive feedback on someone else's brainchild – and to fearlessly share their own.

Performance Perspectives

Putting these into performance perspectives, three types of performance are envisioned. They are innovative performance, quality performance, and performance efficiency. Miron et al. (2004) showed that when the culture is not innovative only high-initiative people reach high levels of innovation, while in an innovative culture there are no significant differences between high and low levels of initiative. This finding is important for developing economies with the implication that in a culture that supports innovation new ideas are considered without efforts having to be invested in to promote them.

On quality performance, they find that creativity also has a bleak side if it is not managed to ensure maintenance of rules and regulations, attention to detail variables because the sources of creativity are more motivated to allocate resources to the innovative aspect of their task and less motivated to allocate their attention resources to the quality aspect of their task.

On performance efficiency, conformity is important for reaching high performance quality, and conscientiousness is necessary for maintaining high levels of work efficiency. Of all the personal characteristics, initiative is the one that contributed both to innovation and efficiency, in both cases by helping to move things forward (Miron et al., 2004).

The study enabled us to see the bright and dark sides of creativity and innovation. On the bright side, this study demonstrated that creativity leads to innovation. Creativity, it was found, does not necessarily preclude attention-to-detail and conformity. People can maintain the balance of being creative and paying attention to detail. The study also showed that an innovative culture does not necessarily compete with a culture of quality and efficiency, and companies may maintain a balance between all three dimensions. In fact, a culture of attention-to-detail was conducive to performance quality when interacting with conformity as a personal characteristic, and it was also complementary to efficiency when interacting with conscientiousness. Innovative performance did not impede quality and efficiency, and in fact these three performance outcomes were found to be positively correlated. Being creative did not necessarily contradict being efficient, as there was no relationship between creativity and efficiency.

On the dark side it was found that creativity was not enough for achieving innovative performance. Initiative was a necessary condition for creativity to affect innovation. Moreover, creative people are not always highly innovative. Their innovative performance depends on the organisational culture in which they operate. Creative people implement their ideas and produce innovative products when working in an environment that supports innovation. Yet, when the organisational culture does not support innovation, creative people do not reach high levels of innovation. Furthermore, creative people may pay the price of poor quality. Although they may have the capabilities to be both creative and pay attention-to-detail, they are motivated to allocate their resources to the creative aspect of their task rather than to the task component that requires attention-to-detail and adherence to rules and standards.

In addition, although creativity does not rule out efficiency, it does not contribute to efficiency. Thus, other personal characteristics become important for the attainment of performance quality and efficiency. Conformity is important for reaching high performance quality, and conscientiousness is necessary for maintaining high levels of work efficiency. Of all the personal characteristics, initiative was the one that contributed both to innovation and efficiency, in both cases by helping to move things forward.

Methodology

The approach adopted in this study was ethnographic in nature. Business owners from the self- employed to Executive Directors were approached about why they have been successful or failed to grow their businesses given their performance from a culture-performance perspective. Those who were satisfied with their current performance were mainly focused on limiting their activities locally (in their community, district or in Ghana). The issue of financial constraint was though important and necessary, yet not sufficient. The desire to grow big and spread the output of the business was the critical driving force and of foremost and fundamental importance. An additional step was to ascertain how corporate cultural issues affected the desire and the rationale behind the success of those who have been able to extend their operations to other developing countries. The outcomes of these studies including their financial performance statements, corporate and industry reports were compared to firm up the findings.

Corporate Culture and Performance in Developing Economies

The above discussions have focused on developed economies with well institutionalised structures driven by large companies and formalised work environments, rules and regulations. Many developing economies in sub-Saharan Africa are characterised by state-dominated firms and small-scale businesses. Many of these are family-owned or one-man businesses which imply that the person or staff culture and the dynamics of the organisational field is the same as the organisation's culture. In developing countries, the culture defines the organisational citizenship behaviour (OCB) which reflects the firm's businesses performance. Individual attitudes influence the team's culture .

231

Performance of these small businesses within the organisational field is defined by their individualism–collectivism where the challenges posed by the environment in the form of unfair taxation, high cost of doing business, unstable macroeconomic variables such as inflation cause the private businessman to place personal goals ahead of group goals, and exhibit attitude-driven behaviour as well as task orientation. Conversely, collectivists view "self" in terms of how connected they are in groups, subordinate personal goals to collective goals, exhibit norm-driven behaviour and are relationship oriented.

A key challenge in developing economies is how culture affects the quality of governance, and accounting and disclosures which practically reflect the overall performance of business entities. The role of managerial discretion over accounting decisions influences business performance through two accounting channels: accounting numbers as numerical quantities and business transparency (Bushman, 2014).

More importantly, financial accounting is an integral component of business transparency, and as such is a powerful point of entry for empirical investigation into the economic consequences of business transparency (Bushman, 2014). Business transparency is defined as the availability to outside stakeholders of relevant, reliable information about the periodic performance, financial position, business model, governance, value, and risks facing the business (Bushman, 2014).

Ratnovski (2013) defines transparency as a set of ex-ante choices that determine the presence of credible communication channels; with the key cost of transparency being lower benefits of control. This definition distinguishes transparency from disclosure which an ex-post action and therefore regulation of disclosure is not sufficient to achieve transparency when businesses can manipulate or obfuscate information especially in cultural settings when the interest is not on tax planning but tax avoidance.

In cultures where performance disclosures lead to extra cost to the business person, performance is understated depending on the purpose for which the information will be used. Case studies in Ghana for example, show that small businesses show three financial statements for the same transaction depending on the person demanding such performance

232

information. Bankers expect the most reliable one for their credit risk analysis and decision making, while the provider of the performance information will benefit from embellishing the information if it projects the business for an acquirer or business partners and it is understated when it is concerned with performance meant for the tax authorities.

The next major relationship is why firms in many developing countries innovate less to improve their performance. The issue is that creativity is not translated into innovation due to lack of standards and weak regulatory structures, and also because governmental support is not provided in a structured way. A major challenge is how these creativities can be translated into national assets in promoting development of new products and services not only for the domestic market but also for the development of the country's diamond (Porter, 1986) to compete effectively. Porter's diamond comprises six dimensions: factor conditions; demand conditions; related and supporting industries; firm strategy, structure and rivalry; government influences; and chance events.

Factor conditions are human resource, physical resources, knowledge resources, capital resources and infrastructure. Specialised resources are often specific for an industry and important for its competitiveness. Specific resources can be created to compensate for factor disadvantages.

Demand conditions in the home market can help companies create a competitive advantage, when sophisticated home market buyers pressure firms to innovate faster and to create more advanced products than those of competitors.

Related and supporting industries can produce inputs that are important for innovation and internationalisation. These industries provide cost-effective inputs, but they also participate in the upgrading process, thus stimulating other companies in the chain to innovate.

Firm strategy, structure and rivalry constitute the fourth determinant of competitiveness. The way in which companies are created, set goals and are managed is important for success. But the presence of intense rivalry in the home base is also important; it creates pressure to innovate in order to upgrade competitiveness.

Government can influence each of the above four determinants of competitiveness. Clearly government can influence the supply conditions of key production factors, demand conditions in the home market, and competition between firms. Government interventions can occur at local, regional, national or supranational level.

Chance events are occurrences that are outside of control of a firm. They are important because they create discontinuities in which some gain competitive positions and some lose.

A country's diamond is always vulnerable. Chance can create discontinuities that enable shifts in competitive positions. The role of government, according to Porter, is to influence the determinants in the diamond.

Interactions between the determinants

The factors in the 'diamond' are interrelated. Competitive advantage in an industry rests on a single determinant. Each factor can affect the behaviour of the others. For example, constructive domestic rivalry can encourage the creation of more specialised supplier industries. It is expected that in creating advantage, factors of production provide the seed corn. The related and supporting industries can also be a foundation, if the competences within them can be configured in a new way. The extraordinary demand in the home market based on national peculiarities and conditions can set the demand conditions determinant in the diamond. Again being first to establish a diamond in a particular industry can raise barriers to entry for others. The critical thinking here is the ability of managers to construct a cluster. A cluster is a linking of industries through relationships which are either vertical (buyer-supplier) or horizontal (common customers, technology, skills). Clusters are supposedly a key factor in the competitive advantage of nations. Examples are London for banks and Bangalore for the Indian software industry.

The culture to grow business needs to be developed. This culture needs to define the minimum quality standards and have a perceptual positional map to refine the core framework within which it intends to grow. This is then followed by the establishment of the resource base to drive the evolving mission to achieve the vision. It revolves always taking the step to challenge existing thoughts and beliefs and put them into its risk management framework to stretch the overall drive. The benefit is to set the tone for skills, training, finance and more importantly the timing of decisions which incorporates in practice real options. Measurement of outcomes becomes a common requirement and granular analysis of occurrences or outcomes; be they in excess or deficient against expected levels is also critical. However, national cultural factors for example might create tendencies to orientate business people to some industries rather than others. For example according to Porter (1986), German firms, have a strong showing in 'industries with a high technical content'.

The challenge is what drives some nationals naturally towards 'high technical content' or 'bigness' against others that do not seem to do more or less? Part of the answer lies in the national culture which also impacts on corporate culture and the foundations on which they are built. The scope of many national cultural foundations revolves around who the architect of the culture was; how the culture is expressed or communicated through inheritance or transfer of power, public sector training curriculum; and which tangible and intangible cues are stressed in the cultural foundations. It should also have systems that reinforce these fundamentals, refine and offer critical thoughts about constructive responses to the changing environment and reformulation of the expected future state of the business.

The two case studies below demonstrate how within the same national cultural context, business managers can possibly respond to cultural and socio-political challenges.

Case Study 1

The first President of Ghana had envisioned that Ghana and Accra would be the London of Africa. He set out setting up key banks with foreign branches in Europe and at least a branch in Togo. It was expected that Ghanaian banks would grow and spread to the USA and other European capitals. Alternatively, Ghanaian banks could spread the culture of quality financial intermediation to other African countries. A special bank training centre was established to complement other tacit strategies to achieve that goal.

By 2016, none of the banks set up by the Ghana government and given the above goal had been able to expand beyond the country's borders except for the joint ownership of Ghana International Bank in London. Foreign banks now control over 54% of Ghana's banking assets. More challenging is that no Ghanaian bank is classified as a Pan-African Bank.

> **Case Study II**
>
> A small business entity decided to improve the Ghanaian environment in the early 2000s. Waste management, a major component of environmental sanitation, has over the years and to date, been a major headache of successive central government and local authorities. The driving force was their desire to minimise the problem that at least 40% of Africans do not have access to basic sanitation and hygiene services. Therefore a garbage collection firm was established in 2006 to provide organised environmental and sanitation services. It now has a total core staff of 3,000 and manages over 85,000 workers under various forms of Public Private Partnerships. Within a period of 10 years, the small firm has been able to establish its own university to train further manpower for environmental cleanliness, set up its own garbage separation processing plan and has set up partnership offices in Equatorial Guinea, Angola, Liberia, Togo and Zambia.
>
> This business has unlimited room to expand now and in the near future, and is expected to enter other African countries like Sierra Leone and Sudan, with a similar approach to environmental cleanliness and environmental management.

The concept of performance is therefore relative and it depends on the dimension one is considering and the issues. The link between culture and performance is that culture helps us to separate performance matrices of managers with high performance lenses from those with 'business as usual' lenses. Performance lenses range from the first or basic level performance target range through the second and third level performance target ranges. The first level performance range is related to issues such as accounting profits, level of assets and liabilities, out of which return on equity (ROE), return on assets (ROA), dividend paid, share value growth and market value can be established. Any firm with a going concern status may show one or two of these financial features.

The second level of performance which cultural dimensions become critical to, is creating the breadth and depth about a business and the ethos for which it stands for, locally and internationally. The firm's culture can influence local and international laws as well as regulations because any change initiated from its creative output affects consumption and lifestyles of many nationals. A typical example is Microsoft.

The third level of performance which cultural dimensions drives is that it innovates and defines the future both locally and internationally. Its ethos protects humanity and the environment. The level of innovation takes into account the first two levels and the distinguishing feature is that it becomes too-big-to fail (TBTF) and global in influence and service.

Figure 13.1 below, depicts the interrelationship between culture and performance. It suggests that cultural foundations affect the performance of organisations, which also drives their appetite to become local, national, transnational or multinational.

The interface between national culture, corporate culture and performance is also seen from the mechanisms used to utilise the individual resources which have cumulative components of innovation and the initiatives as expected in the public sector and parastatal institutions. When the position required to drive the innovation is not held by the person with the three identified characteristics, initiatives are stifled, performance is practically overlooked and performance concept are driven politics, patronage and disregard for quality and promotion of societal advancement.

Conclusions and Implications

This chapter contributes to a strand of literature which examines why businesses in Africa have not been able to cross the global landscape as compared with businesses from other continents. It contributes also to a strand of literature on culture and corporate performance by emphasising how culture, its definition and foundation at national and corporate levels, reflects the quality or grade of developmental lenses managers in various developing countries can potentially cultivate and implement given the socio-political constraints within which they operate. It has introduced in a small way, a different dimension of classifying corporate performance which integrates culture into a performance measurement framework, which in many ways will challenge the thinking of business managers as to what level of performance they are envisaging.

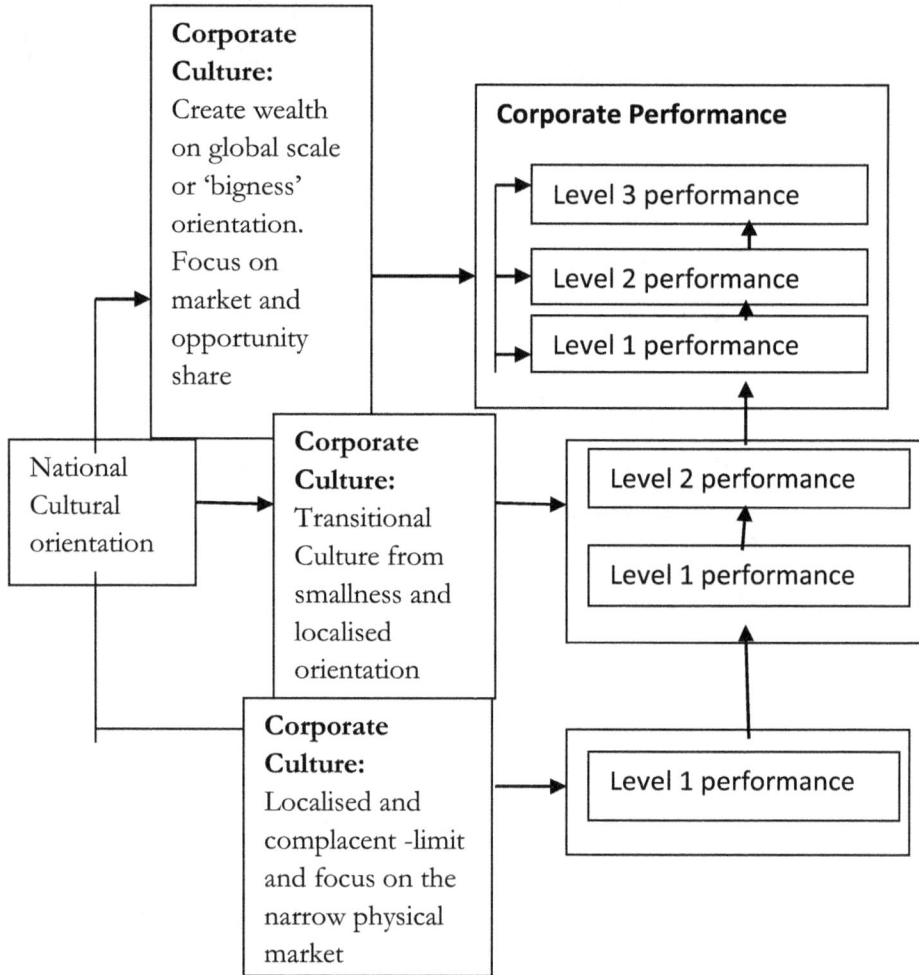

Figure 13.1: National Culture and Performance Range Orientation of Business Managers

The methodology has been ethnographic and there are three suggestions from this research for enterprising managers to: firstly, look for businesses with unlimited markets in Africa; secondly, consider developing a sustainable business cultivated in a culture founded on skills, forward thinking and progress of the society; and finally, prepare for market challenges but always craft the firm's business drive by including risk management dimensions to mitigate cultural risks.

Implications for Managers in Developing Economies

Managers in developing countries should consider instituting organisational culture as the bedrock of organisational survival. Such a foundation should follow from the philosophical construction of what the organisation from top to bottom envisions. The drivers of the business should then cultivate it within the future positional mapping undertaken to ensure that constantly, the organisational culture will be able to capture the drive to stay ahead of competition, contribute to controlling the consumer process of positioning their minds. One common finding cuts across cultures. That is the ability to solve and enhance processes and human prosperity is critical in every small way be it at community, regional, country or continental levels, and globally.

Therefore three suggestions are advanced here. First, create a culture that highlights positive and constructive initiatives. Second, firms should be able to define the philosophical construction of what the future state of their organisations will be able to posit and continue to influence it. Third, the culture should always have in-built dynamic systems or posturing to ensure self-renewal and consistency from its basic philosophical stance. These cultural dimensions will support excellent performance in any expected hostile or competitive environments. Performance should not be driven by greed but with risk management skills which challenge decisions which are long-lasting, sustainable and robust despite potential unexpected challenges.

Limitations and Implications for Future Research

This study's limitations are that: cultural foundational dimensions are largely historical and need to be investigated further; moreover, the bases of the assertions are ethnographic and other methodologies may result in different outcomes. Any research that builds on this work, should explore the motivation for thinking out-of-the-box and forward or ahead, aside the natural instinct in humans to explore their own environment. Future studies should also explore how a constructive culture is sustained and diluted and how they can be revived.

References

- Amabile, T. & Fisher, C. (2009). Stimulate creativity by fueling passion. In E. Locke (ed). *Handbook of principles of organisational behaviour.* 2nd ed. Chichester, UK: John Wiley and Sons Publishing, 481-497.

- Boyce, A., Nieminen, L.R., Gillespie, M., Ryan, A. & Denison, D. (2015). Which comes first, organisational culture or performance? A longitudinal study of causal priority with automobile dealerships. *Journal of Organisational Behaviour* 36 (3), 339 - 359.

- Bushman, R. (2014). Thoughts of financial accounting and the banking industry. *Journal of Accounting and Economics* 58 (November-December), 384-395.

- Hayes, J. & Allinson, C.W. (1998). Cognitive style and the theory and practice of individual and collective learning in organisation. *Human Relations* 51 (7), 847-871.

- Hofstede, G. (1980). *Culture's consequences: International differences in work related values*, 1st ed. Beverly Hills, CA: Sage Publishing.

- Hofstede, G. (2001). *Culture's consequences: International differences in work related values*, 2nd ed. Thousand Oaks, CA: Sage Publishing

- Hofstede, G. (2003). *Culture's Consequences:* Comparing values, behaviours, institutions and organisations across nations. 3rd ed. London, UK: Sage Publishing.

- Hofstede, G. (2011). Dimensionalising cultures: The Hofstede model in context. Online readings in psychology and culture, Johnson, G., Whittington, R. & Scholes, K. (2011). Exploring strategy: Text and cases. 9th ed. Harlow, UK: FT Prentice Hall.

- Kirton, M. (1976). Adaptors and innovators: A description and measure. *Journal of Applied Psychology* 61(5), 622–629.

- Kirton, M. (2003). *Adaptation and innovation in the context of diversity and change*. London, UK: Routledge.

- Miron, E., Erez, M. & Naveh, E. (2004). Do personal characteristics and cultural values that promote innovation, quality and efficiency compete or complement each other? *Journal of Organisational Behaviour* 25 (2), 175-199.

- Ratnovski, L. (2013). Liquidity and transparency in bank risk management. *Journal of Financial Intermediation* 22 (3), 422-439.

- Porter, M. (1986). Competition in global industries: A conceptual framework. Boston, MA: Harvard Business School

- Soares, A., Farhangmeher, M. & Shoham, A. (2007). Hofstede's Dimensions of culture in international marketing studies. *Journal of Business Research* 60 (3), 277-84.

- Schein, E. (2004). *Organisational culture and leadership*. 3rd ed. San Francisco, CA: Jossey-Bass.

Chapter 14

Organisational Structure and Competitive Performance

Ebenezer Ofori Agbettor

Abstract

Organisational structure which tends to form the unseen frame of an entity serves as the basis on which other elements or activities revolve to ensure desired goals are achieved. It therefore goes to say that the appropriate structure in place plays a very significant role in determining the performance and competitiveness of the organisation. This assertion that has been made goes as far back as the classical theorist period and has continued to receive such great attention in contemporary times as expressed in the McKinsey 7-S framework which was developed in the early 1980s by Tom Peters and Robert Waterman. Many companies have found the need to make structural changes that are compatible with use of new technologies i.e. internet for e-business, which requires stronger horizontal coordination. Although there are a number of internal and external forces that determine the appropriate organisational structure to adopt for competitive performance, for the purpose of this chapter, three main factors are discussed, in cognisance of Michael Porter's strategies of cost leadership and differentiation.

Keywords*: Organisation; structure; functions; divisions; strategy; performance.*

Introduction

The problem confronting most organisations or nations is largely one of structural design. Organisations want to use elements of structure to define authority and responsibility for managers, promote accountability, and improve coordination so that the companies can bring out new products/services to gain and maintain competitive edge. Every organisation wrestles with the problem of how to organise. Reorganisation often is necessary to reflect a new strategy, changing market conditions, or innovative technology. In recent years many companies in Ghana, including HFC Bank, Vodafone Ghana, Tullow Ghana, Airtel, Ghana Commercial Bank, Agricultural Development Bank, have realigned departmental groupings, chains of command, and horizontal coordination mechanisms to attain new strategic goals.

Structure indeed is a powerful tool for reaching strategic goals, and a strategy's success often is determined by its fit with organisational structure. The existence of a business organisation is to achieve goals and objectives. The goals and objectives business organisations set to achieve determine how the managers allocate tasks to employees. The allocated jobs are usually grouped into departments. This works out in the same way, when national governments need to form ministries such as Agriculture, Health, Finance, Tourism, Communication, Trade and Industry, etc. Nelson and Quick (2011) opine that departments in organisations can be categorised into various units such as manufacturing, sales, marketing, advertising, and so on. They added that departments are connected to shape the organisational structure. Quangyen & Yezhuang (2013) argued that the structure of an organisation gives it the shape to carry out its purpose in the business environment. Martinelli (2001) argued that the type of organisational structure adopted by a firm will depend on the nature of the particular organisation in question. In other words, the sector or the environment that the firm operates will inform the best structure to adopt so as to create and sustain superior performance and/or maintain competitiveness, thus, also ensuring alliance with appropriate strategy to achieve strategic goals of cost leadership or differentiation as advanced by Michael Porter (1980).

The question of how one goes about analysing how well an organisation is positioned to achieve its intended competitive performance or advantage has attracted many different answers. Some approaches consider internal factors, some consider external variables, some combine these perspectives, and others look for congruence between various aspects of the organisation being studied. Ultimately, the issue boils down to which factor(s) that comes under close scrutiny.

The McKinsey 7-S framework for organisational effectiveness developed by Tom Peters and Robert Waterman (1982) which includes the structure of an organisation can be used in a wide variety of situations where an alignment perspective is useful, for example, to: improve the competitive performance of a company; examine the likely effects of future changes within a company; align departments and processes during a merger or acquisition; and, determine how best to implement a proposed strategy.

Organisational Structure

Classical theories of organisations focus on organisation structure. The view is that if the structure of an organisation is well designed, organisational effectiveness shall be achieved. The popular ideas in the classical school have been provided by historical organisation theory, Frederick Taylor, Henri Fayol and Max Weber. This is the theory of organisations which prevailed during the period before 1900. In ancient organisations the focus was primarily on organisation structure. Ancient organisations were considerably simpler than those in which we live and work today. The typical organisation was the tribe, ruled by a religious leader or authority figure that was obeyed by all. But as society enlarged, so did the complexity of structures to define authority, responsibility, and accountability.

Buchanan and Huczynski (2004) define structure as: "a formal system of task and reporting relationships that controls, co-ordinates and motivates employees so that they work together to achieve organisational goals". Thus, structure is synonymous with a rope that employees hold and which binds all employees towards a unified direction and aids the identification of 'Who is Who' and 'What is What' of organisation. Structure serves as basis for orchestrating organisational activities. Organisations should understand the importance of structure in carrying out business operations. Organisations can choose from a variety of structures like, functional, divisional, project teams, virtual network and matrix structure. Failure to choose an effective structure has its consequences on the organisation as it will not only affect the health of the organisation, but also employees' loyalty, motivation at work and job satisfaction. Thus, when designing its structure an organisation needs to take care of all aspects that relate to people and workings of the organisation.

Mullins (2005) emphasises that structure affects productivity, economic efficiency, morale, and job satisfaction. The important notion stemming from Mullins' assertion is that good structure will not only have tangible effects (i.e., financial) but intangible effects (e.g., motivation) thus impacting organisations' operational effectiveness as employees carry out operations/tasks of organisation. Mintzberg (2009) argued that organisational structure defines how people are organised or how their jobs are divided and coordinated. Greenberg (2011) refers to organisational structure as the formal configuration between individuals and groups concerning the responsibilities, allocation of tasks and authority in the hierarchy, level of horizontal integration, centralisation of authority and patterns of communication.

Indeed, it is the manner in which power and responsibilities are allocated, and work procedures are done, among members of the organisation.

A theoretical model that covers three types of organisational structure is presented as follows: Firstly, centralisation of decision making process can be defined as the degree to which the right to make decisions and evaluate activities is concentrated on the top hierarchy levels of organisations (Fry & Slocum, 1984; Hall, 1977). It can also be seen as an increase of decisions made at higher hierarchical levels within organisations and a decrease of participation of employees in the decision making process (Daft, 1995; Doll & Vonderembse, 1991; Germain, 1996). From another dimension, it can be conceptualised as a locus of authority and decision-making in the organisation. Environment plays an important role for locus of authority since organisations in uncertainty environments should delegate decisions to lower hierarchy levels in order to quickly adjust to changing situations (Doll & Vonderembse, 1991).

Secondly, flatness of organisation hierarchy is conceptualised as the degree to which an organisation has many or few levels of management hierarchy (Burns & Stalker, 1961). Walton (1985) argues that a traditional command and control model is characterised by an expanded hierarchy that may be a by-product of the systems and is justified by the need to control employee behaviour. On the other hand, a commitment model is characterised by a management system that tends to be flat, relies upon shared goals for control and lateral coordination, bases influence on expertise and information rather than position, and minimises status differences. Organic organisations tend to have few levels of hierarchy and is characterised by more efficient and effective flows of information and decision-making. A flat organisation can reduce problems of information delays, distortion and corruption as information flows from one level to another.

Thirdly, specialisation of departments and employees refers to the level of horizontal integration existing within an organisation. In other words, it is the degree to which departments and employees are functionally specialised or integrated. Low levels of horizontal integration reflect an organisation in which the departments and employees are functionally specialised, whereas high levels of horizontal integration reflect an organisation in which departments and employees are integrated in their work, skills, and training

(Davenport & Nohria, 1994; Doll & Vonderembse, 1991). Given that cross-trained employees tend to be responsive to changes in customers' needs (MacDuffie, 1995; Vonderembse, Ragunathan, & Rai, 1997), managers can use horizontal integration to address fast changing environments. At the same time, a great variety of specialists in a horizontally integrated organisation may provide a broader knowledge base (Kimberly & Evanisko, 1981), increasing cross-fertilisation of ideas (Aiken & Hage, 1971). For example, Wiersema and Bantel (1992) found that educational specialisation heterogeneity of the top management team was a significant predictor of organisational change.

Importance of Organisational Structure

Bloisi (2007) highlights the importance of structure as a means of getting people to work towards common goals, thus, acting as facilitators in pursuit of organisational goals. A good structure should provide a right blend of command and control. Designing an organisation structure helps top management identify talent that needs to be added to the company. Planning the structure ensures there are enough human resources within the company to accomplish the goals set forth in the company's annual plan. It is also important that responsibilities are clearly defined. Each person has a job description that outlines duties, and each job occupies its own position on the company's organisational chart

Without a formal organisational structure, employees may find it difficult to know who they officially report to in different situations, and it may become unclear exactly who has the final responsibility for what. Organisational structure improves operational efficiency by providing clarity to employees at all levels of a company. With a good organisational structure in place, departments can work more like well-oiled machines, focusing time and energy on productive tasks. A thoroughly outlined structure can also provide a roadmap for internal promotions, allowing companies to create solid employee advancement tracks for entry-level workers. In a nutshell, a well-designed organisation structure promotes growth, profitability and success.

Types of Organisational Structures

A fundamental characteristic of organisation structure is departmentalisation, which is the basis for grouping positions into departments and departments into total organisation. Managers make choices about how to use the chain of command to group people together to perform their work. Five approaches to structural design reflect different uses of the chain of command in departmentalisation. Functional, divisional, and matrix are traditional approaches that rely on the chain of command to define departmental groupings and reporting relationships along hierarchy. Two innovative approaches are the use of teams and virtual networks, which have emerged to meet changing organisational needs in the turbulent global environment.

Functional Approach

Functional structure is the grouping of positions into departments based on similar skills, expertise, work activities, and resource use. A functional structure can be thought of as departmentalisation by organisational resources, because each type of functional activity - accounting, human resource, engineering, manufacturing - represents specific resources for performing the organisation's task. People, facilities, and other resources representing a common function are grouped into a single department. One example is Kasapreko Company Ghana, which relies on in-depth expertise in its various functional departments to produce high-quality alcoholic beverages for its regional market. The quality control department, for example, tests all incoming ingredients (i.e. herbs) and ensures that only the best go into its products like "Alomo Bitters" and gin. Quality inspectors also test outgoing products and because of their rich experience can detect the slightest deviation from expected quality.

How it Works

As can be seen in the Figure 1, the major departments under the CEO are groupings of similar expertise and resources, such as accounting, human resources, production, and marketing. Each of the functional departments is concerned with the organisation as a whole. The marketing department is responsible for all sales and marketing, for example, and the accounting department handles financial issues for the entire company.

The functional structure is a strong vertical design where information flows up and down the hierarchy, and the chain of command converges at the top of the organisation. In this structure, people within a department communicate primarily with others in the same department to coordinate work and accomplish tasks or implement decisions passed down a hierarchy. Managers and employees are compatible because of similar training and expertise.

Figure 14.1: Functional Organisational Structure

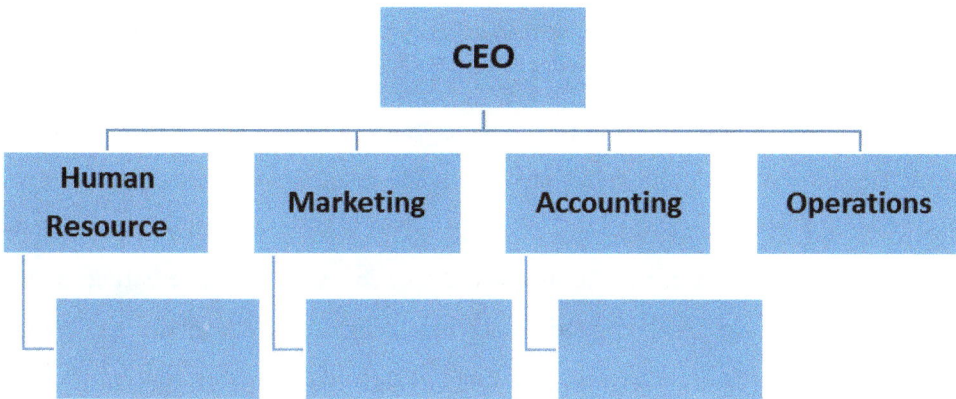

Divisional Organisational Structure

In contrast to the functional approach, in which people are grouped by common skills and resources, the divisional structure occurs when departments are grouped together based on organisational outputs. The divisional structure is sometimes called a product structure, program structure, or self-contained unit structure, geographic territory and function.

Each of these terms means essentially the same thing. Diverse departments are brought together to produce a single organisation output, whether it be a product, a programme, or a service to a single customer. Most large corporations have separate divisions that perform different tasks, use different technologies, or serve different customers. When a huge organisation produces products for different markets, the divisional structure works because each division is an autonomous business.

How it Works

In the divisional structure, divisions are created as self-contained units with separate functional departments for each division. For example in Figure 2, each functional department resource needed to produce the product is assigned to each division. Whereas in a functional structure, all engineers are grouped together and work on all products; in a divisional structure, separate engineering departments are created within each division. Each department is smaller and focuses on a single product line or customer segment. Departments are duplicated across product lines.

The primary difference divisional and functional structure is that the chain of command from each function converges lower in the hierarchy. In a divisional structure, differences of opinion among research and development, marketing, manufacturing and finance would be resolved at the divisional level rather than by the CEO. Thus, the divisional structure encourages decentralisation. Decision making is pushed down at least one level in the hierarchy, freeing the CEO and other top management personnel (directors) for strategic planning. It works in the same way in a global geographic structure where all functions in a specific country or region report to the same division director. The structure focuses company activities on local market conditions where competitive advantage may come from production or sale of a product or service adapted to a given country or region.

Figure 14.2: Divisional Organisational Structure

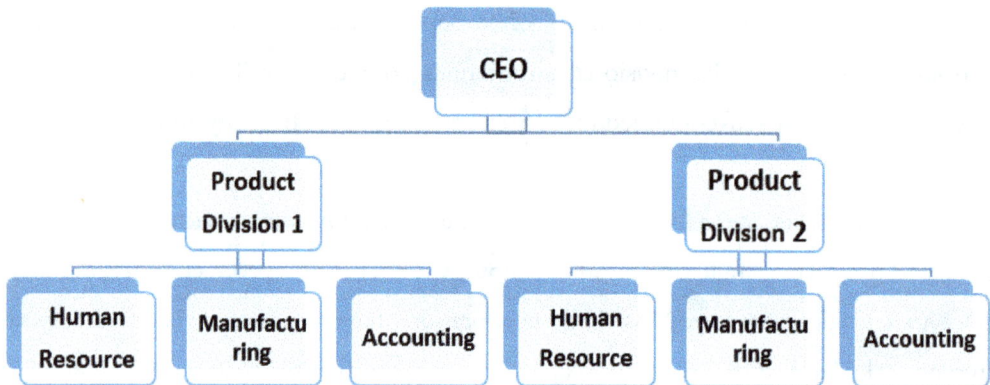

Team/Project Organisational Structure

The vertical chain of command is a powerful means of control, but passing all decisions up the hierarchy takes too long and keeps responsibility at the top. The team/project approach gives managers a way to delegate authority, push responsibility to lower levels, and be more flexible and responsive in the competitive global environment.

How it Works

One approach to using teams in organisations is through cross-functional teams, which consist of employees from various functional departments who are responsible to meet as a team and resolve mutual problems. Team members will still report to their functional departments, but they also report to the team, one member of whom may be the leader. Cross-functional teams are used to provide needed horizontal coordination to complement an existing divisional or functional structure. The project team focuses all its energies, resources and results on the assigned project. Once the project is completed, the team members from various cross functional departments may go back to their previous positions or may be assigned to a new project. Some of the examples of projects are: research and development projects, product development, construction of a new plant, housing complex, service innovation, shopping complex, bridge, etc. A frequent use of cross-functional teams is for change projects.

Figure 14.3.Team/Project Organisational Structure.

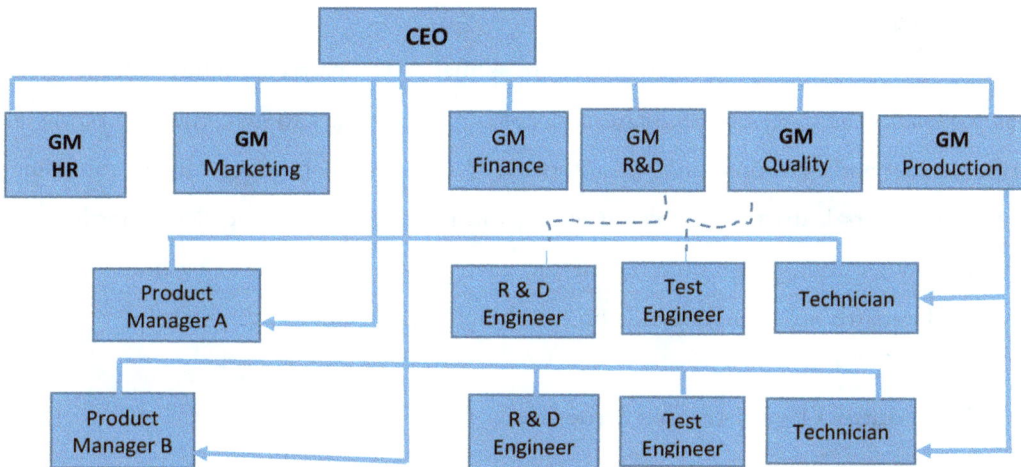

A second approach is to use permanent teams, groups of employees who are brought together in a new way similar to a formal department. Each team brings together employees from all functional areas focused on a specific task or project. Here emphasis is on horizontal communication and information sharing because representatives from all functions are coordinating their work and skills to complete a specific organisational task. Authority is pushed down to lower levels, and front-line employees are often given the freedom to make decisions and take action on their own. Team members may share or rotate team leadership. With team-based structure, the entire organisation is made up of horizontal teams that coordinate their work and work directly with customers to accomplish the organisation's goals.

Matrix Organisational Structure

This combines aspects of both functional and divisional structures simultaneously in the same part of the organisation. The matrix structure evolved as a way to improve horizontal coordination and information sharing (Burns 1989). One unique feature of the matrix is that it has dual lines of authority. In Figure 4 the functional hierarchy of authority runs vertically, and the divisional hierarchy of authority runs horizontally. The vertical structure provides traditional control within functional departments, and the horizontal structure provides coordination across departments. The matrix structure therefore supports a formal chain of command for both functional (vertical) and divisional (horizontal) relationships. As a result of this dual structure, some employees find themselves reporting to two supervisors simultaneously.

How it Works

The dual lines of authority as seen in Figure 4 make the matrix structure unique. This however violates the unity-of-command concept but is necessary to give equal emphasis to both functional and divisional lines of authority. Dual lines of authority can be confusing, but after managers learn to use this structure, the matrix provides excellent coordination simultaneously for each geographic region and each product. It needs to be noted that the success of the matrix structure depends on the ability of people in key matrix roles.

Figure 14.4: Matrix Organisational Structure

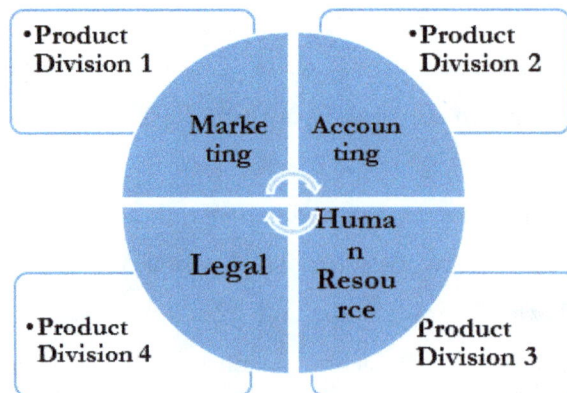

Two-boss employees, those who report to two supervisors simultaneously, must resolve conflicting demands from the matrix bosses. They must confront senior managers and reach joint decisions. They need excellent human relations skills with which to confront managers and resolve conflicts

The matrix boss is the product or functional boss, who is responsible for one side of the matrix, whilst the top leader is responsible for the entire matrix. The top leader oversees both the product and functional chains of command. His or her responsibility is to maintain a power balance between the two sides of the matrix. If disputes arise between them, the problem will be kicked upstairs to the top leader (Davis & Lawrence, 1977).

Virtual Network Approach

This approach extends the idea of horizontal coordination and collaboration beyond the boundaries of the organisation. In a variety of industries, vertically integrated, hierarchical organisations are giving way to loosely interconnected groups of companies with permeable boundaries (Schilling & Steensma, 2001). Outsourcing, which means farming out certain activities, such as catering, cleaning, credit processing, has a significant trend. In addition, partnerships, alliances, and other complex collaborative forms are now a leading approach to accomplishing strategic goals. The virtual network structure means that the firm sub-contracts most of its major functions to separate companies and coordinates their activities from a small organisation headquarters (Miles and Snow, 1995).

How it Works

The organisation may be viewed as a central hub surrounded by a network of outside specialists, as illustrated in Figure 5. Rather than being housed under one roof, services such as distribution, accounting, catering and cleaning are outsourced to separate organisations that are connected electronically to the central office (Miles & Snow, 1986).

Figure 14.5: Virtual Network Organisational Structure

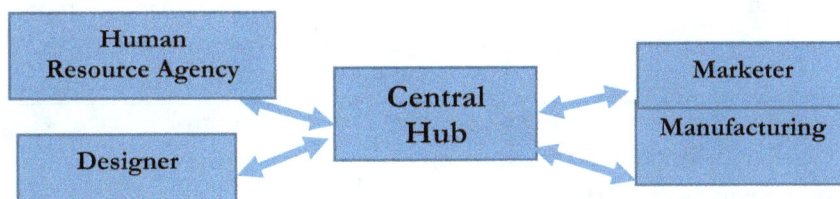

Advantages and Disadvantages of Each Structure

The idea behind networks is that a company can concentrate on what it does best and contract out other activities to companies with distinctive competences in those specific areas, which enables a company to do more with less (Anand & Daft, 2007).

A modular approach in networking usually used by manufacturing companies tend to enable them use outside suppliers to provide entire chunks of a product, which are then assembled into a final product by a handful of workers. Automobile plants, including General Motors, Ford, Volkswagen and DaimlerChrysler, are leaders in using the modular approach.

Structural Approach	Advantages	Disadvantages
Functional	Efficient use of resources; economies of scale; in-depth skill of specialisation and development; top manager direction and control	Poor communication across functional departments; slow response to external changes; lagging innovation; decision concentrated at top hierarchy creating delays.
Divisional	Fast response; flexibility in unstable environment; fosters concern for customer needs; excellent coordination across functional departments.	Duplication of resources across divisions; less technical depth and specialisation; poor coordination across divisions
Team/Project	Reduced barriers among depts; increased compromise; shorter response time; quicker decisions, Better morale; enthusiasm from employee involvement.	Dual loyalties and conflict; time and resources spent on meetings; unplanned decentralisation.
Matrix	More efficient use of resources than single hierarchy; flexible; adaptable to changing environment; inter-disciplinary cooperation; expertise available to all divisions.	Frustration and confusion from dual chain of command; high conflict between two sides of the matrix; many meetings; more discussion than action.
Virtual Network	Can draw on expertise worldwide; highly flexible and responsive; Reduced overhead costs.	Lack of control; weak boundaries; greater demands on managers; Employee loyalty weakened.

The Table above provides information on the advantages and disadvantages on the various organisational structures.

Factors Shaping Organisational Structure

Despite the trend towards horizontal design, vertical hierarchies continue to thrive because they often provide important benefits for organisations (Leavitt, 2003). In response to the question of how a manager knows whether to design a structure that emphasises the formal, vertical hierarchy or one with emphasis on horizontal communication and collaboration, the answer lies in the contingency factors that influence organisational structure. Numerous internal and external forces affect an organisation but for the purpose of this exercise, three main factors will be discussed. The right structure is designed to 'fit' the contingency factors of strategy, environment and production technology as illustrated in figure 14.7.

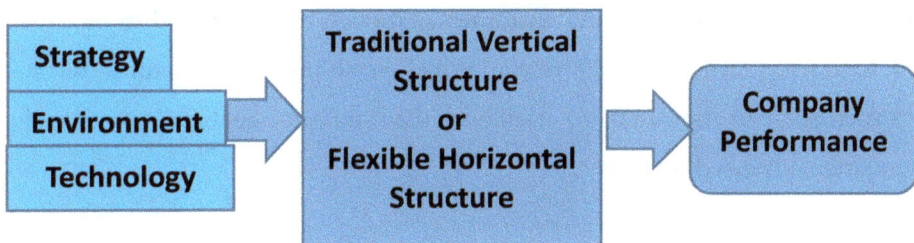

Figure 14.7: Factors That Influence Organisation Structure

Structure Follows Strategy

That strategies that business organisations adopt can impact an organisational structure is advanced by Michael Porter where he proposes two main strategies, first differentiation and second cost leadership (Porter, 1980). With a differentiation strategy, the organization attempts to develop innovative products unique to the market. With a cost leadership strategy, the organisation strives for internal efficiency. The strategies of cost leadership versus differentiation require different structural approaches. A study demonstrated that business performance is strongly influenced by how well the company's structure is aligned with its strategic intent, so managers strive to pick strategies and structures that are congruent (Olson, Slater, and Hult, 2005).

Figure 14.8 clearly shows the continuum that illustrates how structural approaches are associated with strategic goals. The functional structure is appropriate for achieving internal efficiency goals. The vertical functional structure uses task specialisation and strict chain of command to gain efficient use of scarce resources, but it does not enable the organisation to be flexible or innovative. In contrast, horizontal teams are appropriate when the primary goal is innovation and flexibility. Each team is small, is able to be responsive, and has the people and resources necessary for performing its task. The flexible horizontal structure enables organisations to differentiate themselves and respond quickly to the demands of a shifting environment but at the expense of efficient resource use.

Figure 14.8 also illustrates how other forms of structure represent intermediate steps on the organisation's path to efficiency or innovation. The functional structure with cross-functional teams and project managers provide greater coordination and flexibility than pure functional structure. The divisional structure promotes differentiation because each division can focus on specific products and customers, although divisions tend to be larger and less flexible than small teams. Figure 8 does not include all possible structures, but it illustrates how structures can be used to facilitate the strategic goals of cost leadership or differentiation advanced by Porter.

Figure 14.8: Strategic Goals to Structural Approach

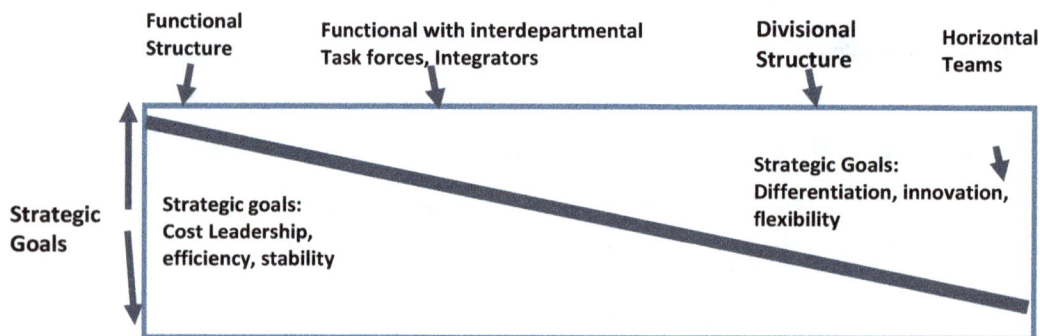

Structure Reflects the Environment

The external business environment can also play an important part in a company's organisational structure. Dynamic environments with constantly changing consumer desires or behaviour cause a great deal of difficulty for decision makers in both corporate and governmental circles. External environmental uncertainties cause the following in organisations: increased differences occur among departments; the need for increased coordination to keep departments together; and increased need to adapt to change. When an environment is stable, the organisation uses a mechanistic system where it has a rigid, vertical, centralised structure, with most decisions made at the top. The organisation is highly specialised and characterised by rules, procedures, and a clear hierarchy of authority. In rapidly changing environment, however, the organisation tends to be much looser, free-flowing, and adaptive, using an organic system. The structure is more horizontal and decision-making authority is decentralised. People at lower levels have more responsibility and authority for solving problems, enabling the organisation to be more fluid and adaptable to changes in the environment (Courtright, Fairhurst & Rogers, 1989).

Figure 14.9 shows the contingency relationship between environmental uncertainty and structural approach. When the external business environment is stable, the organisation can succeed with a mechanistic structure that emphasises vertical control. With little need for change, flexibility, or intense coordination, the structure can emphasise specialisation and centralised decision making. When environmental uncertainty is high, however, a flexible organic structure that emphasises lateral relationships such as teams and horizontal projects is appropriate. Vertical structure characteristics such as specialisation and centralisation should be downplayed. In an uncertain environment, the organisation figures things out as it goes along, departments must cooperate, and decisions should be decentralised to teams and task forces working on specific problems.

Figure 14.9: Relationship between Environment & Structure

	STRUCTURE	
	Vertical	**Horizontal**
Uncertain (unstable)	**Incorrect Fit:** Vertical structure in uncertain environment Mechanistic structure too tight	**Correct Fit:** Horizontal structure in uncertain environment
Certain (stable)	**Correct Fit:** Vertical structure in certain environment	**Incorrect Fit:** Horizontal structure in certain environment Loose Organic structure

ENVIRONMENT

When managers use the wrong structure for the environment, the organisation's competitive performance suffers greatly. A rigid, vertical structure in an uncertain environment prevents the organisation from adapting to change. Likewise, a loose, horizontal structure in a stable environment is inefficient. Too many resources are devoted to meetings and discussions when employees could be more productive focusing on specialised tasks

Structure fit the Technology

Technology which includes the knowledge, tools, techniques, and activities used to transform organisational inputs into outputs impact the competitive performance of both manufacturing and service organisations. Research conducted by Joan Woodward (1965) to determine whether basic structural characteristics, such as administrative overhead, span of control, and centralisation were different across firms, concluded that small batch and continuous process firms have somewhat loose, flexible structures (organic) and mass production firms have tight vertical structures (mechanistic). Woodward stated that different technologies impose different kinds of demands on individuals and organisations and these demands have to be met through an appropriate structure (Woodward, 1965). Her study also concluded that the relationship between structure and technology was directly related to a company's competitive performance.

Likewise, technology application in service organisations directly influences structure which stems from the need for employees to be close to the customer (Chase and Tansik, 1983). Structural characteristics are similar to those for continuous manufacturing technology firms just like service firms that tend to be flexible, informal and decentralised. Here, horizontal communication is high because employees must share information and resources to serve customers and solve problems. Services of banks, post offices, hotels, hospitals are also dispersed, hence each unit is often small and located geographically close to customers. Such dispersed facilities to districts and regions are to provide faster and better service to customers. Indeed, every manager ought to recognise how structure fits the contingency factors of strategy, environment and technology, and design the right mix of structural characteristics to fit the contingency factors. It is worth mentioning that there are other factors like the size and complexity of organisation, the nature of the organisation's work, organisational culture and management style.

Benefits of a Good Organisational Structure

While there are many different structures that organisations can adopt, depending upon the type of organisation including whether it is a service organisation or a manufacturing organisation, a well-structured organisation has many benefits. An article by Smriti Chand (n.d.) provides some of the beneficial outcomes of optimally designed organisational structure and they are discussed as follows:

1. **A good organisational structure facilitates attainment of objectives through proper coordination of all activities:** It has a built-in system of "checks and balances" so that the progress towards the attainment of objectives is evaluated along the way so that any required adjustments can be made and any new decisions required can be taken.

2. **In a good organisational structure, the conflicts between individuals over jurisdiction are kept to a minimum:** Since each person is assigned a particular job to perform, the responsibility of performing that job rests solely with him. It results in traceability of outcomes and the work interdependency of that particular task is reduced to a minimum.

3. **It eliminates overlapping and duplication of work:** Duplication exists when work distribution is not clearly identified and the work is performed in a haphazard and disorganised way. Since a good organisational structure requires that the duties be clearly defined and assigned, such duplication of work is eliminated.

4. **It decreases likelihood of "run-arounds:"** The run-arounds occur when we do not know who is responsible for what and we are not sent to the right people in the first instance for getting some work done. However, in a well-organised company where the responsibilities are clearly established, this does not occur.

5. **It facilitates promotions of personnel:** Since the organisational chart clearly pinpoints the positions of individuals relative to one another, it is easier to know as to which level a person has reached at any given time in the organisational hierarchy. Furthermore, since each job is well described in terms of qualifications and duties, the promotional stages can be more clearly established.

6. **It aids in wage and salary administration:** A fair and equitable wage and salary schedule is based upon the premise that the jobs with similar requirements should have similar benefits. If these requirements are clearly established and the annual increments

or the cost of living increments for each type of job are properly and clearly understood, then compensation administration policies are easier to implement.

7. **Communication is easier at all levels of organisational hierarchy:** Since the lines of communication and flow of authority are clearly identified on the organisational chart, the intercommunication is both clearer and easier and it eliminates ambiguity.

8. **A well-structured organisation provides a sound basis for effective planning:** Since the goals are clearly established and resources clearly identified, both short term and strategic planning become more focused and realistic and such planning contains the provision to permit changes to be made in the right direction including expansion and contraction of facilities, operations and activities when it becomes necessary.

9. **It results in increased cooperation and a sense of pride among members of the organisation:** An employee is given sufficient freedom within the domain of his responsibility and his authority. Since the authority and the extent of exercise of such authority is known, it develops a sense of independence among employees which, in turn, is highly morale boosting.

10. **It encourages creativity:** Because of a sense of belonging and high morale that a well-structured organisation develops among employees and also because of clear-cut accountability, recognition of skill and appreciation for their contribution towards organisational growth, the employees develop their own initiative and a spirit of innovation and creativity.

Competitive Performance

Competitive performance or competitiveness was operationalised and measured using a competitive performance scale comprising ten performance criteria derived from Khandwalla (1995). The ten performance criteria include: profit growth, sales revenue, financial strength, operating efficiency, performance stability, public image, employee morale, environmental adaptation, new ideas, and social impact on the society

The term competitive advantage refers to the ability gained through attributes and resources to perform at a higher level than others in the same industry or market (Porter, 1980 cited by Chacarbaghi and Lynch, 1999). The study of competitive advantage has attracted profound research interest due to contemporary issues regarding superior performance levels of firms in the present competitive market conditions. "A firm is said to have a competitive

258

advantage when it is implementing a value creating strategy that is not simultaneously being implemented by any current or potential player" (Clulow, Gerstman & Barry,2003).

Successfully implemented strategies will lift a firm to superior performance by facilitating the firm with competitive advantage to outperform current or potential players (Passemard and Calantone, 2000). To gain competitive advantage, a firm's business strategy manipulates the various resources over which it has direct control and these resources have the ability to generate competitive advantage (Rijamampianina, Abratt & February, 2003). Superior performance outcomes and superiority in production resources reflect competitive advantage (Lau, 2002).

The above writers signify competitive advantage as the ability to stay ahead of present or potential competition. Also, it provides the understanding that resources held by a firm and the business strategy will have a profound impact on generating competitive advantage. Powell (2001) views business strategy as the tool that manipulates the resources and create competitive advantage, hence, a viable business strategy may not be adequate unless it possesses control over unique resources that have the ability to create such a unique advantage.

Competitive advantage grows out of the company's ability to provide greater value than it costs to create it. Value is what the buyer is willing to pay for. Superior value stems from offering lower prices than competitors for equivalent benefits or providing unique benefits that more than offset a higher price. Porter introduces the concept of the value chain as an analytical framework for strategically thinking about the activities of a company and how their relative costs contribute towards differentiation. The value chain provides a way to understand the sources of buyer value that will command a premium price, and why one product or service substitutes another. By thinking of strategy as a series of activities, it becomes more tangible rather than just a broad vision. The activities required for a low cost strategy is very different from those of a differentiation strategy and the particular configuration one company chooses can be quite distinct from that of its rivals.

Link Between Organisational Structure and Competitive Performance

Overall, the relationship between organisational structure and competitive performance is determined by the appropriate structure adopted in response to organisational strategies, external environment and technology, to mention a few. Woodward's (1965) research on relationship between manufacturing technology and organisational structure concluded that the adoption of appropriate structure is directly related to a company's competitive performance. Thus, when a small batch and continuous process organisations adopt an organic structure where loose, flexible, informal and decentralised structures and high horizontal communication prevail, the competitive performance of an organisation is heightened as it is able to respond speedily to customers' needs. When services can be standardised, a tight centralised structure can be effective, but service organisations in general tend to be more organic, flexible and decentralised.

As indicated earlier, strategies that business organisations adopt can impact an organisational structure as advanced by Michael Porter 1980 (differentiation and cost leadership). With a differentiation strategy, the organisation attempts to develop innovative products unique to the market. With a cost leadership strategy, the organisation strives for internal efficiency. The strategies of cost leadership versus differentiation require different structural approaches. As shown in Figure 8, strategic goals of cost leadership, efficiency in stable environment will provide or ensure competitive performance when the functional structure is adopted. In the same manner, strategic goals of differentiation, innovation, flexibility in an unstable environment will ensure competitive performance when either a divisional or horizontal team structure is adopted. A study demonstrated that business performance is strongly influenced by how well the company's structure is aligned with its strategic intent, so managers strive to pick strategies and structures that are congruent (Olson, Slatter, and Hult, 2005).

A stable or unstable business environment indeed determines the appropriate structure to adopt as one aims to achieve competitive advantage or performance. As discussed earlier, in a rapidly changing environment, the organisation tends to be much looser, free-flowing and adaptive, using an organic structure where a more horizontal and decision-making authority is decentralised. This structure will, in turn, position the organisation to be more responsive to the changing needs of customers or the market, thereby being able to sustain the organisation's competitive performance. On the other hand, in a stable environment, the organisation tends to be characterised by a rigid, vertical, centralised structure, with most decisions made at the top. The organisation is highly specialised and characterised by rules, procedures, and clear hierarchy of authority.

The 7-S model developed by Tom Peters and Robert Waterman (1982) for organisational effectiveness which includes structure of an organisation can be used in a wide variety of situations where an alignment perspective is useful, to improve the competitive performance of a company. This model is based on the theory that for an organisation to perform well, these seven elements need to be aligned and mutually reinforcing. The model, indeed, is most often used as an organisational analysis tool to assess and monitor changes in the internal situation of an organisation. Thus, it is used to help identify what needs to be realigned to improve performance, or to maintain alignment (and performance) during other types of change.

Conclusions

Based on the discussion which made a compelling argument for a relationship between organisational structure and competitive performance, we may conclude that there is a strong likelihood of an association between organisational structure and competitive performance and that organisational structure is likely to be a good predictor of competitive performance. It also indicated that firms with the appropriate organisational structure outperform firms with inappropriate structures. This discussion provides important implications for the management of all organisations in developing economies, including Ghana, irrespective of the sector in which they operate. In order to improve competitive performance, firms need to demonstrate a high level of commitment to the application of appropriate organisational structure. An effective structure facilitates proper working relationships among various sub-units in the organisation. This may definitely improve company efficiency within the organisation's units/departments, thereby, improving on the company's competitive performance.

In a nutshell, the following critical points are worth noting:

- Modifying current strategy or selecting a new one calls for changes to organisational structure

- No one structure is superior to the others

- No best or optimal structure for all firms

- Strategy-structure fit can lead to a competitive advantage or achievement of above average returns.

- Structure must match strategy

- Choice of structure should be based on control, coordination, and motivation issues

- Several structure forms can be used to implement strategies

Implications for Business Executives and/or Policy Makers

The discussion revealed that there is a relationship between specialisation of work process and labour productivity which implies that organisational structure affects the behaviour of employees in the organisation. This means when a clear structure exists people perform better, tasks are divided and productivity is increased. Indeed, having a suitable organisational structure in place, one that recognises and addresses various human and business realities of the company in question is a prerequisite for long term success. It is therefore recommended that business executives/policy makers should critically analyse the effectiveness and efficiency of the organisation by ensuring proper structures are put in place and implemented with the aim of achieving set goals. Organisations should also endeavour to have well-structured mechanisms in order to achieve laid down objectives that will enhance their competitive performance. In other words, structural fitness of an organisation must be such that it enhances performance that ensures competitive advantage by business executives.

Implications for Future Research

This discussion can also help researchers to better understand the relationship between organisational structure and competitive performance in Ghana and developing economies. If organisations in Ghana are to survive, grow, and compete effectively in their national and regional markets, their managers should develop organisational, human, technological and planning attributes and practices that can make them become more sensitive to the significance of adopting appropriate organisational structures for competitive performance. To generalise in a discussion as this, may not apply or match perfectly with every specific case, particularly when most of the references made are from developed nations. It would therefore be prudent to carry out further investigations in Ghana or the African context in order to empirically confirm the propositions made in this chapter. As the factors that influence organisational structure are not mutually exclusive, their interdependence has made scientific analysis difficult but not impossible, hence the need for further investigation.

References

- Aiken, M. & Hage, J. (1971). The organic organisation and innovation. *Sociology, 5*, 63-82.

- Anand, N. & Daft, R. (2007). What is the right organisation design? *Organisational Dynamics, 36*(4), 329-344.

- Burns, T. & Stalker, G. (1961). *The management of innovation.* London: Tavistock.

- Burns, L. (1989). Matrix management in hospitals: Testing theories of matrix structure and development. *Administrative Science Quarterly, 34*, 349-368.

- Bloisi, W. (2007). *Management and organisational behaviour* (2nd European ed.). Maidenhead: McGraw-Hill Education.

- Buchanan, D. & Huczynski, A. (2004). *Organisational behaviour. An introductory text.* (5th ed.). Essex: Prentice Hall.

- Chase, R. & Tansik, D. (1983). The customer contact model for organisation design. *Management Science, 29*, 1037-1050.

- Chacarbaghi, K. & Lynch, R. (1999). *Competitive advantage: Creating and sustaining superior performance by Michael E. Porter 1980*, cited by Chacarbaghi and Lynch 1999, p. 45.

- Clulow, V., Gerstman, J. & Barry, C. (2003). The resource-based view and sustainable competitive advantage: The case of a financial services firm. *Journal of European Industrial Training 27* (5), 220–232.

- Courtright, J., Fairhurst, G. & Rogers, L. (1989). Interaction patterns in organic and mechanistic systems. *Academy of Management Journal, 32,* 773-802.

- Daft, R. (1995). *Organisation theory and design* (5th ed.). Minneapolis/St. Paul, MN: West Publishing Company.

- Davenport, T. & Nohria, N. (1994). Case management and the integration of labour. MIT. *Sloan Management Review,* 35(2), 11-23.

- Davis, S. & Lawrence, P. (1977). *Matrix.* Reading, MA: Addison-Wesley.

- Doll, W. & Vonderembse, M. (1991). The evolution of manufacturing systems: Towards the post-industrial enterprise. International Journal of Management Science, 19 (5), 401–411.

- Fry, L. & Slocum, J. (1984). Technology, structure and workgroup effectiveness: A test of a contingency model. *Academy of Management Journal*, 27, 221-246.

- Germain, R. (1996). The role of context and structure in radical and incremental logistics innovation adoption. Journal of Business Research, 35(2), 117–127.

- Greenberg, J. (2011). *Behaviour in organisations* (10th ed.). Upper Saddle River, NJ: Prentice Hall.

- Hall, R. (1977). *Organisations, structure and process.* Englewood Cliffs, NJ: Prentice Hall.

- Khandwalla, R. (1995). *The management style.* New Delhi: McGraw-Hill Companies Inc.

- Kimberly, J. & Evanisko, M. (1981). Organisational innovation: The influence of individual, organisational, and contextual factors on hospital adoption of technological and administrative innovations. *Academy of Management Journal*, 24, 689-713.

- Leavitt, H. (2003). *Why Hierarchies Thrive. Harvard Business Review,* 81(3), *96-102.*

- Lau, R. (2002). Competitive factors and their relative importance in the US electronics and computer industries. *International Journal of Operations & Production Management,* 22(1), 125–135.

- Martinelli, P.D. (2001). Systems hierarchies and management. *Systems Research and Behavioural Science,* 18(1), 68-82.

- MacDuffie, J. (1995). Human resources bundles and manufacturing performance: Organisational logic and flexible production systems in the world auto industry. *Industrial and Labour Relations Review,* 48(2), 197-221.

- Miles, R. & Snow, C. (1995). The new network firm: A spherical structure built on a human investment philosophy. *Organisational Dynamics,* 23(4) 5-18.

- Miles, R. & Snow, C. (1986). Organisations: New concepts for new forms. *California Management Review,* 28(4), 62-73.

- Mintzberg, H. (2009). *Tracking strategies: Toward a general theory of strategy formation.* New York, NY: Oxford University Press.

- Mullins, J. (2005). *Management and organisational behaviour* (7th ed.). Essex: Prentice Hall.

- Nelson, D. & Quick, C. (2011). *Understanding organisational behaviour*. Mason, OH: South- Western, Cengage Learning.

- Quangyen, T. & Yezhuang, T. (2013). Organisational structure: Influencing factors and impact on a firm. *American Journal of Industrial and Business Management, 3*(2), 229-236.

- Olson, E., Slater, S. & Hult, G. (2005). The importance of structure and process to strategy implementation. *Business Horizons, 48,* (1) 47-54.

- Passemard, D. & Calantone, R. (2000). *Competitive advantage: Creating and sustaining superior performance by Michael E. Porter 1980*, cited by Passemard & Calantone 2000:18.

- Peters, T. & Waterman, R. (1982). *In search of excellence*. New York, NY: Harper & Row, Publishers.

- Porter, M. (1980). *Competitive strategy*. New York, NY: Free Press, 36-46.

- Powell, T. (2001). Competitive advantage: logical and philosophical considerations. *Strategic Management Journal, 22* (9), 875–888.

- Rijamampianina, R., Abratt, R. & February, Y. (2003). A framework for concentric diversification through sustainable competitive advantage. *Management Decision, 41*(4), 362-371.

- Schilling, M. & Stteensma, H. (2001). The use of modular organisational forms: An industry-level analysis. *Academy of Management Journal,* 44(12), 6.

- Smriti, Chand (n.d.). 10 Benefits of a good organisational structure – explained! *Your Article Library, Management.* Retrieved from: http://www.yourarticlelibrary.com/management/10-benefits-of-a-good-organisational-structure-explained/3508/

- Vonderembse, M., Ragunathan, T. & Rai, S. (1997). A post-industrial paradigm: To integrate and automate manufacturing. *International Journal of Production Research, 35*(9), 2579-2599.

- Walton, R. (1985). From control to commitment: Transforming workforce management in the US. In K. Clark, R. Hayes & C. Lorenz (eds.). *The Uneasy Alliance: Managing the Productivity-Technology Dilemma*. Boston, MA: Harvard Business School Publishing.

- Wiersema, M. & Bantel, K. (1992). Top management team demography and corporate strategic change. *Academy of Management Journal,* 35(1), 91-121.
- Woodward, J. (1965). *Industrial organisation: Theory and practices.* Oxford: Oxford University Press.

INDEX